WITTGENSTEIN, EMPIRICISM, AND LANGUAGE

WITTGENSTEIN,
EMPIRICISM,
AND LANGUAGE

John W. Cook

New York   Oxford

OXFORD UNIVERSITY PRESS

2000

Oxford University Press

Oxford   New York
Athens   Auckland   Bangkok   Bogotá   Buenos Aires   Calcutta
Cape Town   Chennai   Dar es Salaam   Delhi   Florence   Hong Kong   Istanbul
Karachi   Kuala Lumpur   Madrid   Melbourne   Mexico City   Mumbai
Nairobi   Paris   São Paulo   Singapore   Taipei   Tokyo   Toronto   Warsaw

and associated companies in
Berlin   Ibadan

Copyright © 1999 by John W. Cook

Published by Oxford University Press, Inc,
198 Madison Avenue, New York, New York 10016

Oxford is a registered trademark of Oxford University Press

Library of Congress Cataloging-in-Publication Data
Cook, John W. (John Webber), 1930–
Wittgenstein, empiricism, and language / John W. Cook.
p.   cm.
Includes bibliographical references and indexes.
ISBN 0-19-513298-X
1. Wittgenstein, Ludwig, 1899–1951.   2. Reductionism.
3. Language and languages—Philosophy.   I. Title.
B3376.W564C65   1999
192—dc21   99-10740

9 8 7 6 5 4 3 2 1

Printed in the United States of America
on acid-free paper

For Carol, Aaron, and Gretchen

Preface

This book could be thought of as a sequel to my *Wittgenstein's Metaphysics* (1994), in which I argued that Wittgenstein undertook to solve a number of philosophical problems by resorting to reductionist solutions, such as phenomenalism and behaviorism. That book roused such hostility and misunderstanding in some readers that I was forced to think long and hard about the source of their reaction. I knew of course that I was stepping firmly on the toes of philosophers who had built careers by endorsing Wittgenstein's later philosophy, and their reaction to my unwelcome interpretation could have been expected. Most of the reactions, however, were philosophical in nature and appear to arise from several sources. One is a failure to understand what reductionism is, resulting in a failure to recognize even glaring instances of it. Another is the assumption that empiricism, far from being a weird view of things, reflects the ways in which we commonly think and talk about ourselves and the world. (One critic, noting my lack of sympathy for empiricism, decided I must be a *rationalist!*) Finally, there is a tendency to look at Wittgenstein's later work as a continuation or development of G. E. Moore's philosophy, and this has led some philosophers to interpret Wittgenstein's aphoristic remarks in a way that might have been congenial to Moore. But this tendency places Wittgenstein in entirely the wrong tradition, thereby obscuring his philosophical aims and the meaning of much that he said.

The present book is my attempt to deal with all of this in a way that goes beyond *Wittgenstein's Metaphysics*. It can, I believe, be read perfectly well by those unfamiliar with the earlier book, but I must warn such readers that they may think I haven't said enough in this book to substantiate certain of my claims, both about Wittgenstein and about various philosophical issues. They are advised, then, to turn to the earlier book where they will, I trust, find their requirements satisfied. On the other hand, those who have read the earlier book and were not convinced by it will, I believe, find that I have now addressed their concerns.

Chapter 11 is a slightly revised version of "Moore and Skepticism," which was my contribution to the *Festschrift* honoring Norman Malcolm, *Knowledge and Mind,* eds. Carl Ginet and Sydney Shoemaker (Oxford University Press, 1983). Chapters 10, 13, and 14 contain parts of paper, "Three Forms of Ordinary Language Philosophy," which I read at the annual philosophy symposium at California State University, Fullerton, in March 1987.

Throughout the book I have identified the sources of my quotations from Wittgenstein by means of the abbreviations listed on pages xi–xii which are arranged in roughly chronological order.

Captiva, Florida   J. W. C.
June 1997

Contents

Abbreviations

Abbreviations used to refer to Wittgenstein's writings, notes, and lectures in roughly chronological order:

NB   *Notebooks, 1914–16,* eds. G. H. von Wright and G. E. M. Anscombe, trans. G. E. M. Anscombe (Oxford: Blackwell, 1961).

TLP   *Tractatus Logico-Philosophicus,* trans. D. F. Pears and B. F. McGuinness (London: Routledge and Kegan Paul, 1961).

RLF   "Some Remarks on Logical Form," *Proceedings of the Aristotelian Society,* supp. vol. 9 (1929), pp. 162–171, reprinted in *Essay on Wittgenstein's Tractatus,* eds. Irving M. Copi and Robert W. Beard (London: Routledge and Kegan Paul, 1966), pp. 31–37.

WVC   *Wittgenstein and the Vienna Circle,* shorthand notes recorded by Friedrich Waismann, ed. Brian McGuinness, trans. Joachim Schulte and Brian McGuinness (Oxford: Blackwell, 1979).

EL   "A Lecture on Ethics," *Philosophical Review,* vol. 74 (1965), pp. 3–12.

PR   *Philosophical Remarks,* ed. Rush Rhees, trans. Raymond Hargreaves and Roger White (Chicago: University of Chicago Press, 1975).

PG   *Philosophical Grammar,* ed. Rush Rhees, trans. Anthony Kenny (Berkeley: University of California Press, 1974).

WL32   *Wittgenstein's Lectures: Cambridge, 1930–1932,* ed. Desmond Lee (Chicago: University of Chicago Press, 1982).

WL35   *Wittgenstein's Lectures: Cambridge 1932–1935,* ed. Alice Ambrose (Chicago: University of Chicago Press, 1982).

BB   *The Blue and Brown Books* (Oxford: Blackwell, 1958).

NFL   "Wittgenmstein's Notes for Lectures on 'Private Experience' and Sense Data,'" ed. Rush Rhees, *Philosophical Review,* vol. 77 (July 1968), pp. 271–320.

LSD   "The Language of Sense Data and Private Experience—I" and "The Language of Sense Data and Private Experience—II," notes taken by Rush

Rhees in Wittgenstein's 1936 lectures, *Philosophical Investigations,* vol. 7 (January 1984), pp. 1–45, and vol. 7 (April 1984), pp. 101–140.

LC *Lectures and Conversations on Aesthetics, Psychology, and Religious Belief,* ed. Cyril Barrett (Oxford: Blackwell, 1966).

CE "Cause and Effect: Intuitive Awareness," *Philosophia,* vol. 6, nos. 3–4 (Sept. and Dec. 1976), pp. 391–408. Selected and edited by Rush Rhees. English translation by Peter Winch.

LFM *Wittgenstein's Lectures on the Foundations of Mathematics, Cambridge, 1939,* ed. Cora Diamond (Hassocks: Harvester Press, 1976).

RFM *Remarks on the Foundations of Mathematics,* revised edition, ed. G. H. von Wright, R. Rhees, and G. E. M. Anscombe, trans. G. E. M. Anscombe (Cambridge, Mass.: MIT Press, 1983).

PI *Philosophical Investigations,* eds. G. E. M. Anscombe and R. Rhees, trans. G. E. M. Anscombe (Oxford: Blackwell, 1953).

Z *Zettel,* eds. G. E. M. Anscombe and G. H. von Wright, trans. G. E. M. Anscombe (Oxford: Blackwell, 1967).

RPP, I *Remarks on the Philosophy of Psychology,* vol. 1, eds. G. E. M. Anscombe and G. H. von Wright, trans. G. E. M. Anscombe (Chicago: University of Chicago Press, 1980).

RPP, II *Remarks on the Philosophy of Psychology,* vol. 2, eds. G. H. von Wright and Neikki Nyman, trans. C. G. Luckhardt and M. A. E. Aue (Chicago: University of Chicago Press, 1981).

LW, I *Last Writings on the Philosophy of Psychology,* vol. 1 eds. G. H. von Wright and Heikki Nyman, trans. C. G. Luckhardt and Maximilian A. E. Aue (Chicago: University of Chicago Press, 1982).

LW II *Last Writings on the Philosophy of Psychology,* vol. 2, eds. G. H. von Wright and Heikki Nyman, trans. C. G. Luckhardt and Maximilian A. E. Aue (Oxford: Blackwell, 1992).

WL47 *Wittgenstein's Lectures on Philosophical Psychology: 1946–1947,* ed. P. Geach (Chicago: University of Chicago Press, 1989).

ROC *Remarks on Colour,* ed. G. E. M. Anscombe, trans. Linda McAlister and Margarete Schattle (Berkeley: University of California Press, 1977).

OC *On Certainty,* eds. G. E. M. Anscombe and G. H. von Wright, trans. D. Paul and G. E. M. Anscombe (Oxford: Blackwell, 1969).

CV *Culture and Value,* ed. G. H. von Wright, trans. Peter Winch (Chicago: University of Chicago Press, 1984).

WR *The Wittgenstein Reader,* ed. Anthony Kenny (Oxford: Blackwell, 1994).

Introduction

During my years as a graduate student in the 1950s, I was introduced to Wittgenstein's writings by Oets Bouwsma and Norman Malcolm, both of whom were great admirers, first of G. E. Moore, and then of Wittgenstein's later work. Under their influence I came to regard Wittgenstein as a revolutionary figure, who had made a radical break with the assumptions that had formerly shaped most philosophical thinking. In consequence, I wrote several articles in which I sought to interpret Wittgenstein in this light. Yet I encountered difficulties in this approach. If his aim was, as he said, "to bring words back from their metaphysical to their everyday use" (PI, §116), why did he pay so little attention to what we actually say? And if, as he claimed, a main source of philosophical confusion is "a one-sided diet of examples" (PI, § 593), why did he so seldom deal with fully developed and realistic examples? Worse yet, why, when he did present examples, did he so often mismanage them?

These became urgent questions for me in the late 1960s as I began to appreciate the insights of my colleague Frank Ebersole, and in time I came to think that I did not understand Wittgenstein at all. Both Bouwsma and Malcolm, I concluded, had profoundly misunderstood him. For several years I gave up trying to fathom Wittgenstein's thinking, but the nagging questions remained. Then in 1969, with the publication of Wittgenstein's *On Certainty*, I was obliged to address those questions again. Malcolm asked me to review the book for *The Philosophical Review*, and without first having read it, I accepted the invitation. For months I struggled with Wittgenstein's thoughts, becoming ever more certain that he was profoundly in error. But although I could see where he was going wrong, I could not discover why he was doing so. In the end, I had to ask Malcolm to relieve me of writing the promised review, which he graciously did.

Several years passed before I went back to thinking about *On Certainty*, and when I did so, I published some of my thoughts in an essay entitled "Notes on Wittgenstein's *On Certainty*.[1] One of the things I said there was that some of Wittgenstein's examples suggest that he thought one's waking experience could take the uncanny twists and turns that we encounter in dreams, as when he suggests that he might see men turn into trees and trees into men (OC, §513). But I could not explain why he had this idea.

The explanation, I soon discovered, could be found in Wittgenstein's writings and lectures of the 1930s, which had recently been published. What I found there was that Wittgenstein remained a phenomenalist throughout the 1930s, after much of *Philosophical Investigations* had been written. This confirmed my suspicion that in *On Certainty* he was wrestling with epistemological problems that uniquely beset phenomenalists.[2] That realization sent me on a long voyage of discovery. As I continued to read Wittgenstein's writings, both early and late, I came to see that his views about many things, and especially about language and the nature of philosophy itself, were a product of his metaphysical views, which he was commonly thought to have disavowed in his later work. Many passages in his writings that had seemed especially inscrutable now found an obvious interpretation. Wittgenstein ceased to be an enigma once his writings were placed in the right historical context.

In *Wittgenstein's Metaphysics* I undertook to show that if one traces his views from his pre-*Tractatus* years onward, one can see that he was doing battle with various forms of philosophical skepticism and that his strategy was to eliminate the things about which skeptics are skeptical. Which is to say that in the matter of material things he resorted to phenomenalism and in the matter of other minds he resorted to (a phenomenalistic version of) behaviorism, which meant that he could overcome skepticism without having to prove that there are (Cartesian) minds and an external world. These and several other reductionist solutions are at the heart of Wittgenstein's philosophy, both early and late.

This, for several reasons, can be difficult to discern, especially in his later writings, where he appears to reject reductionism (see BB, p. 18). But if one reads his works closely, it becomes evident that he meant to reject only one version of reductionism, that which he had espoused in the *Tractatus*. In his later works he developed another, subtler, version of reductionism, one that is often mistaken for something quite different. This new version, which may be the most difficult of Wittgenstein's ideas, is discussed in chapters 2–9.

When I say that Wittgenstein undertook to defeat skepticism by adopting reductionist solutions, I am not denying that he believed himself to be giving correct descriptions of our language. To understand how he could have believed this, some historical background is required. One needs to appreciate the extraordinary influence that Russell's *Our Knowledge of the External World* had upon Wittgenstein's thinking from 1915 onward. I discussed this briefly in three chapters of *Wittgenstein's Metaphysics*,[3] but I did not explore this influence in all its ramifications. I have now remedied this in chapter 2 and in the appendix to the present volume, where I show that important elements of Wtiigenstein's later work are the result of the particular way he reacted to Russell's book. I believe that readers who have been hostile to my claim that Wittgenstein was, first and foremost, an empiricist will find that I have now fully justified that claim.

Chapters 10–14 are concerned with another impediment to understanding Wittgenstein, namely, the misconceptions that arise from viewing his later writings as "ordinary language philosophy." The principal mistake here is the idea that "ordinary language philosophy" is a readily identifiable philosophical method. It is not. There are at least three different approaches to philosophical problems that might be called "ordinary language philosophy," and the differences between them are extremely important. One result of ignoring those differences is that Wittgenstein's views have been mistaken for a type of philosophy he didn't practice and genuinely abhorred. Another result is the widespread belief that the criticisms that can be leveled with deadly effect against the type of ordinary language philosophy associated with G. E. Moore can be leveled against every sort of ordinary language philosophy. This sweeping dismissal of ordinary language philosophy not only rests on a mistake, it has also led philosophers to ignore the one version of ordinary language philosophy that is truly valuable—that practiced, most notably, by Frank Ebersole. The differences between these three versions of ordinary language philosophy are discussed in chapters 10, 13, and 14.

In *Wittgenstein's Metaphysics* I discussed some of the ways in which Wittgenstein's empiricism shaped his views about language—how it led, for example, to his criticism of the idea of a private language. In the present volume I have extended my account of his post-*Tractatus* views about language to show that they were fashioned to subserve his later version of reductionism. For example, although the early sections of the *Investigations* are generally thought to contain a straightforward account of language, an account uninfluenced by metaphysics, this is simply not so. What Wittgenstein says about words and language early in the *Investigations* was designed to pave the way for replacing the *Tractatus* version of reductionism with a new and subtler version.

Why is philosophy so complicated? . . . Philosophy unties the knots in our thinking, which we have tangled up in an absurd way; but to do that, it must make movements which are just as complicated as the knots.

—Ludwig Wittgenstein

Part I

THE WAY OUT OF THE FLYTRAP

The Subject Matter of Philosophy

In his lectures during the 1930s Wittgenstein often commented on the difference between what he was doing and what previous philosophers had done. Yet despite these differences there were also connections, he said. Too often, I believe, the differences have been emphasized and the connections ignored, with the result that his work has been seriously misunderstood. I want, if possible, to rectify this situation.

Two Conceptions of Philosophy

G. E. Moore once began a series of lectures by presenting those in attendance with, as he said, "a general idea of what philosophy *is*: or, in other words, what sort of questions it is that philosophers are constantly engaged in discussing and trying to answer." He said:

> To begin with, then, it seems to me that the most important and interesting thing which philosophers have tried to do is no less than this; namely: To give a general description of the *whole* of the Universe, mentioning all the most important kinds of things which we *know* to be in it, considering how far it is likely that there are in it important kinds of things which we do not absolutely *know* to be in it, and also considering the most important ways in which these various kinds of things are related to one another. I will call all this, for short, "Giving a general description of the *whole* Universe," and hence will say that the first and most important problem of philosophy is: To give a general description of the *whole* Universe. . . . And [this] problem is, it seems to me, plainly one that is peculiar to philosophy. There is no other science which tries to say: Such and such kinds of things are the *only* kinds of things that there are in the Universe, or which we know to be in it.[1]

Moore went on to give his own "description of the universe," saying such things as that people have minds as well as bodies, that there are in the universe a great many material objects, and that these objects often exist when no one perceives them.

The year was 1910, and at that time most philosophers, although they might have quarreled with Moore's description of the universe, would have found nothing to dispute in his characterization of their discipline. This could not be said of many philosophers who came along a decade or so later, following the publication of Wittgenstein's *Tractatus Logico-Philosophicus*. In that book Wittgenstein said: "All philosophy is a 'critique of language'" (4.0031). He also said: "Philosophy does not result in 'philosophical propositions,' but rather in the clarification of propositions" (4.112), meaning that philosophizing, when properly conducted, does not yield *descriptions* of the sort Moore envisioned, which are about "the Universe" and also a priori. (Or as Wittgenstein put it, "We cannot say in logic [i.e., in philosophy], 'The world has this in it, and this, but not that'" (TLP, 5.61).) He not only said these things, of course, but also undertook to show why philosophy could not possibly be the sort of thing Moore made it out to be, why it couldn't possibly be anything like a *science*. The place of philosophy, he said, "is above or below the natural sciences, not beside them" (4.111).

This continued to be Wittgenstein's view of the matter in his post-*Tractatus* years, when he began developing what many took to be an entirely new philosophy. He continued to say that philosophy, when properly done, concerns itself with language and is nothing at all like a science. Thus, in lectures he said that philosophical problems have been

> attacked in the way scientific problems are, and are treated perfectly hopelessly, as if we had to find out something new. The problems do not appear to concern questions about language but rather questions of fact of which we do not yet know enough. It is for this reason that you are constantly tempted to think I am . . . discussing the problems of a science called metaphysics. (WL35, p. 99)

In that same lecture he said: "All I can give you is a method; I cannot teach you any new truths" (WL35, p. 97).

A Grave Misunderstanding

Some people find this extremely puzzling and even distressing. How, they ask, can philosophy do its job if it merely attends to *words?* Isn't Wittgenstein simply ignoring the "big questions" philosophers have grappled with for centuries? Bertrand Russell was especially exercised by this issue and denounced Wittgenstein with considerable vigor. Referring to what he thought Wittgenstein was teaching, he said:

> The new philosophy seems to me to have abandoned, without necessity, that grave and important task which philosophy throughout the ages has hitherto pursued. Philosophers from Thales onward have tried to understand the world. . . . I cannot feel that the new philosophy is carrying on in this tradition. It seems to concern itself, not with the world and our relation to it, but only with the different ways in which silly people can say silly things. If this is all that philosophy has to offer, I cannot think that it is a worthy subject of study.[2]

Wittgenstein, said Russell, "seems to have grown tired of serious thinking and to have invented a doctrine which would make such an activity unnecessary."[3] This appraisal of Wittgenstein is, of course, perfectly ludicrous.

Wittgenstein was quite aware of what people expect from philosophy and said as much: "What is philosophy? . . . . We want a final answer, or some description of the world, whether verifiable or not" (WL32, p. 21). And he acknowledged that his way of going about philosophy "seems only to destroy everything interesting, that is, all that is great and important" (PI, §118). But he also had an explanation. We are, he said, "tempted to think that here are things hidden [and hence unverifiable]. . . . And yet nothing of the sort is the case. . . . All the facts that concern us lie open before us" (BB, p. 6). "In philosophy we know already all that we want to know" (WL32, p. 35), and the reason we pose philosophical questions is *not* because there is something as yet unknown about the universe but because we have fallen into confusion. The "big questions" of philosophy, he was saying, aren't really questions or aren't the questions they appear to be. As he put it in lectures: "This is the essence of a philosophical problem. The question itself is the result of a muddle. And when the question is removed, this is not by answering it" (LSD, p. 139).[4] But how can a question be removed without being answered? And what has language got to do with it?

Wittgenstein's explanation has two parts, the first of which is that our language, although perfectly serviceable for ordinary purposes, is constructed in such a way that it confuses us. The second part is that, in our failure to recognize the linguistic character of our problems, we imagine that what's needed for solving them is some sort of esoteric knowledge of various things. We don't realize that what we actually need is to remind ourselves of something about the words that figure prominently in the formulation of our problems. If, for instance, we are confused about time, we will think that we don't know what time is and need to learn more about it, when all we actually need is to be reminded of how the word *time* and other temporal terms, such as *past* and *present,* are commonly used. "This kind of mistake recurs again and again in philosophy; e.g. when we are puzzled about the nature of time, when time seems to us a *queer thing.* We are most strongly tempted to think that here are things hidden. . . . And yet nothing of the sort is the case. . . . But it is the use of the substantive 'time' which mystifies us" (BB, p. 6). So instead of asking, as Moore would, "What is time?" we ought to be asking: "How are the temporal expressions of our language used?" It is by answering *this* question that we can free ourselves from philosophical perplexity.

Wittgenstein was not, then, *ignoring* the questions that perplexed Russell and Moore; he was recasting them as questions of another kind. As he put it:

> Philosophical investigations: conceptual investigations. The essential thing about metaphysics: that the difference between factual and conceptual investigations is not clear to it. A metaphysical question is always in appearance a factual one, although the problem is a conceptual one. (RPP, I, §949)

If Wittgenstein is right about this, then no one—including Russell—should complain that Wittgenstein wasn't conducting factual investigations. But did Wittgenstein mean that his "conceptual investigations" leave us no wiser about the world? Clearly, he held that philosophy can't make us better informed, but did he think that it can in some way set us straight about the world, about reality?

The Goal of Philosophy

There are sharply differing views about how to interpret Wittgenstein on this point. Many of his would-be followers have taken him to mean that a philosophical problem is just a muddle, so that philosophy has done its job when the muddle is made to go away. In support of this interpretation, they might point to his remark that "the results of philosophy are the uncovering of one or another piece of plain nonsense" (PI, §119). These followers would say, then, that Russell was wrong in thinking that "philosophers from Thales onward have tried to understand the world." And they take Wittgenstein to mean that because philosophical problems are *merely* verbal muddles, *merely* linguistic confusions, their removal doesn't yield anything resembling a philosophical view of the world. I once shared this interpretation of Wittgenstein, but I no longer find it plausible. Wittgenstein was just as metaphysical as Russell wanted him to be.

Russell complained that Wittgenstein concerned himself, not with the world, but only with words—as if these concerns were exclusive of one another. Wittgenstein, however, did not share that view. He held, rather, that the *way* to arrive at a correct philosophical view of the world is by means of an investigation of words that will remove our misconceptions and leave us with an unspoiled view of reality.

Although he said that "philosophy is a battle against the bewitchment of our intelligence by means of language" (PI, §109), he did not mean that when a philosopher, having paid sufficient attention to language, is no longer "bewitched," he or she will revert to being just like people who have never asked themselves a philosophical question—will be like them, that is, in having no philosophical view of the world. He did not think that his way of doing philosophy simply expunges from our thinking any and all philosophical views of the world. On the contrary, he declared that his method enables us to achieve "the [philosopher's] goal of grasping the essence of what is represented" by language (PR, p. 51).

In the *Tractatus*, where Wittgenstein said that "all of philosophy is 'critique of language,'" he also said that at the end of the road a philosopher "will see the world aright" (TLP 6.54), meaning, not that he will see some contingent aspect of the world aright, but that he will see the *essence* of it, "the logical form of reality" (TLP, 4.121) aright.[5] As P. M. S. Hacker has observed, "philosophy, as practiced in the *Tractatus*, has one overarching goal—to render an account of the essence of the world."[6] The common interpretation of Wittgenstein is that he later abandoned this conception, that he ceased to think that there is any such thing as an "essence" for philosophers to grasp. But far from abandoning this conception of philosophy, he gave it fuller expression, saying:

> What belongs to the essence of the world simply *cannot* be said.[7]
>
> And philosophy, if it were to say anything [in the material mode], would have to describe the essence of the world.

> But the essence of language [i.e., *logical* grammar] is a picture of the essence of the world; and philosophy as custodian of grammar can in fact grasp the essence of the world, only not in the propositions of language, but in the rules for this language which exclude nonsensical combinations of signs. (PR, p. 85)[8]

On Wittgenstein's view, when a metaphysical question—a question formulated in the material mode—is recast as a question about language, the *answer* to that question, that is, an answer calling attention to a feature of logical grammar, will show something about the essence of the world and *not* merely something about language.

In the *Investigations* he expresses this idea cryptically as follows: "*Essence* is expressed by grammar" (PI, §371), meaning that we can display the essence of the world by describing the grammar of the relevant words, such as *time*. In his 1946–47 lectures he said: "Grammatical characteristics must characterize *what* it is that we talk about, as opposed to what is said about them" (WL47, p. 293), so by describing the grammar of some word or phrase we can show what *kind* of thing we are speaking of when using that word or phrase. "Grammar tells us," he says, "what kind of object anything is. (Theology as grammar.)" (PI, §373).[9]

Wittgenstein held that, owing to our linguistic confusions, we have a distorted view of the world and that his job was to leave us with an undistorted view. Our view is distorted, he explained, because "we look at the facts through the medium of a misleading form of expression" (BB, p. 31). He also says that our ordinary forms of expression have "prevented us from seeing the facts with unbiased eyes" and that he has "tried to remove this bias" (BB, p. 43). In the *Investigations* he says that a philosophical misconception is "like a pair of glasses on our nose through which we see whatever we look at. It never occurs to us to take them off" (§103). The suggestion is, of course, that Wittgenstein will help us to remove the distorting lenses, thus enabling us to see things for what they are.

So the aim of philosophy, as Wittgenstein saw it, is *not* simply to provide accurate accounts of language—or of the uses of various words—its aim is to enable us to see the world with unbiased eyes, so that we may "grasp the essence of the world," which is to say, the essence of time or mind or existence or whatever we were philosophically perplexed about.

Wittgenstein was promising, then, to deliver exactly what Russell said he wanted from philosophy. This is what is so difficult to understand about Wittgenstein. To further clarify the matter, I will go over this point in a somewhat different way.

The Methods of Wittgenstein's Early and Later Periods

It is possible for a philosopher to hold that there is no such thing as what Wittgenstein meant by "the essence of the world," that there is nothing comprised of those "most important kinds of things" Moore was speaking of in 1910. This is not to say that we might look for those things and come away empty handed. Rather, a philosopher may take the position that philosophical categories, one and all, do more to muddle than to facilitate our philosophical thinking. This means that when we have done philosophy properly we will have nothing resembling a metaphysical theory—we could not, that is, rightly be described as a dualist or a behaviorist or a materialist or a phenomenalist or an empiricist or as anything else of that sort. This, as I have said, was not Wittgenstein's view. He did not think that he should end up with *no* philosophical view of the world. His aim was to get his view of the world—his ontology, if you will—properly figured out and to then display it by means of remarks about language. He went about this in quite different ways in the *Tractatus* and in his later work, but his aim remained the same.

In the *Tractatus* he went about displaying "the logical form of reality" by laying down the specifications for (what he took to be) an ideal language, a language whose grammar, shorn of the misleading features of ordinary language, mirrors directly the logical form of the world. One of his specifications was that the fully analyzed propositions of such a language (which he called "elementary propositions") will consist entirely of *names* (4.22). That means that there will be no verbs and hence no tenses in an ideal language. What, then, does this feature of its grammar show us? According to Wittgenstein's strictest strictures, we shouldn't try to *say*. But if we ignore those strictures, as he himself often did, we can say that the absence of tenses shows that time is not comprised of the past, the present, and the future. This idea, it should be noted, is not peculiar to Wittgenstein. In Book XI of his *Confessions,* Augustine, after much wrestling with the problem, wrote: "What is now plain is that neither future nor past things are in existence, and that it is not correct to say there are three periods of time: past, present, and future." On this point, then, the difference between Augustine and Wittgenstein is that Augustine allowed himself to use the material mode of speech to express a metaphysical idea. Wittgenstein's metaphysics, although the same as Augustine's on this point, must be discerned in his specification that elementary propositions, being comprised solely of names, contain no verbs and hence no tensed verbs.

Unquestionably, then, at the time of the *Tractatus* Wittgenstein was as metaphysically inclined as Russell and Moore, although his scruples against using the material mode of speech made this somewhat difficult to see. And my claim is that in this respect Wittgenstein never changed; he remained a practicing metaphysician—and not unwittingly but of steadfast purpose. I said above, however, that in his post-*Tractatus* years his *means* of showing (or displaying) the essence of the world changed. He abandoned the idea of constructing an ideal language for this purpose and employed other means.

To illustrate this change of method, I will compare his ways of treating the same metaphysical idea in the *Tractatus* and in his later work. In the *Tractatus* he said that "the only impossibility that exists is *logical* impossibility" (6.375). This material mode statement, of course, he regarded as inappropriate; he should instead have displayed the essence of the world by describing an ideal language. And this, in fact, he did. He wrote: "The . . . impossibility of a situation is not expressed by a proposition, but by an expression's being . . . a contradiction" (5.525). This means that in an ideal language there would be no such word as *can't* or *impossible* and hence no sentences of the form "Such and such is impossible" or "That could never happen." It also means that many of the things we presently say could not be translated word for word into an ideal language. For example, in translation the sentences "It would be impossible for a man to survive two hours in water this cold" and "Jack can't run as fast as Jill" would lose the words "impossible" and "can't." This is because there is no *contradiction* in saying "Jack ran faster than Jill." And what this absence of contradiction, in turn, shows is that Jack's running faster than Jill is not out of the question. As Wittgenstein put it, "What can be described can also happen" (TLP, 6.362).

In his post-*Tractatus* years Wittgenstein retained this metaphysical view, but he no longer stated it by saying that in an ideal language an impossibility would be indicated by an expression's being a contradiction. His new method can be seen in The Blue Book, where he discusses the word *can't* in the sentence, "An iron nail can't scratch glass," declaring that "we could write this [sentence] in the form 'experience teaches that an iron nail *doesn't* scratch glass', thus doing away with the 'can't'" (BB, p. 49). This remark about "can't" was not meant to be a specification for an ideal language, which we don't yet have; it was intended to show us something directly about our own language, namely, that "can't" corresponds to nothing in reality. But his point is the same as in the *Tractatus*: We are to see that there are only *logical* impossibilities; nothing is *physically* impossible.

Wittgenstein described in various ways the post-*Tractatus* method he employed here. His most general description is this: he said that, in order to carry out a logical analysis, "all that is necessary is to separate what is essential from what is inessential in *our* language. . . . Each time I say that, instead of such and such a representation [in ordinary language], you could also use this other one, we take a further step towards the goal of grasping the essence of what is represented" (PR, p. 51).[10] This is what he does with the sentence "An iron nail can't scratch glass": he substitutes for it a sentence in which "doesn't" replaces "can't," and he does so to demonstrate that the word *can't* is inessential and hence to show something about the essence of the world—that nothing is physically impossible.

In this instance, then, we can see that although Wittgenstein's metaphysical views did not change, he employed, in later years, a new way of showing (or displaying) the essence of the world. This can be further documented as regards the example just discussed. As late as 1949 he still clung to the Humean view that nothing is physically impossible. Commenting on the sentence "It isn't possible for pears to grow on an apple tree," he explained away the words "isn't possible" by saying that "this only means that . . . apples grow on apple trees and pears grow on pear trees."[11] And in that same year he repeated the methodological principal behind this substitution: "How far do we investigate the use of words? Don't we also judge it? Don't we also say that this feature is essential, that one inessential?" (RPP, I, §666).[12] Here, then, is the *Tractatus* ontology showing up in Wittgenstein's writings of 1949. So it should not surprise us that in 1948, just three years before his death, he remarked to his friend Drury: "My fundamental ideas came to me very early in life."[13] It is commonly claimed that after 1929 Wittgenstein abandoned his early ideas and launched an entirely new philosophy. But he could hardly have spoken to Drury as he did in 1948 if what were *then* his fundamental ideas had come to him only after 1929, when he was forty years of age. While it is beyond doubt that his ideas about language changed during his post-*Tractatus* years, his remark to Drury plainly indicates that his ideas about language were not among those he regarded as fundamental. His fundamental ideas—those that remained constant—were his ideas about the essence of the world.[14] In fact, his ideas about language in his later years are of interest only as they are related to his ideas about the essence of the world.[15]

The Source of Wittgenstein's Views

What I have said here about Wittgenstein leaves us with an important question about his philosophical method: how did he determine *which* features of our language are inessential? How, for example, did he determine that our ordinary use of "can't" is inessential? In a passage already quoted he said that we come to see the essence of what is represented whenever *he* says that a new sentence could be used instead of the ordinary one. But how did he determine that the one sentence *is* as good as the other, that it comes to the same as the other.

Wittgenstein never answered this question—or never did so explicitly. He did, it is true, say that he wanted "to replace wild conjectures and explanations by quiet weighing of linguistic facts" (Z, §447). And he cautioned that "one cannot guess how a word functions. One has to *look at* its use and learn from that" (PI, §340). Remarks such as these would provide an answer to the question I posed *if* Wittgenstein's pronouncements about language were to a fair degree accurate. But they are not. As Frank Ebersole has aptly remarked, Wittgenstein "does not—in truth—ever follow his own advice."[16] So we are still in the dark as to the source of his oracular pronouncements about language. Where did he get those ideas?

Part of the answer is fairly obvious: what he says about language mainly reflects his conviction that empiricism is right about nearly everything. (His idea that nothing is *physically* impossible is clearly a product of his empiricism.) In other words, his way of determining what is "inessential" in our language was to consider whether some feature of it—some "form of words"—conflicts with an empiricist ontology, for instance, phenomenalism. If it conflicts, it's inessential.

But Wittgenstein's preference for empiricism, although it partially accounts for much that he says about language, can't be the whole explanation. We still need to know why he was drawn to empiricism. Why was he less troubled by the failings of empiricism than by those of dualism or rationalism?

The answer can be found in Wittgenstein's pre-*Tractatus* notebooks, in a group of passages that are, very clearly, comments on Russell's *Our Knowledge of the External World*. As I remarked in the introduction, this book had an extraordinary influence on Wittgenstein's thinking from 1915 onward, and in the next chapter I will show how this influence led Wittgenstein to believe that empiricism provided the only way to avoid a calamitous skepticism. (To be more exact, it was a particular form of empiricism that struck him as offering safe haven: the view William James called "radical empiricism." Russell later called it "neutral monism," and that name stuck.) There are those, I realize, who insist that since the later Wittgenstein disavowed all theories, it cannot be right to claim, as I do, that he was an empiricist and thought of the world as being more like what phenomenalists than what dualists think it is like. This objection, as I will demonstrate in chapter 3, involves a non sequitur: Wittgenstein did not think of phenomenalism as a theory.

Empiricism and the Flight from Solipsism

Wittgenstein first read Russell's *Our Knowledge of the External World* in the spring of 1915 and promptly entered in his notebook a number of comments critical of Russell's views. Most of these I will leave for discussion in an appendix. But two of his comments are relevant to my question about why Wittgenstein was drawn to empiricism, and I will therefore make them the starting point for this chapter.

Seeing the Hardness of the Soft

The first is a comment about skepticism. Russell, in his book, had declared skepticism to be "irrefutable,"[1] to which Wittgenstein replied:

> Scepticism is *not* irrefutable, but *obvious nonsense* if it tries to doubt where no question can be asked.
>
> For doubt can only exist where a question exists; a question can only exist where an answer exists, and this can only exist where something *can* be *said*. (NB, p. 44)

This comment, I believe, is pretty much self-explanatory: a doubt can exist only where an *answerable* question can be asked.[2] I will say no more about this except in connection with Wittgenstein's next comment, which is: "My method is not to sunder the hard [data] from the soft, but to see the hardness of the soft."

The terminology (hard and soft data) is of Russell's coinage, and Wittgenstein is using it to dispute Russell's view that one can differentiate hard data from soft data by subjecting the data (i.e., our prephilosophical beliefs) to methodological doubt.[3] So Wittgenstein is saying that *his* method enables one to see that (contrary to Russell) *none* of our prephilosophical beliefs falls into Russell's category of soft data, that is, all of them pass muster when subjected to methodological doubt.

To understand this, we need to look more closely at what Russell called "methodological doubt." He writes:

> It is necessary to practise methodological doubt, like Descartes, in order to loosen
> the hold of mental habits. . . . The naive beliefs which we find in ourselves when
> we first begin the process of philosophic reflection may turn out, in the end, to be
> almost all capable of a true interpretation; but they ought all, before being admit-
> ted into philosophy, to undergo the ordeal of sceptical criticism. Until they have
> gone through this ordeal, they are mere blind habits, ways of behaving rather than
> intellectual convictions. And although it may be that a majority will pass the test
> [and thus be certified as hard data], we may be sure that some will not, and that a
> serious readjustment of our outlook ought to result.[4]

Russell gives two examples of "data" he regards as being inherently "soft," as
lacking philosophical respectability: "Certain common beliefs are undoubtedly excluded from hard data. Such is the belief . . . that sensible objects in general persist when we are not perceiving them. Such also is the belief in other people's
minds."[5] (That Russell regards these as "common beliefs" shows that he, like
Moore, was a realist.)[6] In opposition to this, Wittgenstein says that *his* method is
to see "the hardness of the soft," meaning that his method enables one to see that
all of our common beliefs—in other words, the things we regularly say, such as
"The pot boiled over while no one was watching"—can survive the ordeal of
skeptical criticism.

Methodological Doubt

To understand Wittgenstein's method, we need to reflect on the fact that methodological doubt consists of screening anything you might say or think to see whether
it can survive skeptical scrutiny. Whether it can will depend, of course, on what,
exactly, we mean. For if, as realists claim, we are speaking of something that transcends experience, then what we say will *not* pass muster: the skeptic will declare
it to be unknowable. But if we are speaking of things we can perceive, phenomenal
objects, the skeptic—the skeptic within one's own bosom—will raise no objection.

More importantly, a philosopher who practices methodological doubt is accepting the assumptions that give rise to it, such as the assumption that what can
be perceived is always some phenomenal entity (or sense-datum) and the assumption that what we see of another person is a body. So in practicing methodological
doubt, one is allowing skepticism to dictate how anything we say must be interpreted *if* it's to be deemed philosophically respectable. And a philosopher who *accepts* such interpretations is a hard-core empiricist. Wittgenstein, moreover, was
just such a philosopher: he said that his method consists of interpreting the things
we say in such a way that no skeptic would find them dubious. Thus, writing
about Wittgenstein in 1912 Russell could say of him: "I argued about Matter with
him. He thinks it is a trivial problem. He admits that if there is no Matter then no
one exists but himself, but he says that doesn't hurt, since physics and astronomy
and all the other sciences could still be interpreted so as to be true."[7] Giving such
an interpretation is what Wittgenstein *meant* by seeing "the hardness of the soft."

This method—this principle of linguistic interpretation—appears to be a form
of reductionism, a way of saying: Xs are nothing but Ys. (That's how it induces

the censorious skeptic to accept Xs—by saying that Xs aren't as dubious as you think, for they're really nothing but . . .) Wittgenstein tried to carry out this interpretive program in different ways at different times, and I will discuss these differences in later chapters. Here I want only to show that he did adopt this method and that it had various implications for his philosophy.

Solipsism and the Threat to Language

A philosopher who practices methodological doubt is, as I said, allowing skepticism to dictate how to interpret anything one says *if* it's to be deemed philosophically respectable. Only if it is interpreted to mean something very different from what our words suggest will it survive skeptical scrutiny. Suppose that one resisted that interpretation, what price would one pay? One would be delivering into the hands of the skeptic everything but the contents of one's mind. In other words, the price for adopting a realist interpretation of the things we say is that one is driven straight into solipsism: nothing but one's own inner world can be known to exist. Russell in his 1914 article "On the Nature of Acquaintance" took this a step further:

> How do we come to know that the group of things now experienced is not all-embracing? . . .
>
> . . . At first sight, it might seem as though the experience of each moment must be a prison for the knowledge of that moment, and as though its boundaries must be the boundaries of our present world. Every word that we now understand must have a meaning which falls within our present experience; we can never point to an object and say: 'This lies outside my present experience.' We cannot know any particular thing unless it is part of present experience; hence it might be inferred that we cannot know that there are particular things which lie outside present experience.
>
> . . . On this ground, we may be urged to a modest agnosticism with regard to everything that lies outside our momentary consciousness. . . . Such a view . . . would seem, if rigorously applied, to reduce the knowledge of each moment within the narrow area of that moment's experience.[8]

Wittgenstein called this "solipsism of the present moment" (WL35, p. 25) and acknowledged, according to Moore, that "he himself had been often tempted to say 'All that is real is the experience of the present moment' . . . and [he said] that anyone who is at all tempted to hold Idealism or Solipsism knows the temptation to say 'The only reality is the present moment' or 'The only reality is *my* present experience.'"[9] Reflecting on this in 1949, Wittgenstein remarked: "Imagine what language there could be in such a situation. One could just gape. This!"[10]

Thoughts of being struck dumb like this brought Wittgenstein's thinking to a critical juncture, so that he often alluded to it in later years. In *Philosophical Remarks* he speaks of "that inarticulate sound with which many writers would like to begin philosophy" (p. 98).[11] In the *Investigations* he says that "in the end when one is doing philosophy one gets to the point where one would like just to emit an inarticulate sound" (§261).

In the grip of such perplexing thoughts, Wittgenstein compared himself to a fly in a flytrap: "The solipsist flutters and flutters in the flyglass, strikes against the walls, flutters, flutters further. How can he be brought to rest?" (LSD, p. 300). Finding the way out became Wittgenstein's central concern: "What is your aim in philosophy? To shew the fly the way out of the fly-bottle" (PI, §309).[12]

Here it is important to bear in mind that the way one gets *into* the flytrap is by way of methodological doubt, that is, by allowing the skeptic to dictate how what we say must be interpreted if it's to survive skeptical scrutiny. Couldn't one, therefore, simply avoid the flytrap by refusing to practice methodological doubt? This is the solution Moore attempted, but his efforts in this direction were ill-conceived (see chapter 11), as were later attempts to give Moore's arguments a linguistic turn (see chapter 10). In any case, Wittgenstein was sure that his problem could not be solved in this way, and he was scornful of philosophers who tried to follow Moore's example.

> [P]hilosophers should not attempt to present the idealistic or solipsistic positions . . . as though they were absurd—by pointing out to a person who puts forward these positions that he does not really wonder whether the beef is real or whether it is an idea in his mind, whether his wife is real or whether only he is real. . . . You must not try to avoid a philosophical problem by appealing to common sense; instead, present it as it arises with most power. You must allow yourself to be dragged into the mire, and get out of it. . . . One must not in philosophy attempt to short-circuit problems. (WL35, pp. 108–109)

What lay behind this refusal to follow Moore in simply circumventing the flytrap? Wittgenstein was convinced that this option was blocked by an argument that I will discuss in chapter 7, an argument I will call "Russell's Eliminator." Unlike Moore, then, Wittgenstein thought that he must either fight his way out of the flytrap or surrender to a calamitous solipsism, where language is reduced to an inarticulate sound.

This is why Wittgenstein was drawn to empiricism: it seemed to provide the only way to extricate himself from solipsism, and when it is regarded in that light, empiricism can seem wonderfully liberating.

Some Implications of Empiricism

While it may, in a pinch, seem to a philosopher that empiricism offers the last best hope for mankind, it carries with it some very special requirements. I will here mention just a few of these.

(i) The most obvious requirement is that one must reject the realist's account of common sense and the common sense man. So Wittgenstein says (BB, p. 48) that the common sense man is *not* a realist, that is, does not believe in the existence of things that transcend experience.

(ii) As I pointed out above, a philosopher who practices methodological doubt is allowing skepticism to dictate how to interpret anything one says *if* it's to be deemed philosophically respectable. Only if it turns out, when properly interpreted, to mean something very different from what our words suggest will it survive skeptical scrutiny. But that means that Wittgenstein, by embracing empiricism, was committing himself to the idea that philosophers must distrust the outward form of the things we commonly say in order to arrive at the proper interpretation of them. The outward form of our language leads one to think that a realist interpretation is appropriate, and a philosopher who is gullible enough to adopt that interpretation has failed, according to Wittgenstein, "to understand the logic of our language" (TLP, 4.003). This can happen because "the tacit conventions on which the understanding of everyday language depends are enormously complicated." Because the conventions are tacit, rather than explicitly set out, "it is not humanly possible to gather immediately from [everyday language] what the logic of language is" (4.002).

In keeping with this view of language, Wittgenstein said in The Blue Book that "ordinary language is . . . sometimes misleading" because it requires us to describe visual and tactile sensations "by means of terms for physical objects." Giving as an example the sentence "I see my hand moving," he declares this to be "a roundabout description of our sensations" (BB, p. 52). "It is obvious," he said years later, "that the description of impressions has the form of the description of 'external' objects" (RPP, I, §1092). Wittgenstein is saying that the grammatical form of things we say disguises the fact that ordinary language is a phenomenalistic language, that the things we say require a phenomenalistic interpretation.

Wittgenstein made this explicit when he said (I quote here from notes taken by Alice Ambrose in 1935):

> In philosophy, when people talk of sense-data, they are really only making a kind of translation. . . . The two languages could be characterized roughly in this way, that one [language] would talk about chairs, etc. and the other about 'perceptual objects'. [Philosophers often call this second language "phenomenalistic language."] But these terms are misleading, for they make it appear as though only a further analysis of the known facts could lead us to use such a language, whereas the truth is that there is nothing in the one language which cannot also be said in the other, only it will be said differently. We are talking about the same things in each case.[13]

In other words, talking about chairs and tables is just another way of talking about perceptual objects (sense-impressions). So our ordinary language, although it did not look to Russell like a phenomenological language, actually is such a language.[14] This claim is what Wittgenstein meant when he said that his method was to see "the hardness of the soft."

(iii) What persuaded Wittgenstein that he had found the right interpretation of ordinary language? The answer, as we have seen, was the specter of a ruinous solipsism. To avoid that, he was obliged to see the hardness of the soft and accordingly asked himself: What interpretation of ordinary language would earn for it the skeptic's stamp of approval? He found the answer in something Russell had said, namely, that if something we say is to survive skeptical scrutiny, then its proper interpretation must permit it to be completely verified, which only a phenomenological interpretation can do:

> I think it may be laid down quite generally that, in so far as physics and common sense is verifiable, it must be capable of interpretation in terms of actual sense-

data alone. The reason for this is simple. Verification consists always in the occurrence of an expected sense-datum. . . . Now if an expected sense-datum constitutes a verification, what was asserted must have been *about* sense-data; or, at any
rate, if part of what was asserted was not about sense-data, then only the other
part has been verified.[15]

It goes without saying that if something we say or think is to pass muster with the
skeptic, it must not only be verifiable but must also, as Russell indicates, be
"about sense-data," in other words, only if we can justly put *that* interpretation
on it will it earn the skeptic's stamp of approval.

This means that if I say, for example, that my friend is angry, this must be (in
Wittgenstein's phrase) "a roundabout description of [my] sensations" if it is to
survive skeptical scrutiny. We have already seen that Wittgenstein endorsed that
interpretation, for he was saying as much when he said that his method was to see
the hardness of the soft. But how was he to *justify* such an interpretation? The answer, quite simply, is this: he thought that it need only be pointed out that very
often we know—have *verified*—that a friend is angry. That is, the fact that I know
(have verified) that *shows* that my statement is a roundabout description of my
sensations. For Wittgenstein, then, verification became the key to interpretation.

(iv) This linkage of verification and interpretation is what Wittgenstein was
explaining when he wrote: "How a proposition is verified is what it says. . . .
The verification is not *one* token of the truth, it is *the* sense of the proposition"
(PR, p. 200). He also said: "In order to obtain a clear notion of the meaning of a
word it is necessary to attend to the sense of the propositions in which it occurs, to
the way they are verified" (WVC, p. 227).

The "meaning" of a word that is to be found in this way is not, of course, like
the meaning that is found by consulting a dictionary. Rather, how a proposition is
verified gives us the proper *philosophical interpretation* of a word—for example,
whether a word such as *angry* is to be interpreted as dualists or as behaviorists interpret it. Thus, Waismann, in summarizing Wittgenstein's views as they stood in
the early 1930s, wrote:

A proposition cannot say more than is established by means of the method of its
verification. If I say 'My friend is angry' and establish this in virtue of his displaying a certain perceptible behavior, I only *mean* that he displays that behavior. . . .
The sense of a proposition is the way it is verified. . . . If I specify a method
of verification, I thereby lay down the form of the proposition in question, the
meaning of its words, the rules of syntax, etc. (WVC, pp. 244–245)[16]

Wittgenstein was making the same point when he said: "The causes of our belief in a
proposition are indeed irrelevant to the question *what* we believe. Not so
the grounds [for it], which are grammatically related to the proposition, and tell
us *what proposition it is*" (Z, §437; emphasis added). Why would philosophers need
something to tell them "what proposition it is"? Because they are confused about the
proper philosophical *interpretation* of a proposition—of, for example, "My friend is
angry." Here again, then, we find interpretation being linked with verification.

This idea came out very clearly in Wittgenstein's lectures, where he said:

The question, "What is its verification?" is a good translation of "How can one know it?" Some people say that the question, "How can one know such a thing?" is irrelevant to the question, "What is the meaning?" But an answer gives the meaning by showing the relation of the proposition to other propositions. . . . It gives the grammar of the proposition, which is what the question, "What would it be like for it to be true?" asks for. (WL35, pp. 19–20)

These remarks are very similar to what Wittgenstein says in the *Investigations*: "Asking whether and how a proposition can be verified is only a particular way of ask 'How d'you mean?' The answer is a contribution to the grammar of the proposition" (PI, §353). In both of these passages Wittgenstein is saying that you can discover the proper interpretation of a proposition (or "the way it is meant") by asking whether and how it is verified.

The passage just quoted from the *Investigations* shows how wrong it is to maintain, as it often is, that in his later years Wittgenstein abandoned the idea that the sense of a proposition is given by the method of its verification. What he abandoned, if he abandoned anything, is the idea that what a person says about immediate experience in the first-person is something that that person verifies.[17] (This is reflected in the wording of PI, §353: "*whether* and how.") But with that exception he continued to insist on the connection between verification and meaning. He also continued to insist that philosophy is importantly concerned with giving proper interpretations. As he put it in the *Investigations*, "When we do philosophy we are like savages, primitive people, who hear the expressions of civilized men, put a false interpretation on them, and then draw the queerest conclusions for it" (PI, §194). So in philosophy we are confronted with problems "arising through a misinterpretation of our forms of language" (PI, §111). Although in his later years Wittgenstein mostly spoke of criteria instead of verification, this didn't change anything. In PI, §353, he explicitly said that *one* way of arriving at the correct interpretation of something we say is to ask how it is verified. So these are not ideas he abandoned in his later years.

the sense is given by its forms of life and thus this is verified

I have said that Wittgenstein opted for empiricism, that is, for phenomenalism, behaviorism, and other forms of reductionism, because he thought that there was no other way to extricate himself from a calamitous solipsism. In later chapters I will discuss in detail how he carried this through in his post-*Tractatus* years. Before doing so, however, I must address an objection that has been repeatedly raised by some of Wittgenstein's admirers. They say that I am completely missing the spirit of his later philosophy when I claim that he was an empiricist. In justification of this, they allude to his insistence that philosophers must not advance *theories*, taking him to mean that philosophers mustn't hold a view such as phenomenalism. Deborah Jane Orr, for example, calls attention to "the oft repeated insistence of the post-*Tractatus* Wittgenstein that his philosophy was non-theoretical" and that he "maintained that it is a mistake to look for theories in his work." Instead, his philosophizing "consists in a minute description of the ways in which human beings use language," and this "cannot be expected to issue in a pseudo-scientific (or metaphysical) theory."[18] If I had been aware of this, Ms. Orr informs me, I would

Verify
$Y = x^2 \rightarrow$ *its...*
then prove its meaning
is used meaningful

Scientific Propositions
mathematical Propositions etc
Facts whose grammatical
structures whose verification is not
their meaning

not have made the mistake of "accusing Wittgenstein of developing a metaphysical theory . . . of being a phenomenalist."[19]

The error, as I will show, lies in this syllogism: Wittgenstein eschewed theories in favor of descriptions; phenomenalism is a theory; therefore he eschewed phenomenalism.

Theories and Descriptions

       Wittgenstein repeatedly said that philosophy must be "purely descriptive" (BB, pp. 18, 125; PI, §124), and he undoubtedly thought that he conducted his own philosophizing in that way, by giving descriptions. But what did he regard as a philosophically relevant description? He meant something so different from what is commonly assumed that others who came along afterward, hoping to emulate his practice, not only misunderstood him but attributed to him a style of philosophy that he genuinely abhorred.

Substitutions and New Symbolisms

Commenting on Wittgenstein's mature philosophical method, George Pitcher writes that "this is actually what Wittgenstein himself does in practice: he investigates the uses of words," and he demonstrates his "genius" in "his examination of the uses of individual words."[1] The purpose of this, says Pitcher, is that "a philosopher's descriptions of the uses of words is . . . to give one a clear, over-all view of them, so that [one's] previous puzzlement will be finally dispelled. . . . [T]he philosopher's job is to give a certain sort of description of the uses of words; his task is a purely descriptive one."[2] And here Pitcher quotes from The Blue Book: "Philosophy really *is* 'purely descriptive'" (p. 18).

       Pitcher does not say what Wittgenstein regarded as a suitable description, but he offers some hints. He says that "because a philosopher's job is a purely descriptive one, he does not and cannot put forward any theories."[3] He also says: "In the *Investigations,* [Wittgenstein] was primarily concerned with what we all say and think in the course of our normal daily activities, and his main task was to get these things straight, to understand them."[4] This encourages one to think that giving descriptions of the sort Wittgenstein approved of could be done by giving some homely examples. If a skeptic confronts one with the problem of other minds, one can reply: "Just look at what we actually *say:* we say 'I could tell from the way he was walking that he was still in great pain,' and 'The look he gave me showed that he was very suspicious of me.'" Similarly, to deal with a phenomenalist, one can tell him: "Look at what we actually *say*: we say, for example, 'The pot boiled over while no one was watching' and 'The patient, while left unattended, went into convulsions and died.'" And if we encounter a philosopher who denies that people have free will, we can respond: "Just look at what we actually *say*: we say, for example, 'This time she wasn't fired; she left of her own free will.'"

These are all descriptions, and they are descriptions of (in Pitcher's words) things "we all say and think in the course of our normal daily activities." Also there is nothing *theoretical* about them. So one might think that they are descriptions of the kind that satisfy Wittgenstein's requirements.[5] But they are not. Although he occasionally said such things (e.g., "If we are using the word 'know' as it is normally used, . . . then other people very often know when I am in pain" (PI, §246)), there are few such remarks in his writings. More importantly, remarks of this sort are not what he had in mind when he said that philosophy is purely descriptive. Philosophers who claim that Wittgenstein's method was to report what people commonly say are saddling him with a conception of philosophy of which he was sharply critical. He said that if you merely *repeat* what the common man says, you do nothing to solve the problem and in fact only show what the problem is; what you say "just brings out the difficulty" (BB, pp. 48–49). What is needed, he thought, is something very different from straightforward reports of the things we commonly say. He was sure that philosophical problems can be solved, but "not by restating the views of common sense" (BB, p. 59; see also WL35, pp. 108–109).[6]

One can readily understand why Wittgenstein thought that if you produce examples of what people actually *say*, you are merely presenting us with the raw material, so to speak, that *creates* the problem.[7] For what is it that creates philosophical problems? Ordinary language! "Language," said Wittgenstein, "sets everyone the same traps; it is an immense network of easily accessible wrong turnings" (CV, p. 18). "We are up against trouble caused by our way of expression" (BB, p. 48). Philosophical problems persist, he said, "because our language has remained the same and keeps seducing us into asking the same question" (CV, p. 15). So we must be on guard against "the confusion our language creates" (PR, p. 153). "Philosophy is a battle against the bewitchment of our intelligence by means of language" (PI, §109). With this attitude toward ordinary language, Wittgenstein couldn't have thought that philosophical problems can be successfully dealt with simply by giving descriptions that reproduce what we all say.[8]

We can be sure, then, that when Wittgenstein spoke of giving descriptions he had in mind something unusual. Clearly, such descriptions must be free of those features of ordinary language that cause philosophical confusion, but they must also, presumably, point the way out of such confusion. So these descriptions will have to give us something quite different from anything we ordinarily say. Wittgenstein was indicating this when, late in his life, he wrote: "My difficulty is altogether like that of a man who is inventing a new calculus (say the differential calculus) and is looking for a symbolism" (RPP, I, §134). This will seem baffling to anyone who assumes that Wittgenstein was merely issuing "reminders" about what we commonly say. For if that means giving examples of ordinary people saying ordinary things, that would be nothing like "inventing a new calculus" or "looking for a new symbolism." And yet Wittgenstein was very explicit about what he wanted. In lectures he said: "I am doing a sort of mathematics— mathematics at the stage that precedes calculation [i.e., when new concepts are introduced]. . . . I want to substitute a *new sort* of description—not that the old one is bad, but to remove misconceptions (WL47, p. 68; emphasis added). And in *Philosophical Investigations* he wrote: "Many [misunderstandings] can be removed by substituting one form of expression for another; this may be called 'analysis' of our forms of expression" (PI, §90). An example of this method was cited in chapter 1: Wittgenstein's proposal that we substitute for the sentence "An iron nail can't scratch glass" another sentence that does not contain the word *can't*.

We may call this Wittgenstein's "substitution method." The earliest mention of it in his writings[9] is in *Philosophical Remarks*: "Each time I say that, instead of such and such a representation, you could also use this other one, we take a further step towards the goal of grasping the essence of what is represented" (p. 51). The method is important, he explained, because "one can think for years about a certain problem and make no progress because one never thinks of making up a new language" (WL35, p. 98), that is, making up a "new form of words."

Clarifications

Wittgenstein's reason for wanting to substitute new sorts of descriptions for our present ones is clear enough: our ordinary forms of expression create misconceptions, misunderstandings.[10] But this requires clarification on a number of points.

(i) The substitution is for philosophical purposes only; it is not to be thought of as an alteration of ordinary language (PI, §132). "Sometimes," said Wittgenstein, "an expression has to be withdrawn from language and sent for cleaning,— then it can be put back into circulation" (CV, p. 39). To clean up an expression one says: "Instead of using this (ordinary) form of words one could use this other form of words." And once that has been made clear, we can continue using the ordinary form of words.

(ii) What, then, becomes of Wittgenstein's remark that "the work of philosophers consists in assembling reminders" (PI, §127)? Can a reminder call attention to a "form of expression" different from our present one? What sort of reminder was Wittgenstein thinking of?

The answer lies in his saying: "We remind ourselves . . . of the *kind of statement* that we make about phenomena [*Erscheinungen*]" (PI, §90; see also Z, §543). About *phenomena*? About *appearances*? Did Wittgenstein think that what we talk about in our everyday lives are *appearances*? If so, that would explain both why he thought our ordinary forms of expression are misleading ("talk about sense impressions does not *look* the way you imagine")[11] and why he thought that it would be edifying to substitute a new form of expression, why that would remove misunderstandings.

(iii) Here it may be objected that Wittgenstein *can't* have been a phenomenalist in his later year because he so obviously rejected the idea that one could give a phenomenological description of what one sees, feels, etc. (see RPP, I, §§287, 919, and 1079). This objection sounds plausible, but it's wrong.

It is true that in his later years Wittgenstein was sharply critical of the idea that we are capable of giving phenomenological descriptions (see *Wittgenstein's Metaphysics,* chapter 10). So the foregoing objection would be decisive if the method that I've called the substitution method required that (explicitly) phenomenological descriptions be substituted for our ordinary forms of words. But this is not what that method requires. What is needed is only a new *form* of words. I will presently demonstrate this with some of Wittgenstein's examples.

(iv) By what means did Wittgenstein arrive at the new forms of expression required by his substitution method? This is something that *needs* an explanation, for his conviction that our language is full of traps wouldn't have allowed him to rely on what we actually *say.*

It may help here to recall that, according Wittgenstein, we are constantly talking about phenomena, sense-impressions, but that we do so in a misleading way. ("It is clear," he said, "that the description of impressions has the form of description of 'external' objects" (RPP, I, §1092).) That being so, he took his job to be that of inventing forms of words which make it more obvious that we *are* talking about a phenomenal world. For example, we say such things as "The pot boiled over while no one was watching." If, in saying this, we are speaking of phenomena (appearances, impressions), our phraseology is clearly misleading: it suggests that we are talking about something that existed unperceived, and one couldn't speak of sense impressions that way. We can therefore expect Wittgenstein to offer as a substitute a form of words that makes it more obvious that we *are* talking about impressions. That is how one employs the substitution method. That is also what Wittgenstein had in mind when he compared himself to "a man who is inventing a new calculus."

(v) An important feature of Wittgenstein's view of language is his idea that an expression, despite its misleading form, may be used—*applied*—in a legitimate, a perfectly suitable, way. Why is that? Because, said Wittgenstein, grammar is arbitrary (PG, p. 184); it doesn't determine meaning. Thus, a pair of expressions may, despite having very different grammatical forms, have exactly the same *meaning.* This will be so provided only that the two expressions have the same *use.*

(vi) Wittgenstein thought that the realist views held by philosophers like Moore are foisted on them by certain features of ordinary language. So when he spoke of substituting a new form of expression for our ordinary form of expression, he typically had it in mind to substitute an expression whose form is clearly *non*-realist for our present expression, whose form seduces philosophers into realism. This needs clarification.

Wittgenstein says the following: "In our language there is an entire mythology embedded" (WR, p. 278), and "The primitive forms of our language—noun, adjective and verb—show the simple picture to which it tries to make everything conform" (ibid.). He also speaks of "the philosophy laid down in the forms of each [language]" (RPP, I, §587). This sounds as though he meant what many others have meant in saying such things, namely, that whoever speaks a language thereby gives voice, unavoidably, to a certain philosophy. Lichtenberg, for example, said:

> Our false philosophy is embodied in the language as a whole: one might say that we can't reason without reasoning wrongly. People don't bear in mind that speaking, no matter about what, is a philosophy. Everyone who speaks is a folk philosopher, and our academic philosophy consists of qualifications of the popular brand.[12]

Similarly, Bertrand Russell maintained that the metaphysical category of "substance . . . dominates syntax, through which it has dominated philosophy down to our present day. . . . The conception of substantial identity with varying properties is embedded in language, in common sense, and in metaphysics."[13] In saying here that the metaphysical concept of substance is "embedded" not only in language but also in common sense, Russell meant that the concept is both part of English syntax and part of the common man's way of thinking about all sorts of things.

Although Wittgenstein was strongly opposed to the particulars of Russell's claim,[14] it might be thought that he was expressing agreement with the general view when he spoke of a philosophy being "laid down in a language." In that case he would be claiming that the plain man shares the philosophical views of the realist. That is what G. E. Moore so obviously held, but Wittgenstein did not. He said that "the common sense man . . . is as far from realism and as from idealism" (BB, p. 48). But how can that be? How can the plain man *talk* like a realist without *being* a realist?

The answer lies in the distinction Wittgenstein drew between "surface grammar" and "depth grammar" (PI, §664). Surface grammar—the superficial appearance of our sentences—may seem to warrant a realist interpretation, but it doesn't actually do so; it does not impose metaphysical realism on our thoughts as we go about our practical affairs. Depth grammar, by contrast, truly reflects our thoughts, but it is not freighted with metaphysical realism. That is why we can talk like realists without being realists.

My point, then, about Wittgenstein's substitution method is that he typically employed it when he wanted to substitute for a common expression, whose surface grammar lures us into realism, another expression whose form is clearly nonrealist. He does so because we get into philosophical difficulties when we fail to realize how different the depth grammar of an expression is from its surface grammar. This is what Wittgenstein meant when he spoke of philosophical problems arising "through a misinterpretation of our forms of language" (PI, §111).

I will presently discuss several cases in which Wittgenstein substitutes for a common expression another whose form is clearly non-realist. Significantly, to explain what he is doing in these cases, he invokes his distinction between theories and pure descriptions. In other words, what he treats as a theory is what he fancies a realist would want to say and what he calls a "pure description" is his own nonrealist alternative. But before turning to those examples, I want to examine further Wittgenstein's ideas about grammar and philosophical problems.

Surface Grammar, Realism, and Reductionist Substitutions

Wittgenstein speaks of philosophical problems arising "through a misinterpretation of our forms of language." How did he think such misinterpretations come about? What is it about surface grammar that leads us astray? Not always the same thing. In some cases "a simile that has been absorbed into the forms of our language produces a false appearance" (PI, §112). But there is also this: "One important source of difficulty is that words look so much alike" (WL35, p. 46), which leads us to form mistaken ideas about various things. He constantly cautioned against this by asking us to realize that there can be logically important differences even where the uniform appearance of words makes things look most alike. Nouns, for example, have many different uses: some are names of things, but most are not. And those that are not are the ones that cause philosophical problems, that lure us into metaphysical realism. He said:

> There is no trouble at all with primitive languages about concrete objects. Talk about a chair and a human body and all is well; talk about negation and the human mind and things begin to look queer. A substantive in language is used primarily for a physical body, and a verb for the movement of such a body. This is the simplest application of language, and this fact is immensely important. When we have difficulty with the grammar of our language we take certain primitive schemas and try to give them wider application than is possible. We might say it is the whole of philosophy to realize that there is no more difficulty about time than there is about this chair. (WL35, p. 119)

Realism, Wittgenstein thought, is the result of following the course he describes here: taking a certain primitive schema, namely, nouns used to talk about things, and trying to apply that schema where it's not appropriate—to time, for example. To avoid realism, then, one must come to see that words can have a use without standing for something. It can be 6:00 p.m. and time for dinner even if there is nothing called "time."

Making Realism the Main Target

The passage I have just quoted, with its antirealist message, is taken from the opening remarks of Wittgenstein's Lent Term lectures of 1935. It is noteworthy that from 1933 onward Wittgenstein began many of his writings, lectures, and dictations with this same, antirealist, message. The pattern is clearly present in the opening paragraphs of The Yellow Book (1933), The Blue Book (1933–34), The Brown Book (1934–35), and the *Investigations* (1931–49). Those works are commonly thought to begin with a lesson in the philosophy of language, a lesson unrelated to metaphysics. But that is not so. In the opening paragraphs of all four Wittgenstein is taking aim at the source of realism. This will become apparent if we ask ourselves: why did Wittgenstein, in the opening paragraphs of these works pose a question about the nature of numbers?

The answer is that he believed that numbers provide the best illustration of an extremely important point, namely, that words can, *without our realizing it,* have a use without signifying (or standing for) something. In his 1913 "Notes on Logic" Wittgenstein commented that man possesses an innate capacity for constructing symbols "without having the slightest idea what each word signifies" and then added: "The best example of this is mathematics, for man has until recently used the symbols for numbers without knowing what they signify or *that they signify nothing*" (NB, pp. 95–96; emphasis added).

These remarks did not come from "out of the blue." In 1903 Russell, in *The Principles of Mathematics,* claimed to have reduced mathematics to logic, that is, to have shown, by defining the natural numbers as classes of classes, that mathematics needs only logical terms, that it has no need of uniquely numerical entities. Speaking of this reduction Russell said: "The above definition of pure mathematics . . . professes to be, not an arbitrary decision to use a common word in an uncommon signification, but rather a precise analysis of the ideas which, more or less unconsciously, are implied in the ordinary employment of the term."[15] In the introduction to the second edition of the book (1937) Russell repeated the point as follows: "[S]tatements apparently about . . . numbers . . . need interpretation which shows that their linguistic form is misleading, and that, when they are *rightly* analyzed, the pseudo-entities in question are not found to be mentioned in them."[16]

The pseudoentities Russell meant to banish by means of his reduction are the 'objects' that "one," "two," and "three" would stand for if such words stood for something. Russell explains:

> If you think that 1, 2, 3, and 4, and the rest of the numbers are in any sense entities, if you think that there are objects, having those names, in the realm of being, you have at once a very considerable apparatus for your metaphysics to deal with, and you have offered to you a certain kind of analysis of arithmetical propositions. When you say, for example, that 2 and 2 are 4, you suppose in that case that you are making a proposition of which the number 2 and the number 4 are constituents, and that has all sorts of consequences, all sorts of bearing upon your general metaphysical outlook. If there has been any truth in the doctrines [of analysis] that we have been considering, all numbers are what I call logical fictions. Numbers are classes of classes. . . . Therefore you do not have, as part of the ultimate constituents of your world, these queer entities that you are inclined to call numbers.[17]

Russell acknowledges that he is engaged in metaphysics when he invokes his own analysis to displace the realist's view of numbers, and I want to suggest that Wittgenstein was engaged in metaphysics in the very same way. Russell declared that the objects which realists take numbers to be are, in truth, "logical fictions," and this is what Wittgenstein had in mind when, in 1913, he wrote that numbers are "the best example" of words that we all use without realizing that "they signify nothing." The more general point which this exemplifies is that realists are mistaken in thinking that certain words signify things. The words in question, Wittgenstein thought, require a reductionist, rather than a realist, analysis.[18]

It is clear now why Wittgenstein began the *Investigations* and the other works I have mentioned with a question about the nature of numbers: He regarded the lesson to be learned from numbers as the best way to overcome our partiality for realism. The fact that number words can have a use without standing for anything is instructive, he thought, because it discredits the sort of inference (from substantive to 'substance') that begets realism.[19]

This lesson is prominent in the opening paragraphs of The Blue Book, where Wittgenstein comments (p. 1) on the question "What is the number one?" This and similar questions, he says, express a unique kind of puzzlement, puzzlement that arises from the fact that "we feel that we can't point to anything in reply . . . and yet ought to point to *something*. (We are up against one of the great sources of philosophical bewilderment: we try to find a substance for a substantive.)" This, in other words, is the source of our realist tendencies.

The *Investigations* begins in a similar way, with a quotation from Augustine, who said that he learned language by learning which *objects* are signified by which words. Wittgenstein comments: "Augustine does not speak of there being any difference between kinds of word. If you describe the learning of language in this way you are, I believe, thinking primarily of nouns like 'table,' 'chair,' 'bread,' and of people's names" (PI, §1). Wittgenstein goes on in the very next paragraph to connect this with metaphysical realism. He imagines someone asking: "What is the meaning [*die Bedeutung*] of the word 'five'?" Naturally, if we are disposed to think that words are paired with objects, we will begin wondering about the object that's paired with "five." And in this way we set ourselves on the path to metaphysical realism. But, says Wittgenstein, it's a path we'd never have strayed onto except for a confusion: "What confuses us is the uniform appearance of words when we hear them spoken or meet them in script and print. For their *application* is not presented to us so clearly. Especially when we are doing philosophy!" (PI, §11).[20]

This is a theme Wittgenstein continues to press throughout the opening pages of the *Investigations*. (In section 17 he remarks: "In language (8) we have different *kinds of word*.") Anyone who thinks that these passages were meant to be simply a contribution to the philosophy of language will fail to realize that Wittgenstein, by beginning the *Investigations* as he did, was firing his opening salvo against a realist metaphysics.[21] And that is not all. Defeating realism was not, for Wittgenstein, an end in itself; it was his first step toward realizing his overarching aim in philosophy, that of showing the fly the way out of the fly bottle—out of solipsism.

Escape from the Fly Bottle

As I pointed out in the preceding chapter, Wittgenstein thought that a philosopher who adopts a realist metaphysics will find himself driven into solipsism and even into solipsism of the present moment, wherein language is reduced to "an inarticulate sound." So if Wittgenstein was not going to take a vow of silence, his immediate need was to discredit realism.

We can be more specific about this. Wittgenstein, as I have said, thought that philosophers who take a realist view of things are failing to realize that the words in question require a reductionist, instead of a realist, analysis. Why does that mistake lead to solipsism? It does so because a realist, instead of adopting phenome-nalistic accounts of other minds and material things, assumes that these are real things, existing outside his own mind. And once that is assumed, other minds and material things fall prey to methodological doubt, and the descent through skepti-cism into solipsism becomes inevitable. The only way to avoid this debacle, Witt-genstein thought, is to adopt phenomenalism as regards material things and phe-nomenalistic behaviorism as regards other people. (In *Wittgenstein's Metaphysics* I explained why Wittgenstein did not think that he was drawing all such things into the sphere of his own mind: he followed neutral monism in rejecting the idea that the mind is a sort of container, the idea that the world is divisible into the internal and the external, the public and the private.)

This, then, is how the anti-realist salvo in the opening paragraphs of the *In-vestigations* constitutes a preemptive strike against solipsism. Dismissing Augus-tine's idea that all words stand for objects is the first move in undermining the idea that there must be a substance for every substantive. That, in turn, paves the way for replacing a realist metaphysics with reductionist alternative. And once this program is carried out for those things that we think of as the mental and the physical, it will be clear that there never was a fly bottle, that the "mind" of the solipsist is an illusion.

The Substitution Method at Work

I let us return to Wittgenstein's substitution method. I said that Wittgenstein's sub-stitution method does not require that (explicitly) phenomenological descriptions be substituted for our ordinary forms of words, and I promised to demonstrate this with several of his own examples. His general idea in each case is that our or-dinary, realist-sounding form of words misleads us, and so, for our enlightenment, he will present us with a form of words that is clearly nonrealist but has, he claims, the same meaning. The following passage illustrates this method.

> One of the most misleading representational techniques in our language is the use of the word 'I', particularly when it is used in representing immediate experience, as in 'I can see a red patch'.
>
> It would be instructive to replace this way of speaking by another in which immediate experience would be represented without using the personal pronoun; for then we'd be able to see that the previous representation wasn't essential to the facts. Not that the representation would be in any sense more correct than the old one, but it would serve to show clearly what was logically essential in the repre-sentation [i.e., would show that 'I' wasn't essential]. (PR, p. 88)

Elsewhere Wittgenstein explained this point as follows: "Instead of saying 'I think' or 'I have an ache' one might say 'It thinks' (like 'It rains'), and in place of 'I have an ache', 'There is an ache here'" (WL35, p. 21).

This shows very clearly the important features of Wittgenstein's method: (i) an ordinary "form of words" is declared to be misleading; (ii) to bring out its mis-leading character, Wittgenstein proposes to substitute for it another form—a grammatically different form—of words; (iii) he adds that the new form would not be "more correct than the old one," (i.e., the meaning of the old form is not determined by it grammar); and (iv) he explains that the new form would "show clearly what was logically essential" for representing the facts in question, namely, immediate experiences.

This view of philosophy was repeated many years later (1949) by Wittgenstein when he wrote: "How far do we investigate the use of words? Don't we also judge it? Don't we also say that this feature is essential, that one inessential?" (RPP, I, §666). The significance of this is that Wittgenstein, in his last years, continued to use the substitution method to get rid of the things that realists hold dear, and to justify an ontology acceptable to empiricists.

How should we evaluate Wittgenstein's use of the substitution method in the foregoing example? It leads him to say the following sorts of things:

> The word "I" does not refer to a possessor in sentences about having an experience (WL35, p. 21).
>
> In "I have pain", "I" is not a demonstrative pronoun (BB, p. 68).
>
> To say "I have pain" is no more a statement *about* a particular person than moaning is. (BB, p. 67)

There are, I believe, philosophers who agree with these remarks. They shouldn't. Wittgenstein was wrong—and in more ways than one. First of all, how, in the first of these remarks, is he using the word *refer*? It's not *words* that refer to something or other; rather, a person who is speaking or writing may refer to one thing or another. We commonly ask: "What were you referring to: the dog or the cat?" But only philosophers ask what a *word* refers to or whether a given word refers to something. I don't understand that use of "refer." (While going over a student's essay with him I might point to the pronoun "it" and ask "What does this refer to?" but that is just a way of asking what the student was referring to when he wrote the ambiguous sentence.) There is a more serious error here. For, contrary to Wittgenstein, we do say that someone has *referred to himself* when he says things of the sort Wittgenstein had in mind, such as "I have a headache." Suppose, for example, that I've been reading through the diary of a friend who has recently died. Someone asks me whether I learned much about my friend from his diary, and I answer: "No, he hardly refers to himself at all in his diary. He mostly talks about other people and politics. In the first twenty pages he referred to himself only once, and that's here on page ten, where he wrote, 'I have a migraine headache today'." This is a perfectly ordinary use of the expression "he referred to himself," and there would be no reason to quarrel with it unless one held some theory with which it conflicted.

What about Wittgenstein's other formulation—that saying "I have pain" is not a statement *about* a particular person? If this means that someone who admits to having a headache says nothing about *himself,* this is not true. I might have occasion to say, "The only thing he said about himself is that he had a headache." This is a perfectly ordinary use of the phrase "said about himself," and there would be no reason to quarrel with it unless one held a theory with which it conflicts.

Wittgenstein is right, of course, when he says that in using the first person pronoun we do not identify someone by criteria (PI, §404). He is also right when he says that "there is no question of recognizing a person when I say I have a toothache" (BB, p. 67). But he is wrong when he takes this as proof that we are not, in such cases, referring to anyone and that sensations, therefore, have no owner, that there is no *subject* of pain.

How did Wittgenstein go wrong? I won't try here to trace his confusion to its roots, but I think it is important to realize that his problem results from the way he thought about the first person pronoun in those cases in which we are not saying anything about being dizzy or in pain—cases such as "I am taller than you" and "I'm covered with mud." He thought that in these cases we are referring to a *body* and that this body has (roughly) the same status in our language-game as an overly loyal dog, in that it happens to be in one's field of vision whenever one looks downward, although it could be entirely absent. (See The Blue Book, pp. 61–74.) Once he had this idea, it was easy for him to tell himself that "the word 'I' in 'I have pains' does not denote a particular body" (BB, p. 74)—meaning that in this case the word *I* does not function like the name of an ever-present dog. And that, of course, is true, but having told himself *that,* he was left with no way of understanding how I could be referring to myself *twice* when I say, "I'm covered with mud and I'm miserably cold."

Let us consider another example. Wittgenstein writes: "It is clear that the description of impressions has *the form of description* of 'external' objects" (RPP, I, §1092; emphasis added). I have already mentioned that we say such things as "The pot boiled over while no one was watching." Here, then, is a form of words that Wittgenstein would want to "send for cleaning." But what new symbolism, what new form of words, will he offer as an edifying substitute? Being an admirer of Berkeley, he did not have to look far for an answer. In lectures he said:

> We can actually *transform* a statement about a pencil into a statement about appearances of a pencil—even when no one is there: "If someone *were* there, he would see . . . etc.' One is often tempted: always to use the picture of someone seeing the pencil and then to talk of "a pencil somewhere else" as a pencil seen by someone. (LSD, p. 28)

Here we see Wittgenstein using his method of substituting one form of words for another—in this case substituting a counterfactual form for our ordinary categorical form. This is apparently derived from Berkeley's remark: "The table I write on I say exists, that is, I see and feel it; and if I were out of my study I should say it existed; meaning thereby that if I was in my study I might perceive it, or that some other spirit actually does perceive it" (*Principles,* I, 3). Wittgenstein is agreeing with the analysis Berkeley first offers ("If I were there, I would see it") and is rejecting Berkeley's suggestion that when we speak of something that *we* don't perceive, we mean that "some other spirit" does. In short, Wittgenstein is proposing a phenomenalistic analysis of what we say.

I will discuss this phenomenalistic analysis in chapter 12 (see also *Wittgenstein's Metaphysics,* pp. 111–114), so I will not do so here. I want, instead, to use Wittgenstein's treatment of this case to shed light on certain things he said about his substitution method.

Wittgenstein's 'Descriptions'

Wittgenstein was well aware that many philosophers were not in sympathy with phenomenalism. Moore, for example, had objected strenuously—and more than once—to the phenomenalists' practice of substituting a counterfactual form of words for an ordinary categorical form, such as "The pot boiled over while no one was watching." To understand some of Wittgenstein's remarks, one needs to realize that they are his answer to the realists' objection. Isaiah Berlin formulates the objection in the way that most clearly invites Wittgenstein's response. He remarks that when we say there is a table next door, "common sense . . . cannot accept as fully equivalent in meaning any sentence not asserting that something is now . . . being characterized."[22] In explanation of this he says:

> But common sense and the philosophers who are in sympathy with it, have always felt dissatisfied. The reduction of material object sentences into what we may, for short, call sense datum sentences, seemed to leave something out, to substitute something intermittent and attenuated for something solid and continuous. . . .
> . . . If he is then told that to say that there was a material object—the land bridge in prehistoric times—is to say something about data there would have been if . . . he feels cheated. For these data appear to depend on the activity of observers; so that the material object becomes analysed into a series of either purely hypothetical, i.e., non-existent, or at best, intermittent data occurring and disappearing as the observer observes and ceases to observe. And this seems . . . a different picture of the world from that which he started by believing; and in no sense merely a description of the old picture though in different words.

In other words, where phenomenalism offers us something intermittent, common sense insists on filling the gaps with something solid.

Remarks such as these provide the background against which we can understand Wittgenstein when he says:

> Pure description is so difficult because one believes that one needs to fill out the facts in order to understand them. It is as if one saw a screen with scattered colour-patches, and said: the way they are here, they are unintelligible; they only make sense when one completes them into a shape.—Whereas I want to say: Here *is* the whole. (If you complete it, you falsify it.) (RPP, I, §257).

This passage shows very clearly what Wittgenstein meant by a "pure description," and Berlin would have recognized immediately that Wittgenstein is here not only rejecting the realist analysis but is also insisting that pure descriptions are phenomenalistic descriptions.[23]

I think we can say not only that Wittgenstein's substitution method was designed to generate descriptions favored by phenomenalists but also that he deemed such descriptions to be philosophically edifying. This comes out particularly clearly in what he said about his use of the substitution method to eliminate the first person pronoun (see above). In the last lectures he gave he discussed William James's idea that "the Self is in me, and is to be observed by introspection." If I am told this, said Wittgenstein, "I close my eyes and put my head down. So I see darkness and feel the pressure under my chin—so *that* is the Self!" He continues:

A philosophical problem comes up when you have a limited *morphology* of uses of language. . . . (One first asks what a word stands for—hence [one expects there to be] a body.) Now there begin all sorts of subterfuges. The blunder is to think the word "Self" means something in the way that "body" stands for the body; . . . [that it] stands for something inside the body. If you consider substituting a signal for "I suffer" you see that the first mistake is to take 'I' as *standing* for something. (WL47, pp. 46–47)

In lectures given some years earlier he said:

[W]e think we describe phenomena incompletely if [in a new notation] we leave out personal pronouns. It is as though we had omitted pointing to something, since the word "I" seems to point to a person. But we can leave out the word "I" and still describe the phenomena formerly described. It is not the case that certain changes in our symbolism are really omissions. One symbolism is in fact as good as the next. (WL35, pp. 21–22)

This makes it clear that the purpose of the substitution method is to generate the most parsimonious descriptions possible. Why should that be edifying? Because realizing that such a description is possible will destroy the illusion that our present symbolism reflects the world as it is. And once freed from that illusion, we can see the world properly.

Wittgenstein's Rejection of Theories

This message, which Wittgenstein delivered in various ways, has an obvious bearing on my (much maligned) claim that he was a phenomenalist. In one passage he says: "The difficulty of renouncing all theory: One has to regard what appears so obviously incomplete, as something complete" (RPP, I, §723). Notice the contrast Wittgenstein sets up here. A philosophical *theory* is an account that is dissatisfied with the "gappines" of the phenomenalist's descriptions; a theory tries to "complete" the picture by introducing "hypothetical entities." It is clear that Wittgenstein meant to renounce any such theory, but it is equally clear that he regarded phenomenalism, not as a theory, but as the antithesis of a theory.

The same contrast is set up in PI, §109, where advancing a theory is equated with allowing something hypothetical, that is, unobservable, into one's considerations. Wittgenstein writes: "And we may not advance any kind of theory. There must not be anything *hypothetical* in our considerations. . . . The problems [of philosophy] are solved, not by giving new information, but by arranging what we have always known." In this rejection of theories there is nothing incompatible with my claim that Wittgenstein was a phenomenalist. The "theories" he meant to oppose are those that posit entities—"hypothetical" entities—whose existence can at best be inferred, as the minds of others are supposed to be inferred by means of the argument from analogy. But phenomenalism posits no such entities. It was designed to *banish* such entities. So my accusers are unjust when they say that I attribute to Wittgenstein theories he rejected.

At the end of the preceding chapter I pointed out that there is a way of interpreting Wittgenstein that goes like this: Wittgenstein eschewed theories in favor of giving descriptions; phenomenalism is a philosophical theory; therefore Wittgenstein eschewed phenomenalism. I said that this syllogism contains an error, and it should now be clear that it lies in the claim that what Wittgenstein regarded as a philosophical theory is what today might be so regarded. He did not think that phenomenalism, behaviorism, and other reductionist accounts are theories. He regarded them as the antitheses of theories (See quotation from Kohler on p. 73.)

Wittgenstein's Descriptions of People and What They Can Do

I have said that Wittgenstein thought that he had a compelling reason for embracing phenomenalism, behaviorism, and other forms of reductionism: he thought there was no other way to extricate himself from a calamitous skepticism. But phenomenalism comes at a considerable cost. It is the claim that nothing can exist save for what can be experienced, as a tone or a red circle can. And this is meant to hold for people no less than for other things: there can be nothing to a person but what phenomenalism allows. For a phenomenalist everything is, so to speak, on the surface, out in the open, in plain view. Or, as Wittgenstein was fond of saying, nothing is hidden. ("The activities of the mind," he said, "lie open before us" (BB, p. 6).) This had grave consequences for his account of human abilities, such as knowing how to play chess or the piano. For what was he to say about such abilities? I can play the piano, but there is nothing I would call an *experience* of that ability. Should I say, then, that it's a state that I can't see? No, said Wittgenstein, "to say that the ability . . . is a state, only it cannot be seen, misuses language" (WL35, p. 95). If we are inclined to think of "the fact of . . . someone being able to do something, etc., as the fact that he is in a particular state," that, said Wittgenstein, is because our language misleads us:

> [T]his way of representation, or this metaphor, is embodied in the expressions "He is capable of . . .", "He is able to multiply large numbers in his head", "He can play chess": in these sentences the verb is used in the *present tense,* suggesting that the phrases are descriptions of states which exist at the moment when we speak. (BB, p. 117)

Wittgenstein, having embraced phenomenalism, was bound to be dissatisfied with this use of the present tense, so this was an occasion for him to invent "pure descriptions" which show that, when we speak of a person's abilities, capacities, or powers, we are speaking of a phenomenal world.

This comes out very clearly in two sets of remarks in which Wittgenstein discusses "pure descriptions"—one from The Brown Book, the other from *Zettel*. Both are concerned with human abilities.

Wittgenstein concludes part I of The Brown Book with some remarks about the examples he has just given (of reading, etc.). They "were not," he tells us, "descriptions of [a person's] outside letting us guess at [his or her] inside which for some reason or other could not be shown in its nakedness." And he warns against the temptation "to think that our examples [of reading] . . . *hint* at something which they cannot show. . . . Our method," he concludes "is *purely descriptive;* the descriptions we give are not hints of explanations" (p. 125; italics in the original).

What we are meant to agree to, in regard to reading, is the following. Wittgenstein maintains that when we read aloud from a printed page, "there's no act of memory, *or anything else,* which acts as an intermediary between the written sign and the [spoken] sound" (PG, p. 96; my italics). So when he said that his examples "were not descriptions of an outside letting us guess at an inside" that couldn't be shown, he meant that it would be a mistake to think that there is something—in either your mind or your brain—that accounts for the fact that you read the passage correctly. If you are inclined to ask *why* your audible performance ran as it did (and not, say, as it would have if you had been speaking in tongues), your question has no answer. The question makes "no sense," according to Wittgenstein (PG, pp. 96–97). "What is of interest to us in reading," he said, "can't be essentially something *internal.*" He adds: "Every more or less behaviouristic account leaves one with the feeling that it is crude and heavy handed; but this is misleading—we are tempted to look for a 'better' account, but there isn't one" (PG, p. 100).

This has long been the standard view of empiricists. As Hume put it: "The distinction which we often make betwixt *power* and the *exercise* of it is . . . without foundation" (*Treatise,* I, III, xiv). Wittgenstein, too, insisted that we mustn't think that having an ability—being able to speak French, for example—is something besides the exercise of it.[24] We must not, in other words, think of an ability as "an inside which for some reason or other could not be shown," so that one couldn't give a "pure description" of it.

The fact that Wittgenstein sums up this point by saying (see above) that his method "is *purely descriptive*" shows us that the *purity* of a description is to be judged by how close it comes to satisfying the requirements of empiricism, that is, of phenomenalism, behaviorism, and so forth.

In *Zettel* there is a group of passages (§§310–315) in which the nature of a "pure description" comes up for discussion—this time in regard to describing (in a philosophically relevant way) a child's learning to count. For a phenomenalist the problem is this: because a learner consists, at any moment, of (nothing but) his then-current phenomenal states, that makes it hard to see how he could take much of anything away from a lesson. No phenomenal state lasts very long, and soon after the lesson has ended the learner will most likely have none of the phenomenal states he had at the time of the lesson. So we mustn't think that when we teach a child to count we thereby put him in a state he wasn't in beforehand. We mustn't think that when we say, "He can count to one hundred," we are attributing to him any sort of *state.* All we can mean is that in certain circumstances he will repeat numbers in a certain order, in the order in which other people say them when they count.

To make this point Wittgenstein, in the passages under consideration, asks whether a philosophically relevant description of the learner should stop (as Hume would have it) with a description of the *conduct* of the teacher and the pupil or whether, when the teacher's work is done, we should add: "The pupil can count now." Wittgenstein asks: "And if I do include [that judgment], am I going beyond pure description?" (Z, §310). And then: "What analogy, what wrong interpretation [of that judgment] produces [the desire for something *more* than the description of the child's conduct]?" (Z, §313). We find it difficult, says Wittgenstein, to accept "as the answer something that looks as if it were only a preliminary to it," and we are reluctant to accept this because we wrongly expect an *explanation* of the child's post-instruction handling of numbers instead of being content with a mere description of what he does. We must "not try to get beyond [the description]. The difficulty here is: to stop" (Z, 314).

In this case, then, Wittgenstein's substitution method consists of simply dropping an allegedly misleading form of words (our use of "can count") and insisting that nothing is *lost* thereby, that "can" is inessential, is "a wheel turning idly" (WVC, p. 47; PR, p. 51).

It is not hard to understand why Wittgenstein took this position. He thought that when you watch a schoolboy you see that he, with pencil in hand, *behaves* in a certain way, but you see nothing *more,* no new *state* implanted in him by the teaching. This is how an empiricist sees the world. Wittgenstein claimed to be reminding himself "of the *kind of statement* that we make about phenomena" (PI, §90), about appearances. And this, it seems, is what he was wanting us to do when he recommended that we ask: "In what scenes will [these words] be used; and what for?" (PI, §489). He was wanting us, I mean, to think of a *scene* as an empiricist—as a phenomenalist—would: a scene is composed of *phenomena.* (See chapter 6, Note 15.)

Phenomenological Analysis

Earlier I asked: "How did Wittgenstein come up with the new forms of expression required by his substitution method?" and suggested that he did so by devising forms of words that make it more obvious that we are talking about phenomena (appearances). Thus, in his 1929 paper "Some Remarks on Logical Form," which he later partly repudiated, Wittgenstein wrote:

> Now we can only substitute a clear symbolism for the unprecise one by *inspecting the phenomena* which we want to describe [by means of a clear symbolism], thus trying to understand their logical multiplicity. That is to say, we can only arrive at a correct analysis by, what might be called, the logical investigation *of the phenomena* themselves, i.e. in a certain sense *a posteriori,* and not by conjecturing about *a priori* possibilities. (RLF, p. 32; emphasis added)

Wittgenstein is saying that a philosopher must *inspect reality* in order to learn what can and cannot be said, what does and does not make sense. But how does one do that?

One is reminded of Hume's saying: "[W]hen I enter most intimately into what I call *myself,* I always stumble on some particular perception or other, of heat or cold, light or shade, love or hatred, pain or pleasure. I never can catch *myself* at any time without a perception, and never can observe anything but the perception" (*Treatise* I, IV, vi). The essential thing for Hume is what can and cannot be *observed,* so since he "never can observe anything but the perception," he concludes that he is "nothing but a bundle or collection of different perceptions." Thus, Hume claims to derive his analysis from what he can observe, and this procedure, I am suggesting, is the sort of thing Wittgenstein meant by "the logical investigation of the phenomena themselves," although he would not formulate his results, as Hume did, in the material mode of speech.

So we might describe Wittgenstein's procedure as follows: (i) at the outset we find ourselves perplexed by the proposition p. (ii) We then ask, "When do we say p?" and remind ourselves that we say that p in the scene S (and others like it). (iii) Next, we must (in imagination) inspect S to see whether it contains any of the realists' queer entities. (iv) Upon finding that it contains no such entities, that it contains only *phenomena,* we are to fashion a description of S, making sure that its form contains no suggestion of those entities favored by realists.[25] This is how an empiricist *inspects reality* in order to conduct a conceptual investigation. Or as Wittgenstein stated the matter at the end of his life, in 1950: "Phenomenological analysis . . . is analysis of concepts" (ROC, II, §16).

The crucial step in the aforementioned procedure—inspecting the relevant scenes and finding that they contain only phenomena (appearances)—obviously presupposes Wittgenstein's phenomenalist views. So his method is not philosophically neutral. If we were to adopt it, we would never be in suspense about whether our investigation of a particular word will show it to be the sort of word realists take it to be. The substitution method delivers only the results it was designed to deliver, for the "descriptions" it substitutes are metaphysically prefigured. This is hardly surprising, for Wittgenstein made it abundantly clear. When he first announced that he would henceforth use the substitution method, he also said that because this method allows us to recognize "what is essential and what inessential in our language," it "amounts to the construction of a phenomenological language" (PR, p. 51). How could he have known this in advance, *before* investigating particular concepts? He knew that he would get only phenomenalistic results because he took it as axiomatic that what can't be described phenomenalistically is a fiction.

One result of failing to understand Wittgenstein has been that many philosophers who have tried to emulate him have become caught up, unwittingly, in philosophical problems that assail phenomenalists but can be ignored by others. Perhaps the clearest case of philosophers being drawn into Wittgenstein's phenomenalistic conundrums is the ongoing debate about following a rule. What Wittgenstein says about rule-following and the possibility of a private language was dictated by, and has no other basis than, his phenomenalism and especially his idea that there is nothing *to* a person but phenomenal states.[26] This idea led him into grave difficulties, but instead of questioning his phenomenalist presuppositions, he pushed ahead, following the argument as it led him into the densest of thickets. Unfortunately, a large company of philosophers mistook him for a reliable guide and trooped into the thicket behind him. For most of them, since they didn't share Wittgenstein's phenomenalism, this was quite unnecessary.

Behavioristic Descriptions

Wittgenstein was not only a phenomenalist. He also, as I have said, held a phenomenalistic version of behaviorism. When this came into play, that is, when he wanted to substitute a new and edifying form of words for something we ordinarily say about *people,* he resorted to behavioristic descriptions. For example, at one point he described two people holding a conversation as "making noises at each other" (LFM, p.203). Descriptions of this sort, he said, are philosophically more edifying than our present way of speaking of other people:

> The *facts* of human natural history that throw light on our [philosophical] problem are difficult for us to find out, for our talk *passes over them in silence,* it is occupied with other things. (Thus we tell someone: "Go into the shop and buy . . ."—not: "Put your left foot in front of your right foot etc., etc. then put coins down on the counter, etc., etc.") (RPP, I, §78)

The latter form of description would, I take it, be philosophically edifying, because it is more obviously about a *body.* But it is difficult, Wittgenstein says here, to give behavioristic descriptions. (Elsewhere he says: "If [someone] screams under certain circumstances which are *difficult to describe,* and acts in a way that is *difficult to describe,* then we say he is in pain" (LW, II, p. 29; emphasis added).)[27] But despite its being difficult to describe human behavior, that is, bodily movements, it is *that*—for instance, "making noises at one another," rather than "conversing"— that is philosophically relevant, that will, as Wittgenstein puts it, throw light on our problem. At one point he says: "If I see a person with a piece of paper making marks in a certain sort of way, I may say, 'He is calculating'" (LFM, p. 203), and here it is the making of marks in a certain sort of way that is (properly speaking) the person's *behavior; calculating* is the word we use when we see the bodily movements occur in certain circumstances.[28] This is why we find Wittgenstein, who often spoke of a person's "behavior" or "pain behavior," making the following—extremely important—admission: "[T]he word "behaviour", as I am using it, is altogether misleading, for it includes in its meaning the external circumstances— of the behaviour in a narrower sense (RPP, I, §314). Wittgenstein is saying two things here: (i) I have been using "behavior" in such a way that a piece of behavior includes, in addition to bodily movements, the circumstances in which those movements occur, and (ii) in order to use the word in a way that is not misleading, a piece of behavior should include only bodily movements. When "behavior" is used in the latter, nonmisleading way, then "grimacing," "crying out," "conversing," and "calculating" would *not* be behavior.

Finding that it was not easy to describe bodily movements, Wittgenstein often relaxed his scruples and used words such as *grimace* and *moan,* but when we find him doing this, we must bear in mind that he used such words with a behavioristic interpretation in mind. And that means that these words have ceased to be our ordinary, nonphilosophical words.[29] I do not of course mean that Wittgenstein was aware of this, for he was not. He believed that his behavioristic interpretation captured our ordinary understanding of such words. I will discuss Wittgenstein's behaviorism more thoroughly in later chapters.

Speakers and Noise Makers

Because of the assumptions that give rise to it, methodological doubt has the consequence, as I have said, of allowing skepticism to dictate how anything you say must be interpreted *if* it's to be deemed philosophically respectable and not a fit subject for skepticism. Moreover, when Wittgenstein, borrowing Russell's terminology, said, "My method is to show the hardness of the soft," he was declaring that his method renders the things we commonly say safe from skeptical dismissal. In other words, wherever skepticism appears to threaten something we say, Wittgenstein will declare that what we say can, *when properly interpreted*, be seen to be something no skeptic could doubt. So finding the right interpretation—a skeptic-proof interpretation—is central to Wittgenstein's method.

The Residuum of Methodological Doubt

Let us observe how this method works in a particular instance. How are we to find a skeptic-proof interpretation of the things we say about other people? The first step is to consult skepticism to see what it accepts as indubitable. Russell performs this step for us in *Our Knowledge of the External World*:

> It must be remembered that, at our present level of doubt, we are not at liberty to accept testimony [from anyone]. When we hear certain noises, which are those we should utter if we wished to express a certain thought, we [in ordinary life] assume that that thought, or one very like it, has been in another mind, and has given rise to the expression which we hear. If at the same time [as we hear those noises] we see a body resembling our own, moving its lips as we move ours when we speak, we cannot [in ordinary life] resist the belief that it is alive. . . . We will consider the legitimacy of this belief presently; for the moment I only wish to point out that [this belief] needs the same kind of justification as our belief that the moon exists when we do not see it, and that without [such justification], testimony heard or read is reduced to noises and shapes.[1]

In this passage Russell gives us his interpretation of what we mean when we say that another person made a statement of some sort, for instance, gave directions to a motorist, and he acknowledges that his interpretation makes what we say (e.g., "He gave us directions") vulnerable to skepticism. But Russell also tells us what there is about a person's talking that a skeptic would accept as indubitable: talking and writing are "reduced to noises and shapes." We might call this "the residuum of methodological doubt."

With this in mind, consider how, in this case, Wittgenstein would use his method of seeing the hardness of the soft—his method, that is, of finding a skeptic-proof interpretation of the things we commonly say.

His interpretation, to earn the skeptic's seal of approval, will have to be in terms of the aforementioned residuum: making marks and noises. And this is to be, not an artificially imposed interpretation, but an analysis of what, ordinarily, it *means* to say, "They are having a conversation" or "He gave us directions" or "She scolded the child," and so on. Accordingly, we find Wittgenstein saying:

> But—and this is an important point—how do we know that a phenomenon which we observe when we are observing human beings is what we ought to call a language? or what we should call calculating?
>
> . . . a criterion of people talking is that they make articulated noises. For instance, if you see me and Watson at the South Pole making noises at each other, everyone would say we were talking, not making music, etc.
>
> Similarly if I see a person with a piece of paper making marks in a certain sort of way, I may say, "He is calculating", and I expect him to use it in a certain way. (LFM, p. 203)

We find the same thing in the *Investigations,* where Wittgenstein says that when you *tell* someone something you "make a noise" (PI, §363). Similarly, in the last lectures he ever gave he said: "But consider what happens in giving a report. You make a noise" (WL47, p. 261). And in The Brown Book he wrote that "there is no one relation of name to object, but as many as there are uses of sounds or scribbles which we call names" (p. 173). This means, presumably, that when I say, "The woman called me by name," I am saying that the woman made a sound, the sound that I call "my name."

When Wittgenstein wanted a more general term that would cover both "the sounds (or noises) we make" in speaking and "the marks (or scribbles) we make" in writing he used the word *signs:*

> If I give anyone an order I feel it to be *quite enough* to give him signs. And I should never say: this is only words, and I have got to get behind the words. Equally, when I have asked someone something and he gives me an answer (i.e. a sign) I am content—that was what I expected. (PI, §503)

In all these passages we find Wittgenstein trafficking in the indubitable residuum of methodological doubt, using words metaphysically.

The Road to Reductionism

To understand his reason for doing this, we need to take note of the metaphysical transformation that a person undergoes when he or she falls into the clutches of a philosopher. Where beforehand—before philosophy, that is—we had a man or a woman giving directions or ordering a meal or scolding a child or calling for help, Russell talks about a body making noises and a mind containing a related thought. That's what we are left with—noises and thoughts! But what about ordering, scolding, asking, calling, etc.? These seem to have disappeared. But the realist proposes to reconstruct the scolding, ordering, etc. from the materials available: the noises and their mental accompaniments. Unfortunately, this leaves the realist at the mercy of skepticism, for where he once heard a friend calling for help or overheard a neighbor scolding a child, the realist now finds himself hearing noises but detecting no mental accompaniments: he can't see into the mind of another. So *are* there friends and neighbors or only noise makers, humanoid bodies emitting sounds?

Wittgenstein's solution to this skeptical query was to declare that "a criterion of people talking is that they make articulated noises." But this means that he did not, in order to get scolding, ordering, etc. back into the picture, cast off the realist's philosophical baggage and return friends and neighbors to their rightful place in human discourse. Although, in a bid to avoid skepticism, he dispensed with the realist's mental accompaniments, he then tried to make do with the remainder of the realist's baggage—the bodies making marks and noises.

This is what we find at the beginning of The Blue Book, where he discusses the realist's two-part analysis of language:

> We are tempted to think that the action of language consists of two parts; an inorganic part, the handling of the signs, and an organic part, which we may call understanding these signs, meaning them, interpreting them, thinking. These latter activities seem to take place in a queer kind of medium, the mind. . . .
>
> Frege ridiculed the formalist conception of mathematics by saying that the formalists confused the unimportant thing, the sign, with the important, the meaning. Surely, one wishes to say, mathematics does not treat of dashes on a bit of paper. . . . And the same, of course, could be said of any proposition: Without a sense, or without the thought, a proposition would be an utterly dead and trivial thing. . . . But if we had to name anything which is the life of the sign, we should have to say it was its *use.* . . .
>
> The mistake we are liable to make could be expressed thus: We are looking for the use of a sign, but we look for it as though it were an object *co-existing* with the sign. (BB, pp. 3–5)

Clearly, Wittgenstein thought he could retain one part of Russell's account, bodies making sounds or marks, while jettisoning the other part, the accompaniments in "a queer kind of medium, the mind." He is saying that, contrary to Russell, these sounds and marks don't need a Cartesian mind behind them in order to constitute talking and writing. And to make up for losing the mind, he proposes to substitute the *use*—or application—of the sounds or marks for the dualist's mental accompaniments.

This comes out clearly in his writings, as when he says: "By application [or use] I understand *what makes the combination of sounds or marks into a language at all*" (PR, p. 85; emphasis added). And in the *Investigations* he says that "a sound is an expression only as it occurs in a particular language-game" (§261). And also: "Every sign *by itself* seems dead. *What* gives it life?—In use it is alive" (PI, §432).

Wittgenstein's idea, then, could be put like this: When we speak or write we make sounds or marks; these are not *themselves* language, but they become language when they are *used*, that is, when they are given a certain kind of role in our activities. Thus, in lectures he said:

> If a man makes Chinese noises we don't say he talks Chinese, unless he has done other things first and can do other things afterwards. . . . The rest of the behaviour and the *language* make the noise an expression of [for example] wondering whether a man has pain. (WL47, p. 55; see also p. 180)

So if a man "makes Chinese noises," then, *given these other conditions,* we can say, "He asked for directions" or "He apologized" and so on.

Like the dualist, then, Wittgenstein offers a two-part analysis, but he has replaced the dualist's occult accompaniments with something that he thinks is *not* occult, namely, the use of a word. This is a typical philosophical transaction. Wittgenstein thought that he could simply subtract those "occult" phenomena posited by dualists and then say something significant about what remains, about the indubitable residuum: the "bodily behavior" of making sounds and marks.

It is important to recognize that Wittgenstein and his opposite number—Russell, for example—are in agreement on one point. They share the assumption that speakers have bodies and are making noises. But is this assumption true? At one point Wittgenstein says: "When I talk about language (words, sentences, etc.) I must speak the language of every day" (PI, §120). But is that what he does? Is he speaking "the language of every day" when he describes two people who are conversing as "making noises at each other" and describes a person who is calculating as "making marks"? This is what we must investigate.

A Philosophical Investigation

Let us begin with "making noises." I might have occasion to say: "There are noises coming from the next apartment; I think it's voices." Here it looks as though the noises could turn out to be speaking, for might I not say later on, "What I heard through the wall was Pat and Mike arguing"? But if we are going to say with Wittgenstein that speaking, that is, arguing, lecturing, complaining, etc., involves *noises,* are the noises I heard in this case the ones we want? I don't think so. Wittgenstein says that "a criterion of people talking is that they make articulated noises." But the noises I heard in this case were muffled or blurred. Indeed, isn't that part of the reason why I said I heard noises, rather than people arguing? Come to think of it, if I were in the room with Pat and Mike as they argued, I would *not* say later on that I heard noises—not, I mean, with reference to their arguing. Rather, I would say that I heard Pat accuse Mike of such-and-such and heard Mike denounce Pat for having done so-and-so. But what about the fact that, in the original example, I say that I hear noises and then, later on, might say: "What I heard through the wall was Pat and Mike arguing" or even "Those noises I heard—that was Pat and Mike arguing"? Does this show that their arguing involved making noises? No, what I mean to say is that their arguing was the *source* of the noises I heard. Filtered through the wall, their arguing was heard as muffled, unidentifiable noises. But these are not the noises that figure in Wittgenstein's analysis of speaking.

To find noises of the sort Wittgenstein had in mind, we must find noises made by a speaker. And there are such cases. For example, Dostoevski described one of his characters as making sputtering noises with his lips whenever he spoke. *Those* are noises made by the speaker, but they, too, are not what Wittgenstein had in mind. We do not want noises a person might make *while* speaking. It is the speaking itself that we are to describe with the word "noises."

How about this case? Referring to a man who regularly disrupts city council meeting with diatribes against one thing or another, I say, "He makes a lot of *noise* but never much *sense*." Is this the use of "noise" we are looking for? No, in using the word *noise* here I am characterizing what he says and the manner in which he says it, rather than his saying it. I mean, I don't describe everyone who speaks up at council meetings as "making noise." I say it only of blustering windbags.

Somehow the word *noise* doesn't seem to be the right sort of word for what Wittgenstein had in mind. In the passage quoted above from his 1939 lectures, he says that "if you see me and Watson at the South Pole making noises at each other, everyone would say we were talking." But if we try to think of a situation we could *rightly* describe by saying that two people are "making noises at each other," we are not going to pick a case in which they are *talking*. Rather, we would have to think of something like two teenage boys trying to outdo one another by gargling louder than the other. If we were puzzled by their antics, we might say to someone, "They are making dreadful noises at each other. I can't imagine *why*."

What about the word *sounds,* then? Is that a more suitable word for Wittgenstein's purpose?

My first thought is that we typically *distinguish* making sounds from speaking. We might say of an injured or dying person, "He tried to speak but could only make a few sounds." Or suppose that I were practicing some of the sounds that give me most trouble when I speak French and that someone who overheard this asked what I was saying. I would reply that I was just making those sounds, that I wasn't saying anything. In cases such as these a person is said to make sounds, but these are not cases of speaking at all. Can we find cases that meet Wittgenstein's requirements?

Let us see if we can get at his meaning in the following way. While traveling in Africa, I come upon two people who appear to be speaking to one another in a language I am not familiar with. I notice that they make frequent clicking sounds with their tongues, and I begin to wonder whether they are actually *talking*. Could it be, I wonder, that in their culture there is a game played in this fashion and that

that's what these people are up to? So I ask my guide: "Are they talking?" When he says that they are, I ask: "What about those clicking sounds? Are they part of the language?" He says that they are.

Consider, now, a slightly different scenario, one in which I come upon the same two people but have no guide to answer my questions. Suppose that I wanted to record in my notebook what I observed. Will I do so in a way that shows Wittgenstein to have been right to say that people who are speaking to one another are making sounds?

It certainly seems so. For I might write: "Today I came upon two people who were obviously engaged in some joint activity that involved making sounds, but I couldn't make out whether they were conversing or playing a game." Since, as it happens, they were talking, doesn't this show that talking involves making sounds?

The question is this: If I made the aforementioned notation in my notebook, would my phrase "making sounds" have the meaning Wittgenstein wants? Suppose that soon after making that notation I learn that those two people were talking to one another, not playing a game. If I were to come upon them a second time and overhear them, would I still use the phrase "making sounds" to record what I observe? Of course not. I might write in my notebook, "Once again I observed X and Y talking to one another," but I would not write, "This afternoon I observed the same two people engaged in a joint activity that involved making sounds." I would not use the phrase "making sounds" to record my observation because I would no longer be uncertain about what the two people were doing, and so I wouldn't need a phrase, "making sounds," that is "neutral" between "talking" and "playing a game." What this suggests is that when I used that phrase in my notebook, I was electing a provisional manner of speaking, one that I would drop as soon as I knew what those two people were actually doing. For this reason that phrase of mine does not give us what Wittgenstein wants. For when he says that talking involves making sounds, he does not mean to be giving a merely provisional description. Rather, he wants to be able to say of someone whom he *knows* is talking, "He is making sounds." (Recall here that he is concerned with, as he puts it, a *criterion* of people talking.) It seems, then, that the provisional description in my notebook does not illustrate what Wittgenstein wanted to say about people talking.

And yet I am tempted to say: "But what I wrote in my notebook, namely, that I observed 'two men engaged in a joint activity that involved making sounds,' does not cease to be *true* when I learn that they were talking. So although I now know they were talking and wouldn't now describe them as making sounds, I *could* still repeat the description, and it would be a true description of their talking." Where does this temptation come from? I seem to be forgetting that the "description" in my notebook was not *meant* to be a description of what those two men were actually doing. I didn't *know* what they were doing. And because I didn't know what they were doing, I could just as well have written that I observed two people who "were either conversing or doing something that sounded rather like conversing." Or I might have written that "they appeared to be conversing in a language unfamiliar to me." My actual description, which contained the phrase "making sounds," comes to exactly the same as these alternatives, and what remains true, in other words, what I would not *retract* upon learning that they were talking is that they *appeared* to me to be conversing. But *that* doesn't involve the phrase "making sounds."

Perhaps, however, Wittgenstein would say that, implicitly, it does involve that phrase, that the phrase is implied by the word *conversing*. Should I accept that? If I do, I will be accepting the very idea that I wanted to investigate. I wanted to find out whether Wittgenstein was right to claim that speaking consists in part of making sounds or whether, in so claiming, he was giving a metaphysical redescription of speaking. So if I am to investigate that idea, I can't simply concede that the aforementioned claim is correct, *despite* my finding no support for it.

When might we say of someone whom we *know* to be talking that she is making sounds? We don't want a case like that of Dostoevski character, a case in which someone makes sputtering sounds as he talks. The sounds must not be *incidental* to the talking. It's the talking itself that we want to describe. Suppose, then, that I say, "She spoke with a lisp." Here I am describing the talking itself, but does that get me closer to the right kind of description? I think Wittgenstein would say that it gets me no closer, that lisping is not what a person does—at least not in the sense that making sounds is to be something a person does.

Let's try to understand this. If a person who speaks with a lisp makes a promise, saying, "I will speak to him about it today," does he thereby promise to lisp? Certainly not; he could keep his promise even if he had ceased lisping. Compare with this the following. If I make a promise, saying, "I'll speak to him about it today," do I thereby promise to make sounds? (Assume, if you like, that the only language I know has no written form.) I think Wittgenstein would have to say that I do, that because of the words "I'll speak," I *indirectly* promise to make sounds. On this view, making sounds stands to speaking as spending money stands to buying something (as contrasted with bartering for something). If you aren't bartering and don't spend money you don't make a purchase, and in the same way if you don't make sounds, you don't speak. But let us see whether these cases are really analogous.

Speaking to her stingy ex-husband, who had promised to buy his daughter some clothes, a woman might say reprovingly: "You promised to spend some money on Jill this year, but you haven't." The father responds, "That's true, but I . . ." So although he spoke of *buying clothes* and the mother now speaks of his not *spending money*, what she says is true. But is the other case analogous? If I've failed to keep my promise to speak to the neighbors about their barking dog, could someone say reprovingly, "You promised to make some sounds that you haven't made"? That would be absurd. The two cases are clearly not analogous.

Children, before they begin talking, make a variety of sounds, often in imitation of their elders. And one could easily get the idea that when children eventually begin talking they incorporate these sounds into words, so that their talking involves *making* those sounds. What is clearly right about this is that a child's making more or less random sounds lays a foundation for speech, and parents are encouraged to give their small children lots of sound stimulation, repeating vowel sounds, labial sounds ("b,b,b. . ."), fricatives ("f,f,f . . ."), and so on. These sounds, of course, are not those Wittgenstein is speaking of, for he would not want to say that, for example, fricatives become part of language by acquiring a *use*. His idea, rather, is that *combinations* of these sounds become words by acquiring a use, and it is these combinations he is referring to when he says that, in making a report, you make sounds. Let us try this out with an example.

Friends of mine have a child they call "Baba." Out of curiosity I inquire about his name, and they tell me the following. Before the child had begun talking he went about making various sounds, one of which was "baba," and the family was so charmed by this that they began calling him "Baba." So the parents say that the child at an early age made the sound "baba" and also say that this later became his nickname. Does it follow that when the child, later on, says "Baba wants a cookie," he is making that sound? And what about his mother—if she says "Baba, drink your milk," is *she* making that sound? That is certainly not how we would *describe* what she did. (We would say, "She told him to drink his milk.") The point of saying that the *child,* at the earlier stage, made the sound "baba" is precisely that the child hadn't yet begun talking. It's at that stage that it makes perfect sense to say he made this or that sound ("Today he made the S sound"). But once he's begun talking and says, "Baba wants a cookie," we would *not* say, "There! He made that sound again." At *this* stage he is no longer making sounds; he is asking for cookies, etc.

Why does it seem so obvious that speaking involves making sounds, not incidentally but as an essential part of speaking? I once answered the telephone and mistook the person calling for her sister. When she corrected me, I said, "You sound *exactly* like your sister." How could she sound like her sister if she were not making sounds?

I am not, of course, suggesting that a person, when speaking, remains *silent*. That is not the issue. But if a woman and her sister sound alike, is that owing to something that favors Wittgenstein's analysis of speaking? If they sound alike, so that one might be taken for the other, their voices will have similar qualities. How do we describe voices? They can be high-pitched, nasal, breathy, raspy, and so on. We can also speak of a person's accent: his southern drawl; her Texas twang, etc. But none of these qualities provide what Wittgenstein needs for his analysis of speaking.

It goes without saying that speaking (or talking) is an audible phenomenon. We hear (and overhear) people talking. We ask people to speak louder (so as to be heard in the back of the room) or to speak more softly (so as not to wake the baby). But the question is whether when we speak louder we do so by making louder *sounds*—or whether we simply *speak* louder. We may be tempted to say: "Only if speaking louder involved making louder sounds would it register higher on a decibel meter," but if we say this we are begging the question. (And do you want to complete that thought by saying: ". . . because the meter wouldn't register a change if one merely *spoke* louder"?) The point I've been trying to make is that it's a mistake to think that the way to speak louder is to make louder sounds.[2]

How Philosophers Hear Sounds

What have we learned? This much, at least, that we can't find the sounds Wittgenstein had in mind by noticing something that is right before us when someone speaks to us, as one can notice the person's accent or the timber of his or her voice. To find the "sounds" he had in mind, one must go through the steps he went through, beginning with the passage in which Russell subjects to methodological doubt our saying such things as "He told me that . . ." and "She said that she would . . ." Russell's treatment of the matter involves two steps. First, he gives us his analysis of these ordinary statements: they refer to a body making noises and a thought in the noise maker's mind. Second, he says that since he cannot perceive thoughts in the minds of others, some justification is needed before he can claim to know that there *are* such thoughts. So in the absence of such justification he can't know whether anyone has ever spoken to him. Aside from his own speaking, then, the only thing that's beyond doubt is that certain objects—humanoid bodies—have been making sounds and marks.[3]

Dissatisfied with this, Wittgenstein says that his method is to show the hardness of the soft, that is, to show that what Russell finds doubtful is not doubtful. He does this, in the present case, by rejecting the first step in Russell's procedure, by rejecting Russell's two-part analysis of speaking. But he does not reject it in its entirety. Rather, he retains the residuum of methodological doubt, bodies making sounds and marks, and then replaces the realist's mental accompaniments with something he believes we *can* perceive: the *use* made of the sounds and marks.

This accounts for why we could not find the sounds Wittgenstein had in mind. They can't be found by simply attending to what is right before us when we encounter a person speaking. They can be "found" only by going through the steps I have just outlined, and one can do *that* only by allowing the skeptic to dictate how "He told me that . . ." must be interpreted *if* it is to survive skeptical doubt, that is, only by accepting the residuum of methodological doubt. This is what Wittgenstein did. This is how he came to give, in behavioristic terms, a philosophical redescription of speaking and writing.

There are several additional points I want to make here very briefly.

(i) It would be a mistake to dismiss Wittgenstein's account of speaking and writing only to replace it with some other account of what it is that makes sounds and marks into speaking and writing. To do that would be to perpetuate the mistake Wittgenstein was making.

(ii) The matter we have been examining provides an illustration of what Wittgenstein had in mind when he declared that our ordinary ways of speaking "pass over in silence" the facts that are of philosophical importance (RPP, I, §78). We describe people as scolding a child or ordering a meal or giving directions. We do not, he realized, describe such episodes by saying that the people are making noises. But he thought it necessary to *interpret* such ordinary phrases as "scolding a child" and "giving directions," for only by interpreting them as he does (in terms of making—and using—noises) and not as Russell does (in terms of noises and their mental accompaniments) have we shown that these things we say ("He told me . . .") can pass muster when subjected to methodological doubt. Wittgenstein asks how we *know* that people are talking and answers that "a *criterion* of people talking is that they make articulated noises." So when he wanted to say what our criterion is, when he wanted to describe it in a philosophically edifying way, he described it in a manner that would never ordinarily occur to us. That is why

Wittgenstein says that the facts that ordinary ways of speaking "pass over in silence" contain the solution to our problem: they do so because they alone provide an interpretation of the things we say that can earn for them the skeptic's seal of approval.

(iii) Empiricists are confident that they have rid their philosophy of the "occult" entities that dualists and others accept. They are confident of this because they have allowed the skeptic to dictate what will and will not be treated as philosophically acceptable. But their confidence is misplaced. It is simply not the case that empiricists add nothing—no peculiar extra entities—to what we assuredly have. For example, Wittgenstein's "sounds" and "marks" are certainly peculiar extras. And so are such things as (Cartesian) bodies, sense-data, and Hume's constant conjunctions, all of which are happily accepted by empiricists as parts of their—supposedly bare-boned—ontology. While they may think that the residuum of methodological doubt is free of everything "occult," this only shows that they haven't looked critically at their own assumptions. In the next chapter I will discuss this matter in greater detail.

Reductionism and Inflationism

I have said that Wittgenstein very often dealt with philosophical problems by proposing reductionist solutions to them. To see that this is so, it is essential to understand what reductionism is and also what it is not. In this chapter, with the help of what is sometimes called Ramsey's maxim, I will try to shed some light on this.

Ramsey's Maxim

Frank Ramsey remarked that in the case of seemingly intractable disputes "it is a heuristic maxim that the truth lies not in one of the two disputed views but in some third possibility, which has not yet been thought of, which we can only discover by rejecting something assumed as obvious by both disputants."[1] This, as I will show, provides a useful way of looking at those philosophical problems that some philosophers have tried to solve by proposing reductionist solutions. They propose such solutions in order to avoid the peculiar entities that other philosophers have claimed to be present in the world. The problem, as they see it, is whether to embrace those peculiar entities or to replace them with something very different in a more stringent—or "reduced"—ontology. Since both alternatives have consequences that will strike some philosophers as unacceptable, this dilemma creates seemingly insoluble disputes of the sort to which Ramsey would apply his maxim.

This can be illustrated by the dispute between dualists and behaviorists. The latter propose a reductionist account of human beings as a means of avoiding the immaterial minds—and their private contents—that are introduced by mind-body dualists. But since many philosophers find a behavioristic account of human beings unacceptable, while others regard immaterial minds as relics of superstition, we are left with a seemingly intractable dispute between the contending parties.

If Ramsey's maxim can be usefully applied to such a dispute, we will have not only to find, but to reject as untrue, something that is "assumed as obvious by both disputants." This cannot be an easy thing to do. If philosophers of such divergent views agree that something is *obvious*, who is going to suspect that it isn't even *true*? In dealing with this difficulty, we will do well to begin by recalling a few points about reductionist solutions.

Types of Reductionism

When we survey the history of reductionism, we find that there have been several versions of it. Prior to Wittgenstein's *Tractatus*, reductionists formulated their views in the material mode of speech, saying, "There aren't any Xs really, but only Ys" or "Xs are a fiction" or "Xs are nothing but Ys." (For example, Hume, in opposing the Cartesian view of the mind or self, said that a person is "nothing but a collection of perceptions.") This version I will call "material mode reductionism."

Wittgenstein, because he held that philosophy must avoid the material mode of speech, rejected such formulations and in the *Tractatus* adopted a linguistic version of reductionism; he maintained that propositions about Xs are equivalent in meaning to (can be analyzed into) propositions about Ys, thus eliminating Xs as elements of reality. This version I will call "analytic reductionism."

In his later years Wittgenstein replaced this analytic version of reductionism with a third version, which I will describe in detail in later chapters. Because Wittgenstein claimed, in this version, to be supplying reminders about how certain ordinary words are actually *used*, it is often mistaken for something other than reductionism. Some have regarded it as a great philosophical advance. But this, as I will show, overlooks the fact that it shares with the other two versions of reductionism a common metaphysical point of view, which I will illustrate by means of an example.

Whereas early opponents of Cartesian dualism might have been content with saying, in the material mode, "There are no minds, really, but only bodies," the influence of the *Tractatus* led philosophers to say instead, "Propositions about 'other minds' (i.e., about the thoughts, feelings, etc. of other people) are analytically equivalent to propositions about bodies and the behavior of such bodies." In his post-*Tractatus* years Wittgenstein abandoned this analytic version of behaviorism, but he retained, as I will show, the metaphysical idea that what we see of other people are their bodies and the behavior of those bodies. He continued, that is, to think that the proper alternative to dualism is one that dispenses with Cartesian minds but retains Cartesian bodies. I want to say that it is this ontology, and *not* his earlier view of analysis, that makes Wittgenstein a reductionist. Let him be ever so observant of the things we say in speaking of other people, if he proposes to map all of this onto "bodies" and "bodily movements," he is advancing a reductionist account.

It may be objected that if Wittgenstein, in his later years, abandoned analytic reductionism, then we can't say that he remained a reductionist—as if "reductionism" is synonymous with "analytic reductionism." But this surely cannot be right, for everyone acknowledges that there were reductionists—material mode reductionists—long before philosophers thought of proposing reductive analyses of propositions. What is it, then, about those two versions that makes them both reductionist? Clearly, they are called "reductionist" because they lead to—are invoked in defense of—a particular sort of (reduced) ontology. Conceivably, then, there could be a third version of reductionism, for the only requirement is that it share with the first two versions the aim of preserving a certain (reduced) ontology. And this is what I am saying about Wittgenstein. Although in his later years he abandoned the analytic reductionism of the *Tractatus,* he retained his original ontology.[2]

Reductionism and Inflationism

Something needs to be said here about the word *reductionism.* It is typically used as a pejorative term and is therefore more likely to be used by a philosopher's opponents than as his label for his own view. Empiricists are commonly denounced as reductionists by those who think that empiricism robs us of all the important things: causality, rationality, minds, moral truths, etc. Empiricists, of course, have their own pejorative terms: *metaphysical* and *metaphysician.* Platonism, Cartesian dualism, vitalism, and the like are declared to be "metaphysical" by empiricists on the grounds that these views add unnecessary and unknowable extras (Platonic forms, immaterial minds, vital principles, etc.) to what we assuredly have. In these disputes, each party declares that the other misrepresents something, either by adding to it or by subtracting from it.

This is not a useful way of treating such issues, and I propose, for starters, that we rescue the term *metaphysics* and its cognates from the clutches of empiricists. Therefore, rather than singling out Platonism and dualism to be called "metaphysical theories," I will coin a term and call them "inflationist theories." Furthermore, I want to declare that such theories and their empiricist counterparts are *all* metaphysical theories, so that reductionists as well as inflationists can be said to hold metaphysical views.

What makes these contending views alike for my purposes is that (and this is where Ramsey's maxim comes in) they *both* misrepresent what they are meant to be about, whether it be people or my desk or whatever. The important thing to recognize here is that in the rivalry between reductionists and inflationists there is generally some shared premise that neither party thinks to question. As regards the nature of man, for example, both parties—both dualists and behaviorists—take it for granted that *at least* people have bodies and that these bodies are what we *see* of other people. Again, in disputes over the nature of physical objects both parties—say, a phenomenalist and a realist, such as Moore—share the premise that *at least* we perceive sense-impressions. It is only after some such shared premise is agreed upon that disputes break out between reductionists and inflationists—reductionists insisting that the shared premise gives, if not the whole, then at least the important part, of the truth about the entities in question (e.g., that people are nothing but bodies), while inflationists insist that the shared premise, although true, does not even begin to give the important part of the truth about the entities in question, for example, that people are not bodies but minds (or souls) that may, for a time, be related to bodies.

So the first thing to realize about disputes between reductionists and inflationists is, as I said above, that their disputes break out only after both parties have accepted—have treated as indisputable—a common assumption or premise.

The second thing to be aware of is that these disputes are generally carried on by a curious form of argument: each side defends its own position principally by attacking the other, by accusing the other of misrepresenting something.[3] Neither party considers the possibility that Ramsey's maxim may apply, that is, that *both* parties are mistaken and mistaken for the same reason, namely, because they accept the shared premise.

There is one other thing we can say about such disputes. Reductionists seem to have the easier time of it because they are content with an ontology comprised solely of those entities that their inflationist opponents readily agree to: bodies, sense-impressions, constant conjunctions, and the like. And because it is now rather widely agreed that the extra entities required by inflationist theories cannot be shown to exist, reductionist theories have come to dominate the philosophical scene.[4] Reductionists, then, seem to emerge from the old disputes as philosophers who sensibly stick to the plain, unvarnished facts. This is the pattern we find in the dispute between Berkeley and Hume over causation: they agreed that what is given in experience are "sensible qualities" and that these are, as Berkeley put it, "inert," that is, they cannot *cause* anything. Berkeley, wanting to account for the fact that the world we perceive is not entirely static, invoked a Spirit as the moving power: It is only because of that Spirit's actions, he said, that anything happens. Hume made quick work of this and maintained that if we stick to the plain, unvarnished facts (stick to Berkeley's "inert sensible qualities"), we find ourselves in a world without causation, in a world without (in Hume's deceptive phrase) "necessary connections." Hume then proceeded to assign the word *cause* an ersatz *reductionist* meaning in terms of constant conjunctions and human expectations and claimed, in addition, that in this way he was bringing the word *cause* back from its metaphysical to its everyday use.[5]

Here we see the typical pattern: an empiricist claiming to stick to what we assuredly have and rejecting unknowable and unnecessary extras.[6] But the important thing to realize is that Ramsey's maxim can be applied here: the shared premise in this case being Hume's agreement with Berkeley that the things we perceive, being sensible qualities, aren't fit to bring about changes in the world. It was only by starting from this assumption that Hume reached his view that all events are, as he put it, "entirely loose and separate," that they are "never connected."[7]

If this is typical of reductionist theories, they are very far indeed from sticking to any plain, unvarnished facts. On the contrary, reductionists are guilty of the *same* error as their inflationist cousins, the error which lies in the premises shared by the two parties—the premise, for example, that we perceive "inert sensible qualities" or that what we perceive of other people are their (Cartesian) bodies.

Rejecting Shared Premises

These shared premises are the keystones of the old metaphysical rivalries, and if they could be removed, we could avoid having to choose sides in those disputes.

Moreover, if there are good reasons (and I think there are) for rejecting these shared premises, there is no important or interesting difference between inflationist and reductionist theories, for the *only* points that deserve attention are those on which both are agreed. In other words, philosophers, instead of trying to defend or repair their reductionist or inflationist theories, should reexamine the premises they share with their opposite number, asking whether it is true that what we see of other people are (Cartesian) bodies, whether it is true that by speaking we make sounds, whether it is true that we have sense-impressions (or perceive sense-data or appearances), and so on. This is what Ramsey's maxim proposes, that "the truth lies not in one of the two disputed views but in some third possibility, which has not yet been thought of, which we can only discover by rejecting something assumed as obvious by both disputants."[8]

This is not the way Wittgenstein approached philosophical problems. Instead of challenging his own most fundamental assumptions, he set about practicing therapy on those who rejected his reductionist solutions. And although he professed that his therapy would bring "words back from their metaphysical to their everyday use," he accomplished nothing of the sort. As I will show in the chapters that follow, the most we can say is that he tried to bring words back from one metaphysical use (inflationism) to another metaphysical use (reductionism) that an empiricist might *take* to be their everyday use.[9]

This, incidentally, is where, for a good many philosophers, "ordinary language philosophy" entered the picture—as a way of staking a claim on the reductionist side. Of course, these philosophers wanted their views to sound plausible, reasonable, even conciliatory, and so they put aside the iconoclasm of earlier reductionists.[10] And they found it easy to adopt the following line: "If only you will let yourself be instructed by the ordinary use of the terms in question, you will find that their use is *not* what inflationists imagine; you will find that a review of ordinary usage reveals the *errors* in Cartesian dualism, Platonism, etc., etc." One might think that philosophers who propose to settle philosophical problems in this way would themselves have taken a close look at the actual use of words, at what people actually *say*. But under Wittgenstein's influence many of these philosophers proceeded, instead, to think and talk like empiricists—to talk about bodily movements (renamed "behavior"), sense-data (renamed "appearances"), constant conjunctions (renamed "regularities"), and the like. And they did so under the guise of clarifying ordinary language. But they gave us instead an empiricist version of "ordinary language." In this way reductionism has survived (without acknowledgment) in the writings of linguistic philosophers.[11]

To avoid a misunderstanding I should emphasize here that when I recommend applying Ramsey's maxim to philosophical disputes I am not suggesting that this is easily done. As I remarked above, since the shared assumptions on which those disputes rest have been accepted as obvious by philosophers of the most divergent views, it is going to be difficult, first, to become suspicious of these assumptions and, second, to show that they are not even true. Moreover, it would hardly be a philosophical approach to such matters to simply browse through the history of philosophy, pick out shared premises and, without due consideration, discard them. Instead, one must inquire (and this would be a *genuine* "revolution in philosophy") whether there are any good reasons for accepting those shared premises and must conduct this inquiry from a position that is as unencumbered as possible, that is, that takes for granted no philosophical baggage (see chapter 15). This means that one will have to transfer one's attention from philosophy's grand conclusions (e.g., "Time is unreal," "Nothing can be known about the external world") to the roots of philosophical thinking, and this may be difficult for some philosophers to do. Moreover, this method cannot be successfully employed by someone who has a tin ear for the language. To employ it successfully, one may need a good deal of what Oets Bouwsma used to call "ear training," so that one can hear the difference when one begins to slip unwittingly into using a word in conformity with the very philosophical idea one was hoping to critically examine. I will discuss these matters further in chapter 14.

Part II

REDUCTIONISM AND CRITERIA

The Ontological and Linguistic Aims of Reductionism

I have said that in his later years Wittgenstein replaced the analytic reductionism of the *Tractatus* with a subtler version of reductionism. In this chapter I want to explain how these two versions differ. I will also try to show how Wittgenstein's later version of reductionism might be mistaken for something else.

Reductionism, Ontology, and Ordinary Language

In the *Tractatus* Wittgenstein purged his ontology of all inflationist entities by maintaining that the only *possible* language is one that does not allow for speaking of (or thinking of) such unseen entities. (It is a language whose propositions either are, or are analyzable into, "elementary propositions," which are comprised solely of names standing for things the speaker is directly acquainted with.) In such a language one could neither ask "Do Ns exist?" nor say "No one knows whether Ns exist," where "N" is supposed to stand for something that transcends experience. Skepticism, in other words, is "nonsense" (TLP, 6.51).

We might be inclined to object to these claims on the grounds that philosophers have repeatedly used English (and German, etc.) to express philosophical doubts about various things. We might protest, then, that possible languages are not as limited as Wittgenstein claimed. This would not have impressed Wittgenstein. For he coupled his account of what any possible language must be like with the additional claim that our everyday language is constructed in such a way that someone might *appear* to have meaningfully expressed philosophical doubts. Our language, he said, does not explicitly prohibit us from putting words together in that (nonsensical) way.[1] If ours were an ideal language, there would be readily surveyable rules that show that anything we can *meaningfully* say can be analyzed into elementary propositions. English and German certainly contain such rules, but they are merely "tacit" (TLP 4.002). Once they are made explicit it will be evident that words such as *chair* and *man* are analyzable into names for items given in immediate experience, that they can be defined by names for "sensible qualities."

Wittgenstein, by making these claims was obviously dismissing inflationism (Moorean realism), which in turn enabled him to dismiss philosophical skepticism as nonsense (TLP, 6.51). But what were his grounds for these claims? Was he able to demonstrate in at least a few instances that an ordinary noun, such as "chair," can be analyzed in the prescribed manner? No. Even in the *Tractatus* he admitted (5.55) that he could not produce a single example of an elementary proposition. For that very reason, however, he had no way of demonstrating that his projected analyses could be carried out. He later said (1931) that it had been a mistake to think that he could leave "elementary propositions [to be] specified at a later date" and said that his claims about the analyzability of ordinary language had been "dogmatic." In the future, he said, he would proceed differently: instead of specifying the requirements for an ideal language that we do *not* have, he would carry out his philosophical projects "in the realm of the grammar of our ordinary language, and this grammar is already there" (WVC, p. 182–184). He did *not* say that he had changed his mind about ordinary language being a (covert) phenomenological language or that his new method would lead to different results.

Analytic Reductionism and Its Replacement

It is this change of mind that I am referring to when I say that Wittgenstein replaced the *Tractatus* version of reductionism with a new version. To see how these two versions differ, we can usefully begin with a passage from *Philosophical Grammar*, in which he repudiates his *Tractatus* conception of language and philosophical analysis:

> Formerly, I myself spoke of a 'complete analysis', and I used to believe that philosophy had to give a definitive dissection of propositions so as to set out clearly all their connections. . . . I spoke as if there were a calculus in which such a dissection would be possible. I vaguely had in mind something like the definition that Russell had given for the definite article, and I used to think that in a similar way one would be able to use visual impressions etc. to define the concept say of a sphere. . . . At the root of all this there was a false and idealized picture of the use of language . . . . [I]t is not a definition of the concept of a physical sphere that we need. (PG, pp. 211–212)

It is clear that Wittgenstein is here rejecting his earlier idea of analysis. But does this mean that he was no longer a reductionist?

To answer this, we need to understand the role of definitions in the type of reductionism he was explicitly rejecting. Consider, then, some remarks he made in a discussion of Russell's definition of number:

> A definition is a transformation-rule. It specifies how to transform a proposition into other propositions *in which the concept in question no longer occurs.*
>
> A definition reduces one concept to another or to several others, which again are reduced to others, and so on. (WVC, p. 221; emphasis added)

The analytic reductionism of the *Tractatus* proposed to reduce concepts in the manner Wittgenstein speaks of here: it proposed to *eliminate* concepts (or terms) by substituting for them a "reduced" terminology. Thus, the word *chair* would be analyzed into—and hence replaced by—words for colors and shapes. But eliminating concepts is not an end in itself. The whole point of the reduction is to show that things like chairs are not among the building blocks of reality. By embracing this sort of reductionism, then, a philosopher can eliminate from his ontology whatever is reductively defined. So we can say that analytic reductionism is eliminative in two ways: linguistically and ontologically. By means of transformation-rules that are (so it is claimed) implicit (or "tacit") in ordinary language, analytic reductionism eliminates terms, and thereby (and most importantly), it eliminates unwanted entities from a philosopher's ontology.

If we designate these as the two aims of analytic reductionism, we can say that Wittgenstein, in his post-*Tractatus* years, very explicitly abandoned its first—or linguistic—aim. But instead of abandoning the second—and most important—aim, he merely found a new way to achieve it, a new way to keep his ontology free of those unwanted entities.

A New Form of Reductionism

Wittgenstein's post-*Tractatus* position, as I will show, is that (a) analytic reductionism is misguided because (in the relevant cases) our ordinary term "X" cannot be defined by means of—cannot be *replaced* by—"Y" terms, but that (b) when the meaning of "X" is given a proper philosophical elucidation, we find that ontologically speaking there are only the Ys of reductionism and no inflationist Xs. These points require additional explanation.

As for (b), the question to ask is this: how is the meaning of a word to be given a proper philosophical elucidation, and how does such an elucidation justify a reductionist ontology? I gave a partial answer to this question in chapter 3, where I discussed Wittgenstein's substitution method. The elucidation consists of Wittgenstein's announcing, "Instead of saying *p*, you could say *q*," where the reductionist ontology is already built into *q*. I will presently discuss some of his other elucidations.

As for (a), the question to ask is this: why is it that our ordinary term "X" cannot be defined by means of—cannot be *replaced* by—"Y" terms? Wittgenstein's answer is that the words that analytic reductionism would eliminate are words that have a unique use in our language, a *use* that would be lost to us if those words were replaced by a "reduced" terminology.[2]

One of Wittgenstein's clearest explanations of this was given in a lecture in which he distinguished his new view from his earlier analytic reductionism. Referring to analytic reductionism as "idealism," he said:

> There is a mistaken conception of my view concerning the connection between meaning and verification which turns the view into idealism. This is [the view] that *a boat race = the idea of a boat race*. The mistake here is in trying to explain something in terms of something else. . . . The difficulty with these explanations

in terms of something else is that the something else may have an entirely different grammar. Consider the word "chair". If there could be no visual picture of a chair, the word would have a different meaning. That one can see a chair is essential to the meaning of the word. But a visual picture of a chair is not a chair. What would it mean to sit on the visual picture of a chair? Of course we can explain what a chair is by showing pictures of it. But that does not mean that a chair is a complex of views. The tendency is to ask "what is a chair?"; but I ask how the word "chair" is used. (WL35, pp. 29–30)[3]

What Wittgenstein speaks of here as a mistake is his earlier Tractarian view. It is the mistake, he says, of failing to realize that Xs cannot be *analytically* reduced (the sign "=" in the above passage warrants the term *analytically* here) to Ys because the word "X" has a different use or grammar from the word "Y." The difference is that it belongs to the grammar of "chair" that we speak of sitting on a chair, whereas we do not speak of sitting on a visual picture (or on a complex of views).

Here, then, we see why Wittgenstein thought that the linguistic aim of analytic reductionism is mistaken. His explanation, or an important part of it, is that there are words and phrases in our language that have a *unique* use, that is, they play a role in our lives that would go unfilled if we were to substitute for them a "reduced" terminology.[4]

This is connected with the fact that Wittgenstein, in his later years, placed his stamp of approval on certain words that reductionists have typically proposed to define away—the word *mind*, for example. These displays of approval could easily be misunderstood. They might be taken to show that Wittgenstein was rejecting the diminished ontology of reductionists and approving of a realistic ontology, like Moore's. This would be a mistake. Wittgenstein is merely saying that the words in question have a use, play a role in our activities; he is not accepting a realist ontology.

In The Blue Book, for example, he says: "'Is there then no mind, but only a body?' Answer: The word 'mind' has meaning, i.e., it has a use in our language . . ." (BB, pp. 69–70). Someone might, naively, take this to be a repudiation of behaviorism. The naive interpretation would be that Wittgenstein was repudiating the behaviorist's ontology and was saying, in Moorean fashion, that people have minds *as well as* bodies. But this was not his meaning. He meant to say only that the word *mind* has *a* use, not that it is used, as dualists think, to speak of some nonmaterial entity. This is why his sentence continues: ". . . but saying this doesn't yet say what kind of use we make of it."

A similar passage occurs in notes he made near the end of his life, where he wrote:

> Then is it misleading to speak of man's soul, or of his spirit? So little misleading that it is quite intelligible if I say "My soul is tired, not just my mind". But don't you at least say that everything that can be expressed by means of the word "soul" can also be expressed somehow by means of words for the corporeal? I do not say that. *But if it were so—what would it amount to? For the words . . . are nothing but instruments, and everything depends on their use.* (RPP, I, §586; emphasis added)

His point here is the following: the substitution, if legitimate, wouldn't amount to anything, because, for it to *be* legitimate, the "words for the corporeal" would have to be *used* in the way we presently use the words they are to replace. Why? Because a substitution won't be legitimate unless the substituted word either has or is given *the same meaning* as the word it replaces, but meaning is determined by use, that is, by the role played in our lives. So if a philosopher proposes a substitution of the sort the *Tractatus* envisioned, he will in most cases be proposing an illegitimate substitution because the *analysandum* has a use not duplicated by the *analysans*. In other words, analytic reductionism fails to recognize that words are different kinds of *instruments,* so that two expressions may not be interchangeable (without loss) as analytic reductionism supposes.[5]

Elsewhere he writes: "Am I saying something like, 'and the soul itself is merely something about the body'? No. (I am not that hard up for categories)" (RPP, II, §690). The categories he has in abundance are, of course, various *uses* of words or, if you like, language-games.[6] Thus, he could chide Rudolf Carnap, whom he no doubt thought of as an analytic reductionist, by saying: "There just are many more language-games than are dreamt of in the philosophy of Carnap and others" (RPP, I, §920). By this he meant: I can allow that a word such as *soul* has a unique use, a use that analytic reductionism would deprive us of.

At this point someone might very well wonder how the two themes in these passages can be reconciled. It is clear that Wittgenstein was approving our using a word such as *soul,* but it is also clear that he wasn't just being charitable toward "Old King Cole was a merry old soul," for he said that he understood the word *soul* in religious teachings (see note 22, this chapter). But how could he approve of our using the word *soul* while holding that it does not stand for (and is not needed for speaking of) a particular kind of (nonmaterial) thing? Conversely, if he is not approving of a realist ontology, complete with souls (or minds), how can he also claim that a word such as *soul* (or *mind*) is not *superfluous,* as analytic reduction claims?

Reality and Our Conceptual World

Part of the answer is that he made a distinction between reality and the world we talk about—the difference being that the latter, which is comprised inter alia of (so-called) minds and (so-called) tables and chairs, as well as supernatural beings and doings, has no ontological significance. Thus, in his 1931–32 lectures he said: "The world we live in is the world of sense-data; but *the world we talk about* is the world of physical objects" (WL32, p. 82; emphasis added). He meant, not that there are *two* worlds, but that the "world" of physical objects is a construct of our language—what he spoke of elsewhere as "our conceptual world" (RPP, II, §672). The world we "live in"—the world of sense-data—he also called "reality," as when he began a remark by saying: "It is clear that reality—I mean immediate experience— . . ." (PG, p. 222).

This is where we can best understand something Wittgenstein said in his 1936 lectures. Addressing the question "Which is real: the foot or the sense-datum of it?" he said: "I have never experienced the temptation to realism. I never said 'What exists is the foot', but I have been strongly tempted to idealism."[7] (As Cora

Diamond explains, "philosophical realism is taken by Wittgenstein to be tied to the idea that our language reaches to things *beyond what is given in experience* (so it contrasts with forms of empiricism, including empiricist idealism and solipsism).")[8] Wittgenstein's position, then, is that things such as feet and tables belong, not to reality, but to our conceptual world, as do God and the devil.

Wittgenstein's distinction between reality and our conceptual world had various consequences in his post-*Tractatus* thinking, some of which I will mention here.

At the time of the *Tractatus* he had not made this distinction, with the result that he then held that reality *is* the world we talk about. This meant that there could be little or no latitude between language and the essence of the world: grammar and ontology had to be congruent, on pain of our talking nonsense. But later, having introduced the distinction between reality and "the world we talk about," Wittgenstein could allow that the words *mind* and *soul* have a nonreducible use while also cleaving to behaviorism, that is, to a reductionist ontology. Minds and souls belong to our conceptual world and, like numbers, are not elements of reality.[9]

Having introduced this distinction, Wittgenstein could raise the following question: "Is there some reality lying behind the notation, which shapes its grammar?" (PI, §562). At the time of the *Tractatus* he was so committed to an affirmative answer that he could not have entertained this as a genuine question. (The logical form of the "simple objects," which make up "the substance of the world," determines logical grammar (TLP, 2.0123–2.0141).) Thus, referring to his *Tractatus* view, Wittgenstein would later say: "We have the idea that language is kept in bounds by reality, or by the connection with reality, in the way in which the motion of the planets controls the falsehood and truth of our statements about them" (WL32, p. 103). But once he abandoned the *Tractatus* view of language, he could say that "grammar is not supported in the sense that a sentence is supported by [the facts]. . . . [T]he rules of grammar are not deducible from the nature of reality" (WL32, p. 104). Or, as he also puts it, "Grammar is not accountable to any reality," so that the rules of grammar "to that extent are arbitrary" (PG, p. 184). And in the *Investigations* he says: "The rules of grammar may be called 'arbitrary,' if that is to mean that the *aim* of the grammar is nothing but that of the language" (PI, §497). But what *is* "the aim of the language"? Wittgenstein's answer comes, apparently, in his remark that "Concepts . . . are the expression of our interests" (PI, §570), which suggests that grammar is "shaped" by our interests, not forced on us by reality.[10] This is why we can have a concept like "soul," which figures in our conceptual world but has no standing in ontology.

This is connected with Wittgenstein's remark: "My attitude towards him is an attitude towards a soul. I am not [as realists think] of the *opinion* that he has a soul" (PI, p. 178). In Wittgenstein's philosophy there are no *people* as we normally understand this. Instead, there are humanoid bodies. By this I do not mean that his philosophy is littered with corpses. The bodies in question are the residuum of methodological doubt—but doubly so: people are reduced, first, to "bodies" and then to phenomenal entities, so that they are what Kohler called "perceptual bodies."[11] So we can say that in Wittgenstein's philosophy there are (phenomenal) "bodies" and Wittgenstein's *attitude* toward them. His attitude is the source of (gives rise to) those concepts we apply to human bodies but not to sticks and stones.[12]

The difference between Wittgenstein's early and later views could be described as follows: if his early view of the relation of language and reality is correct, then we are entitled to use the word *soul* only if either (a) souls exist in their own right, that is, are among the things comprising reality, or (b) there are transformation rules allowing the word *soul* to be reductively defined; whereas if his later distinction between reality and our conceptual world is warranted, then we can use the word *soul* even though neither (a) nor (b) is true, for the word can still have a role in a language-game.

With these points in mind, we can address some rather perplexing questions about Wittgenstein's later work.

Some Clarifications

(i) In The Blue Book Wittgenstein said that "it can never be our job to reduce anything to anything" (BB, p. 18). Why should we not take this as proof that he was washing his hands of reductionism altogether? We must pay attention to what he says here. What does it *mean* to reduce something to something (else)? It means that one claims that Xs are really Ys or that the term "X" can be reductively defined by (and hence *replaced* by) "Y" terms. (In the boat-race passage Wittgenstein said that it is a "mistake . . . to explain something in terms of something else" (WL35, p. 29).) This is what Wittgenstein was opposing when he rejected the *linguistic* aim of analytic reductionism. But to think that he was thereby *also* rejecting the ontological aim of reductionism is to make the mistake, discussed in chapter 5, of equating reductionism with analytic reductionism, as if there could be no other version.

(ii) Many commentators have claimed that Wittgenstein in his later years completely rejected the views set forth in the *Tractatus*. This could not be true if he continued to embrace the ontological aim of reductionism. So what are we to think: did he or did he not reject the *Tractatus* in its entirety? Anscombe reports: "Wittgenstein used to say that the *Tractatus* was not *all* wrong."[13] This is the position I have taken. I have tried to show that Wittgenstein in his later years thought that the *Tractatus* had been partly right and partly wrong: it was wrong in claiming that our ordinary concepts are amenable to reductive definitions, but (if we throw out the idea of the simplicity of objects) there was nothing wrong with its (reductionist) ontology.[14]

(iii) If Wittgenstein continued to subscribe to an important part of the *Tractatus* position, why did he not say so more explicitly? The answer, I suspect, is that he thought that he had said enough to enable another philosopher to figure this out. ("Leave to the reader anything he can do for himself" (CV, p. 77).) As Wittgenstein understood it, his post-*Tractatus* transition was from the demand for reductive definitions to the project of describing the use or grammar of philosophically troublesome words. This is a constant refrain in Wittgenstein's later writings and lectures. Here, for example, is a passage from a 1935 lecture:

There is certainly something tempting in Russell's idea of number. But the idea of defining number at all springs from a misunderstanding. We do not *need* a definition of "number" any more than of "the king [in] chess." All a definition can do is to reduce the idea to a set of indefinables. And this was not the reason for which the definition was given; it would have been unimportant to do that. The reason was the insistent question "*What is* a number?" We can get rid of the puzzlement of this question in a different way: by getting clear about the grammar of the word "number" and of the numerals. Don't ask for a definition; get clear about the grammar. By getting clear about the use of the word "number" we cease to ask the question "What is a number?" Nor do we seek for something intangible which is, for example, the number 3, as contrasted with the digit "3". To observe that *the digit "3"* is not the same as *the number 3* only means that the italicized expressions have different uses. (WL35, p. 164)

He is saying: we don't need a definition, for if we describe the *use* of the word *number,* we will stick to what is observable and not go looking, as realists do, for "something intangible."

Notice how he concluded the boat-race passage: "The tendency is to ask 'what is a chair?'; but I ask how the word 'chair' is used." His point is that by doing this—by describing the use of philosophically perplexing words—we can remove that difficulty that, formerly, we *thought* we could remove only by reductive definitions. This is his point also in The Blue Book where he says that "it can never be our job to reduce anything to anything. . . . Philosophy really *is* 'purely descriptive'" (p. 18). His point is that the task for which analytic reductionism was once thought necessary can still be accomplished—but only by describing the *use* of words. The way to get rid of the inflationist's ghostly entities is, not by defining words in terms of a "reduced" terminology (as the *Tractatus* envisioned), but by describing the use or grammar of the relevant words.

In the *Investigations* Wittgenstein makes the same point about definitions:

[T]he game with these words, their employment in the linguistic intercourse that is carried on by their means, is more involved—the role of these words in our language other—than we are tempted to think.

(This role is what we need to understand in order to resolve philosophical paradoxes. And hence definitions [i.e., reductive definitions] usually fail to resolve them.) (PI, §182)

This passage neatly captures what Wittgenstein took to be one of the most important difference between the *Tractatus* and the *Investigations*. Wittgenstein believed that anyone who followed his advice about describing the use of words would arrive at the same results as he did.

(iv) Why did he believe this? Did it not occur to him that a realist might claim that he *has* investigated the words in question and that the results of *his* investigation favor a realist, not phenomenalist, ontology?

The answer, I believe, lies in the way Wittgenstein explained to himself how a philosopher is lured into realism and how one can cast it off. He thought of realists as mistaking our conceptual world for reality, which is to say that they get their ontology wrong because they take it from our language—and more particularly, from "the misleading forms of words" in our language. Our language creates confusion because its surface grammar covers up important logical differences. Especially confusing are the nouns of our language:

> A substantive in language is used primarily for a physical body, and a verb for the movement of such a body. This is the simplest application of language, and this fact is immensely important. When we have difficulty with the grammar of our language we take certain primitive schemas and try to give them wider application than is possible. We might say that it is the whole of philosophy to realize that there is no more difficulty about time than there is about this chair. (WL35, p. 119)[15]

This idea is reflected in many things Wittgenstein said. Here is a sampling:

> This kind of mistake recurs again and again in philosophy; e.g. when we are puzzled about the nature of time, when time seems to us a *queer thing*. We are most strongly tempted to think that here are things hidden. . . . And yet nothing of the sort is the case. . . . But it is the use of the substantive 'time' which mystifies us. (BB, p. 6)
>
> Where our language suggests a body and there is none: there, as we should like to say, is a *spirit*. (PI, §36)
>
> Let us look at the grammar of ethical terms, and such terms as 'God', 'soul', 'mind'. . . . One of the chief troubles is that we take a substantive to correspond to a thing. Ordinary grammar [unlike the grammar of an ideal language] does not forbid our using a substantive *as though* it stood for a physical body. The words 'soul' and 'mind' have been used as though they stood for a thing, a gaseous thing. 'What *is* the soul?' is a misleading question. . . . What happens with the words 'God' and 'soul' is what happens with the word 'number'. Even though we give up explaining these words ostensively, by pointing, we don't give up explaining them [to ourselves] in substantival terms. (WL35, pp. 31–32)

This, then, is Wittgenstein's explanation of how philosophers become realists. And we can see why he would have thought that one can cast off realism by looking at the use of words. After all, if you look at the use of the word *five,* you can *easily* see that we do not teach the word by pointing to something that it's the name of. Nor do we point and say, "There is five; it is right next to the . . ." Moreover, this is something each one of us already *knows.* As I remarked in chapter 1 Wittgenstein rejected the idea that philosophy is a quest for *new information,* and he rejected it because he thought we *already know* everything that is of philosophical significance.

This is borne out by what he says we already know about the nature of the mind:

> The mental world in fact is liable to be imagined as gaseous, or rather, aethereal. But let me remind you here of the queer role which the gaseous and the aethereal play in philosophy,—when we perceive that a substantive is not used as what in general we should call the name of an object, and when therefore we can't help saying to ourselves that it is the name of an aethereal object. I mean, *we already know the idea of 'aethereal objects' as a subterfuge,* when we are embarrassed about the grammar of certain words, and when all we know is that they are not used as names for material objects. (BB, p. 47; emphasis added)

In other words, Wittgenstein thought that we *already* know that it is a mistake—a subterfuge—to think of the mind as some sort of entity.

More generally, Wittgenstein held that we already know that *all* the entities introduced by inflationists are a subterfuge. ("In philosophy we are always in danger of giving a mythology of the symbolism . . . : instead of simply saying *what everyone knows and must admit*" (PR, p. 65); emphasis added.) Wittgenstein's view of the matter could perhaps be described as follows. Ontology is concerned with reality, and Wittgenstein, as we have seen, equates reality with immediate experience. That being so, he would have thought: since nothing about immediate experience can be *hidden,* there is nothing of ontological significance that's unknown, nothing that a philosopher has to *discover.* According to Wittgenstein, then, "All the facts that concern us lie open before us" (BB, p. 6) or, as he says in the *Investigations,* "Everything lies open to view" (PI, §126).[16]

Answering the Unrepentant Realist

So it was Wittgenstein's position that if a realist would only look at the *use* of the words in question, he would see that their role is *not* that of signifying an element (or feature) of reality. Let us suppose, however, that some unrepentant realist were to reject Wittgenstein's reasoning on these matters. What then? Take, for example, Wittgenstein's treatment of "can't" in "An iron nail can't scratch glass." He says that we could do away with "can't" and say instead "Experience teaches that an iron nail does not scratch glass." While this might satisfy an empiricist like Hume, not all philosophers are empiricists and many would be critical of Wittgenstein's substituting the one form of words for the other. An unrepentant realist might object by saying: "If you drop the word 'can't,' you miss the whole point of saying that a nail can't scratch glass." Or the realist's objection might run: "You may say it your way if you like, but if you do you will be using an elliptical form of words, as we do when we say 'Help!'instead of 'Help me!'—so you won't have gotten rid of 'can't'; you will only have glossed over it."

The same sort of dispute could arise over the pronoun "I." Wittgenstein held that it could be omitted from sentences about the speaker's sensations, emotions, and the like. But a realist might reply that if the pronoun is dropped from such sentences, the resulting form, if it is not merely elliptical, will *not* have the same meaning (or sense) as the original English sentence. Wittgenstein was aware of the fact that realists might respond in this way, and he acknowledged this as follows:

> Now it is a confusion to persist in the idea that in omitting something from our language we have thereby mangled the other [i.e., the proposed new] language, i.e., that certain changes in our symbolism are really omissions. Thus we feel that if "I" were left out, the language which remains would be incomplete . . . as though we would thus omit pointing to something, the personality, which "I" in our present language points to. But this is not so. . . . I have tried to convince you of the opposite of Descartes' emphasis on "I." (WL35, p. 63)[17]

Here Wittgenstein acknowledges the reaction of the unrepentant realist, but what exactly is his reply?

This question requires two answers: one for the *Tractatus* period, the other for the later years. These answers, although different, are fundamentally alike: both are answers of the sort we are familiar with from the writings of earlier empiricists. Hume, for example, says that there are no ideas without impressions, meaning that if you go in search of something, such as the self (or ego) and can find no experience of it, then it's no more than a fiction. Wittgenstein's way of putting this point was, naturally, not nearly as simple, and he put it in slightly different ways in his pre- and post-*Tractatus* years.[18] Let us begin with his early views.

At the time of the *Tractatus* he thought that his reductionist view of ordinary language (that it is a phenomenalistic language in disguise) is justified by the possibility of translating it into an explicitly phenomenalistic language. He was certain, in other words, that such a translation is possible, and his reasoning, in broadest outline, ran somewhat as follows:

(a) In order for a proposition to represent, it must have in common with the fact or facts it represents a form, which is to say that what enables a proposition to represent a particular state of affairs is its logical form. (b) So if what at first *looks* to us to be a proposition should turn out not to have a "form" that is isomorphic with the form of *any* possible state of affairs, it wouldn't *be* a proposition at all, that is, it would be nonsense masquerading as language. (c) The logical form of our everyday propositions is not explicit, in other words, the transformation rules are not overtly stated anywhere, but since we manage to say all sort of things *despite* this, we can infer that those rules are merely hidden, not absent. (If they *were* absent, then we'd have not language, but gibberish.) So, from the fact that we manage to say things in ordinary language, we can infer that it is translatable into a language whose syntax directly mirrors the essence of the world. (d) The way we will know that we have arrived at the complete analysis of a proposition is that we will have got down to the sparest possible language, that is, one that contains no unnecessary signs. (e) And the way we will know that all unnecessary signs have been eliminated is that we will have reached propositions comprised of simple names, in other words, names that stand immediately for simple objects, such as colors. (f) Or conversely, we will know that we have *not* yet achieved a complete analysis if, in our chain of transformation rules, we still have one or more words for which we cannot, as it were, point and say, "This word stands for *this*." (For example, if we are analyzing the ordinary sentence "I haven't made up my mind about where to go next year," and if our first step is to drop the word *mind* by analyzing the sentence into "I haven't decided where to go next year," we will know that this proposition, which still contains the word 'I,' is not yet completely analyzed because we cannot point to something and say "The word 'I' stands for *this*.") (g) More generally, since we *can* point to something only if it is given in immediate experience, we will know that we haven't achieved a complete analysis until we have arrived at an explicitly phenomenological language. (h) So, since the things we say in our everyday language *must* be analyzable into an ideal language, and since an ideal language *must* be a phenomenological language, our everyday language is, despite its misleading grammar, a phenomenological language in disguise.

This, as I said, is what Wittgenstein initially took to be his justification for dismissing those replies that I attributed to an unrepentant realist. So the final step in this chain of reasoning should be the following:

> Therefore, it is a mistake to think, as an unrepentant realist might, that if the pronoun were dropped from "I'm dizzy," the resulting sentence would lack something essential to the sense of the original. More generally, it is a mistake to think that our ordinary language—or *any* language—could be used to refer to something that is not given in experience.

In his post-*Tractatus* years Wittgenstein abandoned part, but not all, of the foregoing justification. The part he abandoned is step (a), which says that in order for a proposition to represent, it must have a form in common with what it represents. (See PG, pp. 210–212, for his rejection of this view.) But with this step abandoned there could no longer be a justification for going on from step (c) to say that the propositions of ordinary language *must* (if we ever actually *say* anything) be translatable into a language whose syntax directly mirrors the essence of the world. So Wittgenstein abandoned the idea that the job of philosophy is to *define* the terms of ordinary language in such a way as to show that they belong to phenomenological language. He abandoned, in other words, the linguistic aim of analytic reductionism.

Although Wittgenstein, in his post-*Tractatus* years, abandoned step (a), he retained an idea found in step (d), which says that the way we will know that we have arrived at the complete analysis of a proposition is that we will have got down to the sparest possible language, that is, one that contains no unnecessary signs. In the *Tractatus* he had explained the relevant idea as follows:

> Ockham's razor is, of course, not an arbitrary rule, nor one that is justified by its success in practice: its point is that unnecessary sign-units have no reference.
> Signs that serve *one* purpose are logically equivalent, and signs that serve *none* are logically meaningless. (5.47321)

The idea, then, is that if a sign unit is unnecessary, that is, if we could without loss eliminate it, it has no reference, and therefore if the *same* purpose is served by both a proposition of ordinary language that contains a sign unit, "W," and another proposition that does not contain "W" (or a synonym of "W"), that shows that "W" in our ordinary form of words has no reference, which means that a proper ontology will include no Ws.

So when Wittgenstein, in 1929 or 1930, began wracking his brain over how, having abandoned the Tractarian idea of logical form, he could still display the essence of the world, the idea came to him that perhaps he didn't need the apparatus of his earlier view to show which sign units are unnecessary—which signs, as he later said, are "inessential" or "idle wheels in our language." And what then came to him was the idea of simply saying, in opposition to realist interpretations:

"Instead of saying that p, as we commonly do, we *could* say 'q,' from which the sign unit 'W' is eliminated." This method, he thought, achieves exactly what he had wanted to achieve with an explicitly phenomenological language:

> Each time I say that, instead of such and such a representation [in ordinary language], you could also use this other one, we take a further step towards the goal of grasping the essence of what is represented.
>
> A recognition of what is essential and what inessential in our language if it is to represent, a recognition of which parts of our language are wheels turning idly, amounts to constructing a phenomenological language. (PR, p. 51)

Notice what this method is said to achieve. It will achieve, says Wittgenstein, the very thing that was to have been achieved by constructing an explicitly phenomenological language: it will show that in speaking our everyday language we are speaking of phenomenal entities, not (as Moore thought) of entities that transcend experience. In other words, he is saying that our ordinary language is a phenomenological language *despite* its containing words such as *mind* and *chair* that cannot (he now admits) be defined away by substituting a "reduced" terminology.

So Wittgenstein, although rejecting here the linguistic aim of analytic reductionism, was retaining its ontological aim, which he now proposes to carry out by a different philosophical method.[19] And in his later years Wittgenstein continued to think that the justification for his method comes down, in the end, to an appeal to experience.[20] (See p. 35.)

This can be seen in a variety of ways. Consider once more the first-person pronoun. In *Philosophical Remarks* Wittgenstein says: "The experience of feeling pain is not that a person 'I' has something. I distinguish an intensity, a location, etc. in the pain, but not an owner" (p. 94). This is a very Humean sort of appeal to experience.

Clearly, Wittgenstein thought he had a justification for his method, for treating a "reduced" symbolism as equivalent to our present one, but the justification appeals, not to our use of words, but to metaphysics.

Consider also Wittgenstein's treatment of "can't" in "An iron nail can't scratch glass." Clearly, "can't" is one of the words that he took to be an idle wheel in our language. But what was his justification for this? Here we must bear in mind that the "idle wheels" in our language are those that fail to engage with experience. Apparently, then, Wittgenstein thought that "can't" does not engage with experience. This is borne out in something he said in lectures about a related concept, necessity. He said: "There is *no experience* of something necessarily happening" (WL35, p. 15; emphasis added). He could also have said: "There in no *experience* of something being impossible" or "Nowhere does experience show us that something *can't* happen." So in the last analysis, Wittgenstein thought that the way to tell whether some word or phrase of our language is inessential is to consider what experience, if any, corresponds to it.[21]

In a more general way Wittgenstein gives the following advice: "Ask yourself: on what occasion, for what purpose, do we say this? . . . In what scenes will [these words] be used; and what for?" (PI, §489). His thought here would seem to be that if we describe (or remind ourselves of) these *scenes,* we will realize that there are not in these scenes any of those queer entities that inflationists would have us include in our ontology.

This, I am suggesting, is what Wittgenstein would have regarded as the appropriate response to an unrepentant realist who dismisses his substitution of one form of words for another, who says that the substituted form either omits something essential to the original form or is merely an elliptical way of saying what we say with the original form of words.

There is one other element in Wittgenstein's prescription for removing the temptation to realism. He also assured us that he is not robbing us of anything we formerly had; that we may go on talking and reasoning in all the familiar ways. ("Philosophy may in no way interfere with the actual use of language. . . . It leaves everything as it is" (PI, §124).) In other words, despite his attack on realism, he is content to have us go on playing our present language-games with words such as *soul*. Thus, when he advises philosophers who have realist propensities to look at the *use* of words such as *God* and *soul*, he is saying to them something like this: I am not taking away what you *do* with these words, and so long as you can retain *that*, you shouldn't feel deprived when I show that in the normal course of our lives we never actually speak of those queer things conjured up by your inept philosophizing.

Wittgenstein stated his post-*Tractatus* position in various ways, one of which was this: "Sometimes an expression has to be withdrawn from language, in order to disinfect it,—and then it can be put back into circulation" (CV, p. 39), that is, one needn't *eliminate* the expression from the language, but one must cleanse it of its realist associations by giving it a benign interpretation.[22]

A Russellian Argument and Wittgensteinian Criteria

I have explained how Wittgenstein's post-*Tractatus* version of reductionism was implemented, in part, by his substitution method. Equally important in this regard was his concept of criteria. In chapter 8 I will explain this concept in detail. In the present chapter I want to explain why Wittgenstein invented it.

Repudiating Analytic Reductionism

In the *Investigations* we find Wittgenstein stating his opposition to the Tractarian version of reductionism in several different ways. I will begin by mentioning three of them.

First, he says: "Does it *follow* from the sense-impressions which I get that there is a chair over there?—How can a *proposition* follow from sense-impressions? Well, does it follow from the propositions which describe the sense-impressions? No" (PI, §486). This negative answer distinguishes his later from his earlier version of phenomenalism, for it means that "There is a chair over there" is not completely analyzable into propositions that describe sense-impressions, for if it *were* so analyzable, "There is a chair over there" *would* follow from the propositions that describe sense-impressions. So this passage signals *a* change from the *Tractatus* position, but it also tells us that in an important respect Wittgenstein's thinking had *not* changed, for the passage contains the phrase "the sense-impressions which I get." It not only contains this phrase but fails to treat it as the error in his earlier view that is most in need of criticism. From this, then, we can infer that Wittgenstein continued to think that we are in some way relying on sense-impressions when we say such a thing as "There's a chair over there." We are only being told here that the relation isn't an analytic one.

Second, Wittgenstein says: "It is like the relation: physical object—sense-impression. Here we have two different language-games and a complicated relation between them.—If you try to reduce their relations to a *simple* formula you go wrong" (PI, p. 180). The simple formula is that of the *Tractatus*, which says that "There's a chair" means the same as (can be analyzed into) a fixed number of sense-datum propositions. Wittgenstein now says that that *simple* formula is an error—meaning, presumably, that a less simple formula is required.

Third, Wittgenstein says that it is mistake to want "to define the concept of a material object in terms of 'what is really seen.'" He continues: "What we have rather to do is to *accept* the everyday language-game, and to note *false* accounts of the matter *as false*. The primitive language-game which children are taught needs no justification; attempts at justification need to be rejected" (p. 200).

It is important to understand why Wittgenstein brings up justification here. He does so because in the *Tractatus* his idea had been that the only way to banish skepticism regarding "the external world" is to show that a word such as *chair* is defined in terms of "what is really seen." So in the passage just quoted he is saying two things. He is saying that his earlier analytic reductionism won't work for a word such as *chair*. But in addition he is saying: abandoning analytic reductionism does not open the door to philosophical skepticism and create a *need* for justification.

This second point is important. Let us ask: why isn't the door to skepticism opened (and a need for justification created) by rejecting analytic reductionism? Such a rejection would create the need for justification if it left Wittgenstein with no alternative but to hold that things such as chairs are beyond (or behind) sense-data, which would place them in the ranks of the inflationists' unseen entities. So from his remark about there being no need for justification we can infer that Wittgenstein did not adopt that alternative.

Russell's Eliminator

There is an important reason why he did not adopt that alternative, a reason that can be found in Russell's 1914 article "The Relation of Sense-data to Physics," which Wittgenstein was very likely familiar with. In that article Russell stated the following objection to the causal theory of perception:

> But how is the correlation itself [between physical objects and sense-data] ascertained? A correlation can only be ascertained empirically by the correlated objects being constantly *found* together. But in our case, only one term of the correlation, namely, the sensible term, is ever *found*: the other term [i.e., the supposed physical cause] seems essentially incapable of being found. Therefore, it would seem, the correlation with objects . . . is itself utterly and for ever unverifiable.[1]

I will refer to this argument henceforth as "Russell's Eliminator."

This argument, which Wittgenstein was later to state as his own (see WL32, p. 81, quoted below), played a critical role in his thinking. For the argument can be generalized as an objection to *any* view that holds that we have inductive evidence for something that is "essentially incapable of being found." Stated in the terminology Wittgenstein later adopted, the generalized argument is this: one could not have a reason to treat Xs as *symptoms* of Ys unless Xs and Ys had been regularly observed to go together, which would be possible only if Xs and Ys are *both* observable phenomena. This formulation is incorporated into Wittgenstein's explanation of the term *symptom* in The Blue Book: "I call 'symptom' a phenomenon of which experience has taught us that it coincided, in some way or other, with the phenomenon which is our defining criterion" (BB, p. 25). Given this definition, there *could* not be a symptom of X if there is no criterion for X. There cannot, then, be *evidence* for the existence of anything that transcends experience. One is guilty of self-contradiction if one so much as *thinks* he has evidence of something that transcends experience. This means, for example, that it's an utter confusion to appeal to the argument from analogy for the existence of other minds.

Some Consequences of Russell's Eliminator

Russell's Eliminator, in this generalized form, had numerous consequences for Wittgenstein's philosophy. The most important of these are the following.

(i) In the *Tractatus* Wittgenstein said: "Scepticism is *not* irrefutable, but obviously nonsensical" (6.51). Why *obviously* nonsensical? Because, in light of Russell's Eliminator, skepticism is seen to be self-contradictory, which is what Wittgenstein goes on to say: "For doubt can exist only where a question exists, a question only where an answer exists" (Ibid). This comes to: "One can lack evidence of (and thus be in doubt about) something's being the case only if it's possible to *settle* the question whether it's the case. So professing to have doubts that *cannot* be settled is obvious nonsense." This was Wittgenstein's position at the time of the *Tractatus*, and this convinced him that there *must* be a way to avoid skepticism in regard to all those things realists treat as transcending experience. His solution was to embrace analytic reductionism. (If chairs and tables, for example, can be analytically reduced, in phenomenalist fashion, to what is experienced, skepticism is clearly banished, but also, if "There's a chair over there" follows *logically* from the description of certain sense-impressions, then it's a contradiction (obvious nonsense) to say that one has those sense-impressions but doesn't know if there's a chair there.) When Wittgenstein later abandoned analytic reductionism, he did not do so by applying Ramsey's maxim and challenging the very idea of sense-impressions. Consequently, he thought he was still obliged by the generalized form of Russell's Eliminator to combat skepticism by reductionism in *some* form. So he set about devising a new version, one that allowed him both to retain his phenomenalistic ontology, so that there's nothing "beyond" or "behind" sense-data, and to avoid the error (as he now saw it) of the linguistic aim of analytic reductionism, which by defining away our ordinary words neglects—and fails to accommodate—their unique uses. His new version, as we will see, relies on his notion of *criteria*.

(ii) If, as Russell's Eliminator seems to prove, there cannot be *evidence* for the existence of anything that transcends experience, then (assuming that beliefs arise from evidence) it can't be the case that anyone *believes* in anything that transcends experience. Accordingly, when Wittgenstein explained the *Tractatus* to Frank

Ramsey in 1923, he said that it is "nonsense to believe in anything not given in experience."[2] Or, as he said later, "It isn't possible to believe something for which you cannot imagine some kind of verification" (PR, p. 89). This is not, of course, because it is so *difficult* to believe in something that transcends experience; rather, a phrase of the form "X transcends experience" makes no sense. As Wittgenstein put it: "It is only apparently possible 'to transcend any possible experience'; even these words only seem to make sense, because they are arranged on the analogy of significant expressions" (Z, §260).

(iii) The previous point has an obvious bearing on what Moore and Russell held in regard to "common sense." Both of them maintained that the plain man holds a dualistic view of the world, which makes him out to be a realist. Since this saddles the plain man with beliefs in a variety of transcendent entities, Wittgenstein was obliged to dismiss this account as nonsensical. In The Blue Book, he was most explicit about this, saying that "the common-sense philosopher [i.e., Moore] . . . *n.b.* is not the common-sense man, who is as far from realism as from idealism" (BB, p. 48). This comes to: the commonsense man is not a realist in that he does not speak of things that transcend experience but is also not an idealist in that he does not doubt (or deny) the existence of tables and chairs and other people.[3]

(iv) What, then, was Wittgenstein's view of the commonsense man? As regards the "external world," Wittgenstein was in agreement with Hume, who said in the *Treatise* (I, iv, ii) that "however [dualistic] philosophers may distinguish betwixt the objects and perceptions of the senses . . . ; yet this is a distinction which is not comprehended by the generality of mankind, who as they perceive only one being, can never assent to the opinion of a double existence. . . . Those very sensations, which enter by the eye or ear, are with them the true objects; nor can they readily conceive that this pen or paper, which is immediately perceiv'd, represents another, which is different from, but resembling it."[4] The American New Realists,[5] to whom Russell gave the name "neutral monists" and whose writings Wittgenstein appears to have been familiar with, supported the Humean view of common sense by depicting the dualists' alternative as grotesque. In their 1912 manifesto they said that dualists regard it as

> necessary to infer a world of external objects resembling to a greater or less extent the effects, or ideas, which they produce in us. What we perceive is now held [by dualists] to be only a picture of what really exists. . . . The only external world is [on their theory] one that we can never experience. . . . [Yet] the world in which all our interests are centered is the world of experienced objects. Even if, *per impossibile*, we could justify the belief in a world beyond that which we could experience, it would be but a barren achievement, for such a world would contain none of the things that we see and feel. Such a so-called real world would be . . . alien to us.[6]

Wittgenstein was expressing his concurrence with this when he said that the commonsense man is not a (Moorean) realist. Echoing the neutral monist's manifesto, he said that if realists—philosophers who "ascribe reality only to things and not to our representations"—were right, then our sense-impressions would be "something accidental and inessential, while something to which I never normally give a thought should be reality" (WR, p. 276).

There is a related point to be made about the realists' view of people. Russell and Moore, as I have said, maintained that dualism is the common man's way of regarding people. This was disputed by Wolfgang Kohler, the Gestalt psychologist, who described dualists as *theorists* and criticized them as follows:

> To a theorist, who sharply distinguishes between perceptual data and facts of subjective ['inner'] experience in others, a step from the former to the latter may seem to be entirely necessary if men are to understand each other. But in common life we pay no attention to the philosophical premises which lead to this conviction. First of all, in common life we are Naive Realists. It does not occur to us to regard the things around us as mere perceptual counterparts of physical things. This also holds for the particular objects which we call other persons. As a consequence, all characteristics which things and persons owe to perceptual organization are commonly taken as characteristics of these [perceptual] things and persons as such. But we also ignore a second [philosophical] distinction: we draw no sharp dividing line between subjective phenomena in the narrower sense of the term [i.e., as being 'inner'] and such perceptual facts as constitute human bodies. . . . [W]e take it as a matter of course that directions [of attention], tensions, efforts, excitements, and so forth, of other persons appear in or on their [perceptual] bodies.
>
> This, it seems, is the reason why in the social contacts of common life the final step from perceptual facts to the mental processes of others is seldom taken. From the point of view of naive phenomenology, it need not be taken. If I refer to the calmness of a man before me, I refer to a fact which I perceive. . . . Similarly, if the man "gets excited," . . . the perceptual event *is*, or *contains*, what I call the man's excitement. I do not ask myself [as a dualist must ask] whether something that belongs to a different world accompanies the impressive display [of behavior].[7]

Although Kohler rejected traditional behaviorism on the grounds that it mistakenly holds that we directly perceive the physical bodies—rather than the perceptual bodies—of other people, he is clearly enunciating, in the above passage, a form of behaviorism. (He says, N.B., that when another person gets excited, the agitated *behavior* we observe "*is* . . . what I call the man's excitement.") Just as Wittgenstein shared Hume's view of the "external world," so he shared Kohler's (phenomenalistic) form of behaviorism.[8] He says that the *behavior* that is our criterion for another's having a toothache is what (in suitable circumstances) we *call* "his toothache." I will discuss this point in chapter 8.

(v) He not only shared the views of Hume and Kohler on these two matters but recognized that Russell's Eliminator, in its generalized form, mandates that he do so. In lectures he said as much. In regard to the "external world" he said this:

> There is a tendency to make the relation between physical objects and sense-data a contingent relation. Hence such phrases as 'caused by', 'beyond', 'outside'. But the world is not composed of sense-data and physical objects. The relation between them is one in language—a necessary relation. If there were a relation of causation, you could ask whether anyone has ever seen a physical object causing a sense datum. . . . All causal laws are learned by experience. We cannot therefore learn what is the cause of experience. If you give a scientific explanation of what happens, for instance, when you see, you are again describing an experience. (WL32, p. 81)

This passage contains Russell's original argument in condensed form, and Wittgenstein repeats it here for the purpose of demonstrating that the relation between physical objects and sense-data is a necessary, not a contingent, relation, that is, that it is a relation fixed in language. It is from the failure to realize this, says Wittgenstein, that we get such dualistic "phrases as 'caused by', 'beyond', 'outside.'"

(vi) Here is where Wittgenstein's notion of criteria comes in. In the *Investigations* he says:

> Asking whether and how a proposition can be verified is only a particular way of asking "How d'you mean?" The answer is a contribution to the grammar of the proposition. (§353)
>
> The fluctuation in grammar between criteria and symptoms makes it look as if there were nothing at all but symptoms. We say, for example: "Experience teaches that there is rain when the barometer falls, but it also teaches that there is rain when we have such-and-such sensations of wet and cold, or such-and-such visual impressions." In defence of this one says that these sense-impressions can deceive us. But here one fails to reflect that the fact that the false appearance is precisely one of rain is founded on a definition [of 'It's raining']." (§354)
>
> The point here is not that our sense-impressions can lie, but that we understand their language. (And this language like any other is founded on convention.) (§355)

Clearly, Wittgenstein is here addressing himself to philosophical skepticism regarding "the external world." The skeptic is the one who says that there is "nothing at all but symptoms" for such-and-such, which comes to saying that we can never *know* that (or whether) such-and-such. In reply to the skeptic, then, Wittgenstein is saying the following. A falling barometer is a *symptom* of rain, that is, we learn from experience that it rains when the barometer drops to a certain point, but it is a mistake to say that experience "also teaches that there is rain when we have such-and-such sensations of wet and cold, or such-and-such visual impressions," for *this* we learn, not from *experience*, but from learning the word *rain*, in other words, we learn the convention that "rain" is used to describe certain sensations of wet and cold and also certain visual impressions.

Could we say, then, that those sensations, rather than being *evidence* of rain, are what we *mean* by "rain"? At an earlier time in his life Wittgenstein would have answered in the affirmative, saying that if you have certain sensations of wet and cold and also certain visual sensation, then *necessarily* it is raining. This is what he meant to suggest when, in 1930, he introduced the following analogy to make his point. In explaining his objection to the idea that sense-data are caused by (and hence are evidence of) physical objects, Wittgenstein remarked: "You can't say that a cyclone causes this sort of weather; because to say there is a cyclone *is* to say that there is this sort of weather" (WL32, pp. 81–82). This analogy was meant to suggest the following: you cannot say that such-and-such sense-impressions are *evidence* (or symptoms or signs) of rain, because sense-impressions of *this* sort *are* the rain. But the passage I have quoted from the *Investigations* is worded very cagily. It says, not that sense-impressions of that sort *are* the rain, but only that "the false appearance is precisely one of rain [because it] is founded on a definition [of 'It's raining']." This way of stating the matter allowed

Wittgenstein room for maneuvering, for he could allow that one might have those *same* sense-impression when it was *not* raining, for instance, when a lawn sprinkler has run amok. But this caveat only meant that Wittgenstein's theory of knowledge had to allow that if one has certain sense-impressions, then those impressions *are* the rain, *unless* it turns out to be something else, such as spray from a lawn sprinkler. Thus, Wittgenstein could still say: "What is common to sense-experiences?—The answer that they acquaint us with the outer world is partly wrong and partly right. It is right inasmuch as it is supposed to point to a *logical* criterion" (RPP, I, §702).[9] We will see in the next chapter why it is also wrong.

Criteria and Wittgenstein's New Form of Reductionism

I quoted Wittgenstein above as saying that "the world is not composed of sense-data and physical objects. The relation between them is one in language—a necessary relation." We now see how, in his post-*Tractatus* years, he thought of this relation "in language": certain visual impressions are, given the right circumstances, a *criterion* of rain. But we also now see that his notion of criteria provides him with a new version of reductionism, for it achieves what I earlier called the *ontological aim* of reductionism, that is, it allowed Wittgenstein to say in the same passage: "The world is not composed of sense-data *and* physical objects."

But how does this version differ from analytic reductionism? The difference is that Wittgenstein no longer held that our language contains rules specifying both necessary and sufficient conditions for there being a chair in the corner or a tree in the yard (see PI, §80). Or as he put it in the *Investigations*: "It is only in normal cases that the use of a word is clearly prescribed; we know, are in no doubt, what to say in this or that case. The more abnormal the case, the more doubtful it becomes what we are to say" (§142). This is why, as Wittgenstein saw it, it can sometimes *look* as though it's raining although for one or another reason, not all of which reasons can be specified in advance, it is *not* raining.

In lectures, as I said above, Wittgenstein also showed how Russell's Eliminator, in its generalized form, mandates Kohler's behavioristic view of "other minds." In his 1936 lectures Wittgenstein said:

> On the one hand we are inclined to say that your behaviour is [for us] the only *clue* to whether you see or not.
>
> On the other hand [we are] inclined to say: Whether you see or not is independent of [i.e., is not *necessarily* connected with] your behaviour.
>
> I say there is a contradiction here.
>
> Suppose you say, "The eye turns yellow when the liver is out of order." This we know from the correlation of two experiences. And here the clue is [logically] independent of the sense of the proposition "the liver is out of order". But we can say it is a clue because we have the correlation of the two experiences.
>
> But in the other case we have not the two experiences to correlate. And if (a) the two are [logically] independent, and if (b) we have ex hypothesi no experience correlating them, how could we say one was a clue to the other?
>
> In the case of a new disease, "flu", we might say "having flu is simply defined by his having fever etc."—But in our [philosophical] case we say he might be blind

and behave as if he were not blind. And you might say this shows that *seeing* and *behaving* are independent.

But this does not follow. (LSD, pp. 12–13)

The point he makes here about seeing can be expanded: It is, as he puts it, "a contradiction" to hold both that (i) we cannot see or hear or in any other way perceive the mental states of other people and that (ii) we believe, on the evidence of their bodily behavior, that they have mental states like our own. In other words, he is saying that a philosopher is guilty of self-contradiction if he says: "I cannot *know* whether there are others with a mental life like my own, but I believe that there are because I take their bodily behavior to be evidence of such."
He makes the same point in the following passage:

"Of course the psychologist reports the words, the behaviour, of the subject, but surely only as signs of mental processes."—That is correct. If the words and the behaviour are, for example, learned by heart, they do not interest the psychologist. And yet the expression "as signs of mental processes" is misleading, because we are accustomed to speak of the colour of the face as a sign of fever [where the fever can be discovered directly by feeling the person's brow]. And now each bad analogy gets explained by another bad one, so that in the end only weariness releases us from these ineptitudes. (RPP, I §292)

Here again Wittgenstein is rejecting the idea that in observing another's behavior we see only "signs"—*symptoms*—that they are worried, in pain, angry, etc. What we observe—or at any rate can observe—are *criteria* for another person's being worried, etc. But there is much that remains to be explained about Wittgenstein's criteria.

Wittgenstein's Concept of Criteria

Wittgenstein's concept of a criterion is a highly specialized and rather complicated concept, one whose "grammar" is difficult to describe. Getting it correctly described, however, is extremely important for the following reason. Wittgenstein declares that philosophy must be "purely descriptive" and that what needs to be described is the use or grammar of the words that create philosophical perplexities. So we can't understand Wittgenstein unless we understand his descriptions, and these often mention criteria. It is essential, therefore, to appreciate why he introduced this concept and what he meant by it. This has particular relevance to the question of whether Wittgenstein's philosophical descriptions leave us with no ontology or with an ontology of the reductionist sort. I have already given reasons, and in this chapter I will give additional reasons, for thinking that his descriptions are designed to yield a reductionist ontology.

Defining the Concept of Criteria

I once asked Oets Bouwsma what he thought Wittgenstein meant by the word *criterion*. He said he wasn't sure but he supposed he meant something like "a particularly good sort of evidence." This interpretation is very widely accepted,[1] but it is also, as I will argue, disastrously wrong. Criteria are not to be understood as differing from symptoms by their being better—or even the best—evidence. The difference is not one of degree but of kind. A symptom is evidence of something else; a criterion is not.

There is a very definite reason why Wittgenstein's concept of criteria is highly specialized and quite complicated. It is because Wittgenstein, having failed to apply Ramsey's maxim in a way that would eliminate Cartesian bodies, still hoped to steer a course between (dualistic) realism and the analytic reductionism of the *Tractatus*. His concept of criteria was designed for this purpose, and its complexities merely reflect the problems confronting anyone who would steer this course. I will elucidate these complexities by tabulating them as rules governing the concept.

> Rule #1: If Y is a criterion for X, the "relation" of X and Y is (to use Wittgenstein's phrase) "one in language" (WL32, p. 81); it is established by a convention (BB, p. 24; PI, §355).

This is the easiest rule to discern in Wittgenstein's writings, and in consonance with it he speaks of "defining criteria" (BB, p. 25; Z, §438) and of "logical criteria" (RPP, I, §702; Z, §466 and §477). He also speaks of criteria as being "fixed" (BB, p. 55, PI, §322) or "adopted" (BB, p. 64) or "introduced" (PI, pp. 212 and 222) by us.

It should be clear from Rule #1 that a criterion cannot be anything like *evidence*, for the fact that one thing, smoke, is evidence of another, fire, is learned from experience; it isn't a matter of convention. This is why Wittgenstein distinguished criteria from symptoms (BB, pp. 24–25; PI, §§354–355; Z, §466): there are, he thought, cases in which we have grounds that are not evidential grounds. His concept of criteria was designed for describing these grounds that do not consist of evidence.[2]

Once we are clear about this first rule, certain others become obvious, rules that make criteria a suitable vehicle for avoiding realism, on the one hand, and analytic reductionism, on the other.

> Rule #2: If Y is our criterion for X, then there is *a* sense in which X and Y cannot be two distinct things.

This rule steers Wittgenstein past realism, and as we will see there is a parallel rule that steers him past analytic reductionism. The sense in which X and Y *cannot* be two distinct things is that they cannot differ as smoke and fire differ. This becomes obvious when we consider the following. If X and Y were two distinct things (or states of affairs), there is no way in which, by laying down a definition or convention, we could bring it about that when Y occurs X occurs. We can't sensibly say: "Let's make it our convention that when Y occurs, then this entirely distinct phenomenon X will occur." Whereas when we make Y our criterion for X, the convention we thereby establish is such that when, in certain circumstances, Y occurs, X necessarily occurs.[3]

We should expect, then, to find Wittgenstein insisting that where Y is our criterion for X, these are not two different things. And this is what we do find as regards both his later version of phenomenalism, wherein sense-data are our criteria for facts about material things, and his later behaviorism, wherein bodily movements are our criteria for the mental states of other people. I will discuss each of these, beginning with the way in which this rule figures in Wittgenstein's later phenomenalism.

In lectures he stated Rule #2 explicitly, saying that "to talk about the relation of object and sense-datum is nonsense. *They are not two separate things*" (WL32, p. 109; emphasis added). He also said that "there is no fact that this is a physical object over and above the qualities and judgements of sense-data about it" and went on to say that "the world is not composed of sense-data and physical objects" (WL32, p. 81). In The Blue Book Wittgenstein warns against violating Rule #2: "And now don't think that the expression 'physical object' is meant to distinguish one kind of object from another" (BB, p. 51) and a few pages later adds that "it confuses everything" to say that "a sense-datum is a different kind of object from a physical object" (p. 64). In 1938, in notes he made for his own use, Wittgenstein wrote:

> It is not a question here at all whether names of physical objects signify one thing and names of sense impressions another, as if one successively pointed to two different objects and said "I mean this object, not that one." The picture of the different objects is here used entirely wrongly.
>
> Not, the one is the name for the immediate object, the other for something else; but rather the two words are used differently. (CE, Appendix B, pp. 435–436, my translation)

This is the role of Rule #2 in Wittgenstein's phenomenalism: he was clearly intent on dismissing Moore's realist view of physical objects.

Rule #2 plays a similar role in Wittgenstein's behaviorism; it is his way of dismissing mind-body dualism. We see this when he takes issue with the following aspect of dualism. Dualists hold that if a man is angry and shows it, his anger is one thing and his display of anger is another. For dualists these are two things going on, as it were, side by side: the one is an episode in the mind and the other is a bodily phenomenon. This makes for trouble when the skeptic asks: "What would it be like if it were only in *your own* case that these parallel events occur? What if all around you there are bodies doing what yours does but without the accompanying mental episodes? How can you be sure that that's *not* what you actually observe in the 'people' around you: bodily movements *without* mental accompaniments?" The dualist, regardless of how he responds to this question, insists that in his dealings with those around him he very often *believes* that he is encountering bodily movements in tandem with a mental accompaniment, such as anger or joy or fear. The dualist also insists that when she says that her friend was furious, she *means* that her friend's (unfeigned) tirade was accompanied by a mental episode, anger.

It is in opposition to this that Wittgenstein applies Rule #2, which is to say that Wittgenstein, in declaring that the friend's tirade is our *criterion* for his being angry, is saying, in part, that his behavior and his anger are *not* two distinct things, as smoke and fire are. We find this in, for example, Wittgenstein's discussion of a child's feeling of shame. He imagines a dualist asking him: "But do you assume that [the child] has only the facial expression of shame, for instance, without the feeling of shame? Mustn't you describe the inside situation as well as the outside one?" To which Wittgenstein responds:

> But what if I said that by 'the facial expression of shame' I meant what you mean by 'the facial expression + the feeling,' unless I explicitly distinguish between genuine and simulated facial expressions? It is, I think, misleading to describe the genuine expression as a *sum* of the expression and something else. (NFL, pp. 302–303)

Here we have a formulation of Rule #2: Wittgenstein says that when a child genuinely displays shame there are not two things, a facial expression *plus* something else. Stated in terms of criteria, his point is that where such-and-such behavior is our criterion for another's mental state, the behavior and the mental state are not two distinct things, as smoke and fire are.

The passage just quoted continues in a way that brings us to a third rule, one that guides Wittgenstein, as I said above, past analytic reductionism. The passage continues: ". . . though it is just as misleading—we get the function of our expressions wrong—if we say that the genuine expression is a particular behavior and nothing besides" (ibid). The third rule, then, is the following.

> Rule #3: When Y is our criterion for X, X and Y are not the *same* thing, as my mother-in-law and my spouse's mother are, that is, "X" and "Y" are not synonymous.

How can this rule be reconciled with Rule #2? It looks as though Wittgenstein has contradicted himself. An analogy drawn from the terminology of poker will be helpful here. If there were no playing cards distinguished by suits, there could be no poker hands dealt and hence no royal flushes or straights. But a group of five cards, even if they're all of the same suit, is not a flush. A bridge player with five hearts left in his hand is not holding a flush. The discard pile in a gin rummy game is not a flush, even if it consists of five spades. But if I held those same five cards in a poker game, I would be holding a flush. This is not because something has been *added* to those five cards. We don't have to be inflationists about flushes and say that those five cards, to become a flush, must be supplemented by something mysterious, perhaps a faint corona of some sort. What distinguishes five spades from a flush is, not the addition of an extra entity, but the circumstances: the cards have been dealt to a player in a poker game.

So the analogue for Rule #3 is this: "A group of five cards of the same suit and a flush are not the same thing." And we would not be contradicting this if, on analogy with Rule #2, we said: "A flush is not a group of five cards of the same suit *plus* some extra entity." Both are true.

This enables us to see why Wittgenstein was not contradicting himself when he said that a child's feeling shame and showing it shouldn't be thought of as being either "a *sum* of the [facial] expression and something else" or "a particular behavior and nothing besides." By combining these Wittgenstein, as I said, is merely steering his way between (dualistic) realism and analytic reductionism. (He states this metaphorically: "It is just as misleading to say that there is just the surface and nothing beneath it, as that there is something below the surface and that there isn't just the surface" (NFL, p. 304).) He is saying that the child's feeling shame and showing it is to be thought of neither as dualists think of it (for they introduce something *behind* the behavior) nor as analytic behaviorists think of it (for they propose to analyze "He feels shame" in terms of behavior *alone*, i.e., without taking circumstances into account). Rule #2 is the behaviorist (or antirealist) rule, and #3 precludes the reductive elimination of concepts. So in the terminology of chapter 6, Wittgenstein uses these two rules to preserve the ontological aim, while rejecting the linguistic aim, of analytic reductionism.

We find Wittgenstein formulating—or giving expression to—these two rules in various ways. For example, Rule #2 comes out as follows: "'But aren't you saying that all that happens is that he moans, and that there is nothing behind it?' I am saying that there is nothing *behind* the moaning" (NFL, p. 302). And in the *Investigations* he endorses Rule #3 thus: "'But you will surely admit that there is a difference between pain-behaviour with pain and pain-behaviour without pain?'— Admit it? What greater difference could there be?" (PI, §304).[4] Clearly, it is essential for understanding Wittgenstein that these two passages (and others like them) be taken together. For if either one by itself were thought to tell the *whole* story, Wittgenstein could be mistaken for either a dualist or an analytic reductionist.[5]

If I am kibitzing in a poker game, my seeing that N holds a flush requires only that I see that N holds five cards of the same suit, in other words, I don't have to infer some *additional* entity that makes his cards into a flush. This is the kind of point Wittgenstein was making when, in regard to sense-data and physical objects, he said that "it confuses everything to say 'the one is a *different kind* of object from the other'" and then explained as follows what the confusion consists in:

> [T]hose who say that a sense datum is a different kind of object from a physical object misunderstand the grammar of the word "kind", just as those who say that a number is a different kind of object from a numeral. They [i.e., realists, like Moore] think they are making such a statement as "A railway train, a railway station, and a railway car are different kinds of objects", whereas their statement is analogous to "A railway train, a railway accident, and a railway law are different kinds of objects." (BB, p. 64)

He meant that realists make the mistake of treating things that are categorically different (like a railway train and a railway law) as though they were alike in being *objects* and differed only in their material properties. This, says Wittgenstein, "confuses everything."[6]

Rules #1 and #2 have a corollary, which can be stated as follows:

> Corollary: If Y is our criterion for X, then if you describe the relation of X to Y in ways that suggest that they are two distinct things, such descriptions will give rise to conceptual confusions, such as skepticism.

Let us consider what Wittgenstein regarded as some of the wrong and misleading ways of describing the relation, beginning with the mental states and sensations of other people. I have already quoted a passage in which Wittgenstein dismisses the idea that a man's pain is somehow "behind" his moaning. He makes similar criticism of other such characterizations. For example, we must not picture sensations or mental states as "inner" phenomena. "This simile of being 'inside' or 'outside' the mind is pernicious" (WL32, p. 25), said Wittgenstein. He also said, "What misleads us here [in thinking about toothache] is the notion of 'outside' plus the 'inside'" (LSD, p. 10). And in the last notes he made on this topic he wrote: "The 'inner' is a delusion" (LW, II, p. 84). This is why he places the phrase "inner process" within scare quotes when he says in the *Investigations*: "An 'inner process' stands in need of outward criteria" (§580).

Similarly in the matter of physical objects Wittgenstein objected to certain philosophically inspired descriptions. He said:

> There is a tendency to make the relation between physical objects and sense-data a contingent relation. Hence such phrases as 'caused by', 'beyond', 'outside'. But the world is not composed of sense-data and physical objects. The relation between them is one in language—a necessary relation. (WL32, p. 81)

Here Wittgenstein contrasts criterial relations with relations that might be described using a word such as *beyond* or *causes* or *behind*. He was opposing here the sort of thing Russell was saying when he wrote: "What we directly see and feel is merely 'appearance', which we believe to be a sign of some 'reality' behind." Russell continues: "But . . . have we any means of knowing whether there is any reality at all?"[7] One can imagine Wittgenstein responding: "No, if you think of the real world as something *behind* your sense-data, you must conclude that there's no possible means of knowing it exists." In chapter 7 I quoted Wittgenstein's remark that it "is partly wrong and partly right" to say that sense-experiences "acquaint us with the outer world." It is right, he says, "inasmuch as it is supposed to point to a *logical* criterion." How is it wrong? Wittgenstein doesn't say, but the phrase "outer world" is a clue to his meaning: if sense-experiences were related to, for example, rain as something inner to something outer, then sense-experiences *could not* be a logical criterion for rain.

These and similar passages confirm the corollary I am suggesting, which is that if there is a criterial relationship between X and Y, their relationship must not be described in ways that, by suggesting that it is some *other* kind of relationship, invite a variety of philosophical muddles, such as philosophical skepticism. This brings us to a fourth rule.

> Rule #4: If Y is our criterion for X, then although we *know of* X by observing Y, we do not *infer* X from Y.

Wittgenstein designed his concept of criteria for dealing with skepticism. But why did he think he needed such a concept? The answer has two parts, the important part being that he failed to see that, when faced with skepticism, one ought to apply Ramsey's maxim. He failed, that is, to realize that it's a mistake to share with realists the premise that what we perceive are sense-impressions (sense-data, appearances, or whatever) and also the premise that what we see of other people are their (Cartesian) bodies and the movements of those bodies.[8] (This, I say, is the *important* part of the answer because once Wittgenstein accepted those premises his plight was hopeless.) The second part of the answer is that the generalized form of Russell's Eliminator (see chapter 7) told him that it's a *contradiction* to say, as realists do, that we make *inferences* from things we perceive to the existence of things that we cannot perceive. But this meant that if he was to explain how, from observing bodily movements, we can know that another person is frightened or in pain, he needed a way to avoid that contradiction, and his concept of criteria was designed for precisely that purpose. But avoiding that contradiction required him to hold that if we know from a person's bodily movements that he is in pain, then the relation of the movements to the pain must be a noncontingent one. It was this noncontingent relation that the concept of criteria was meant to describe.

We can once more call upon the poker analogy for assistance. In order to see that a poker player is holding a flush, I would have to see that he holds five cards of the same suit. (If he were holding his cards so that some covered others, I couldn't see that he is holding a flush.) Moreover, I could answer the question "How did you know Jack was holding a flush?" by saying, "I caught a glimpse of his cards, and all were spades," in other words, *that* is how I knew he was holding a flush. Now clearly this is not a case of inferring the existence of one thing from the existence of another (or one state of affairs from another). It is not, I mean, like inferring that a house is on fire from seeing smoke pouring from the windows. When an inference of this sort is made, it depends on our having learned something from experience, but it wasn't by watching cards being shuffled, dealt, and played that I learned to answer "How did you know . . . ?" by saying "I caught a glimpse of his cards, and . . ." Rather, I learned to answer that way by learning the terminology of poker, including the definition "A flush is a poker hand in which all cards are of the same suit." And this, according to Wittgenstein, is how it is with sense-impressions and material things: we don't infer the latter from the former; rather, as he puts it, we understand the language of sense-impressions (PI, §355). "And this language like any other," he adds, "is founded on conventions."

If Wittgenstein is to steer between (dualistic) realism and analytic reductionism, he needs, in addition to the antirealist Rule #4, a rule that opposes the linguistic aim of analytic reductionism—one that distinguishes Wittgenstein's criteria from the "transformation rules" (see chapter 6) he had taken for granted in the *Tractatus*. Thus we have a fifth rule.

> Rule #5: If we make Y our criterion for X, we thereby establish a logical relationship, but it is not a relation of logical equivalence between sentences (or propositions) of one sort and those of another sort, although in a given circumstance there can be such a logical equivalence.[9]

At the time of the *Tractatus* Wittgenstein held that the mentalistic words of ordinary language are *defined* in terms of bodily behavior. This means that the rules governing mentalistic terms specify both necessary and sufficient conditions for their use and that therefore I cannot be in doubt whether someone is worried or in pain if I have closely observed his bodily movements. This was rejected by Wittgenstein in his post-*Tractatus* years.

So if Y is our criterion for X, this doesn't mean that it is possible to specify necessary and sufficient conditions for the occurrence of X. This opens up the following possibilities. Someone may *behave* exactly like someone in pain and yet *not* be in pain—in case he is, for example, feigning pain at an accident scene in order to defraud an insurance company. Also we might observe someone's behavior very carefully over an extended period of time and yet be unable to say what he is thinking or feeling—in case, for example, this person comes from a culture very different from our own.[10] Analytic reductionism does not allow for either of these possibilities, and that was one of Wittgenstein's reasons for abandoning that sort of reductionism. Thus, in his 1930 lectures he said:

> Behaviourism must be able to distinguish between real toothache and simulated toothache, between a man who is pretending to have toothache and a man who really has it. If I see you reading I can only say that you have certain symbols be-

fore you and do something. But I must be able to distinguish between reading and not reading. (WL32, p. 46)

Wittgenstein is saying here that behaviorism must be modified so as to avoid the absurd implication that an actor who acts the part of a man with toothache *is* in pain. To avoid this, Wittgenstein adopted the view that bodily behavior is not *by itself* a sufficient condition for a person's being in pain (or being angry or sad, etc.), for we must also take into account the *circumstances* of the behavior— whether, for example, he is faced with an unpleasant chore he can avoid by pretending to be in pain. Thus we find Wittgenstein contrasting his earlier and later views of this matter as follows: "It is not the case that every time someone screams he is in pain; rather, if he screams under certain circumstances that are difficult to describe, and acts in a way that is difficult to describe, then we say he is in pain, or is probably in pain" (LW, II, p. 29). What we say, in other words, depends on the circumstances: "Under these circumstances one *knows* that he is in pain, or that he isn't; under those, one is uncertain" (LW, II, p. 32).

Wittgenstein is again explaining his later view when he writes: "If someone behaves in such-and-such a way *under such-and-such circumstances*, we say that he is sad" (Z, §526). He also says: "I observe pain in another man if I watch his behaviour, e.g. holding his cheek and groaning *in certain circumstances*" (WL47, p. 35). I have italicized the phrases in these quotations that distinguish Wittgenstein's later view from his earlier one. But to this it must be added that Wittgenstein rejected the idea that, for example, "toothache" could be *defined* in terms of certain behavior (holding one's cheek and groaning) together with a complete list of the circumstances in which such behavior is genuine. He held that such a list could not be "completed" (see Z, §§439–441).

So what distinguishes Wittgenstein's new version of behaviorism is this: he abandoned the Tractatarian view that the words of ordinary language must be governed by rules that dictate their use for every circumstance. In the *Investigations* he states this point as follows: "It is only in normal cases that the use of a word is clearly prescribed; we know, are in no doubt, what to say in this or that case. The more abnormal the case, the more doubtful it becomes what we are to say" (§142). To illustrate this point, he invites us to consider the case in which a chair seems to disappear and reappear, and he asks whether we have rules ready for such a situation, "rules saying whether one may use the word 'chair' to include this sort of thing" (PI, §80). His implied answer, of course, is that we do not. The word *chair*, therefore, cannot be defined as he had supposed in the *Tractatus*. Analytic reductionism is ruled out. But this does not mean that Wittgenstein had become a realist and expanded his ontology to include objects of a kind he had formerly repudiated.

This same point is to apply to our mentalistic terminology as well: these words, too, are not everywhere bounded by strict rules. Thus, in a passage quoted above Wittgenstein says that in some circumstances we will—and in others we won't—know whether to say that someone is in pain. But again this does not mean that he had become a realist and expanded his ontology to accommodate objects of a kind he had formerly repudiated. Although he rejected the linguistic aim of his earlier reductionism, he remained faithful to its ontological aim.

Wittgenstein's concept of criteria is a philosophical concept, not one used in everyday life, but he intended it to be used by philosophers to *describe* various things we say in everyday life. This, of course, is what he himself frequently did, as when he said: "Now—judged by the usual criteria—the pupil has mastered the series of natural numbers" (PI, §185). This refers back to the pupil mentioned by Wittgenstein in §§143–145, and when we consult these passages we find that the "usual criteria" are that the pupil, after some instruction, "continues the series correctly, that is, as we do it" (§145). In this case, then, the criterion is that the pupil, with pencil in hand, writes certain numbers on a sheet of paper. This description does not *seem* to be carrying any philosophical baggage. And yet if we are to understand Wittgenstein, we need to realize that although he often described criteria in ordinary terms, it is essential to his view of criteria that those descriptions be *interpreted* in a particular way. The interpretation must conform to the stricture discussed in chapter 2, namely, that if we don't want to end up as solipsists, we must allow skepticism to dictate how anything we say is to be interpreted. If it's to be deemed philosophically respectable and not end up on the skeptic's discard pile, it must be interpreted in a way that permits complete verification. Thus, we arrive at a sixth rule governing Wittgenstein's concept of criteria.

Rule #6: If Y is our criterion for X, then Y must be something no skeptic would regard as unknowable.

A criterion, we should recall, is to be a phenomenon by which we can *judge* that something is so (PI, §185), a phenomenon that *tells* us that something is so (BB, p. 24). Therefore, when a philosopher cites some state of affairs as our (Wittgensteinian) criterion for something's being so, that state of affairs mustn't be something skeptics deem to be unknowable, for otherwise the skeptic could justly charge that the criteria being invoked beg the question. So for Wittgenstein nothing may count as a criterion unless it is given in (immediate) experience.[11] For example, when Wittgenstein describes another person's behavior as being our criterion for something, we are to understand that the other person is (in Kohler's phrase) a "perceptual body," a phenomenal object.[12]

It may be objected that if Wittgenstein had really intended that his concept of a criterion should be governed by Rule #6, then he would not have used ordinary words and phrases to describe the things he cites as criteria. But this ignores an important element in Wittgenstein's philosophy, namely, that he thought that in everyday life ordinary words and phrases are *regularly* used with a phenomenalistic (or behavioristic) meaning, and there is no reason to think that he regarded the words we regularly use to describe criteria as being an exception. So when Wittgenstein cites some phenomenon as our *criterion* for something, his description must be understood to be a phenomenalistic (or behavioristic, etc.) description even if he describes it in the most ordinary terms. For example, if he specifies a criterion by saying that a pupil wrote down some numbers, one must be prepared to interpret the words *pupil* and *wrote down some numbers* in a particular way—in accordance with Wittgenstein's reductionist ontology.

Although Wittgenstein typically used ordinary words and phrases to specify the criteria for something, he sometimes proceeded quite differently, and in chapter 4 we examined such a case. Wittgenstein asks, "How do we know that a phenomenon we observe when we are observing human beings is what we ought to call language?" and answers that "a criterion of people talking is that they make articulated noises," so that if we saw two people "at the South Pole making noises at each other, everyone would say [they] were talking, not making music, etc." (LFM, p. 203). Undoubtedly, Wittgenstein did not think that "making noises at each other" is an *ordinary* way of describing two people conversing, but he did think that such a phrase suited his philosophical purpose. That purpose (in the present instance) was to show that (and how) we can *know* that two people are talking, and he thought that "two people making noises at each other" is less likely to raise the skeptic's hackles than "two people telling jokes" or "two people arguing."[13]

We can get a better idea of how Wittgenstein understood this by considering a group of passages from part II of the *Investigations*. One paragraph runs:

A doctor asks: "How is he feeling?" The nurse says: "He is groaning." A report on his behaviour. But need there be any question for them whether the groaning is really genuine, is really the expression of anything? Might they not, for example, draw the conclusion "If he groans, we must give him more analgesic"—without suppressing a middle term? Isn't the point the service to which they put the description of behaviour? (PI, p. 179)

The term "criterion" does not occur in this passage, but it is clear enough that Wittgenstein intended that term to be used for describing a case such as this in the following way: "The nurse, in reporting the patient's behavior, is reporting what, in this situation, is a criterion for his being in pain."

The nurse says, "He's groaning," and Wittgenstein calls this "a report on his behaviour." Immediately preceding this paragraph we find the following lines:

Then psychology treats of behaviour, not of the mind?

What do psychologists record?—What do they observe? Isn't it the behaviour of human beings, in particular their utterances? . . .

"I noticed that he was out of humour." Is this a report about his behaviour or his state of mind? . . . Both; not side-by-side, however, but about the one *via* the other. (Ibid.)

So when, in the next paragraph (quoted above), Wittgenstein says that the nurse's remark about the patient's groaning is "a report on his behaviour," he means that her report is about his state of mind *via* his behavior—but *not* as if these were side-by-side [*nicht im Nebeneinander*]. Anscombe's English translation here is not wrong, but it is not as suggestive as would be the literal translation "not in juxtaposition" or "not as coexisting." The philosophical relevance of this is clear: Wittgenstein is excluding here just what Rule #2 excludes; he is saying that the pain and the groaning are not two distinct things, as they would be if they were, so to speak, side-by-side. The poker analogy is helpful once more, for it provides the following parallel to Wittgenstein's wording: "If I tell you that a poker player was dealt five spades, is this a report about the cards he drew or about the kind of hand he holds. Both; not side-by-side, however, but about the one *via* the other." Similarly, the man's behavior and his pain are no more two distinct and coexisting things than are a poker hand of five spades and a flush. This, then, is Wittgenstein's response to the original question, whether "psychology treats of behaviour, not of the mind." His response is to reject the question as resting on a misconception about the relation of mental states and bodily movements.[14]

What does this tell us about criteria? This much is clear: Wittgenstein is using his concept of criteria to formulate a version of behaviorism. That, in turn, tells us that, in cases like the one just discussed, the behavior Wittgenstein cites as criteria is what behaviorists mean by "behavior": it is the behavior of—or better yet, *the bodily movements* of—a Cartesian body. This is just what Rule #6 requires.

One other thing is clear. Wittgenstein, I said, meant his concept of criteria to be used for saying the following sort of thing: "The nurse, in reporting the patient's behavior is reporting a criterion for his being in pain." But this means that he thought that the nurse—and all the rest of us—employ behavioristic terminology in speaking of other people. But how can that be? A strictly behavioristic terminology would contain words that could also be used to describe something inanimate, such as a machine. It would contain words like *turn* and *move* and *stop* but not words like *write* and *flee*. It would contain words for describing sounds made by inanimate objects, such as *squeak* and *creak,* but not words like *cry out, argue,* and *groan.* So Wittgenstein can't have thought that we regularly employ a strictly behavionistic terminology in speaking of other people (See RPP, I, §78). But would he have thought that when we speak of someone groaning, for example, we are using *groan* in the same sense in which we speak of an inanimate object groaning—as when we say: "The ship's timbers groaned as it was tossed about in the heavy seas"? Perhaps he did, but when we use the word *groan* in this way, we mean "sounds resembling a groan" We are using *groan* in a figurative sense.[15] Did Wittgenstein think that words such as *groan* are used figuratively when we are speaking of other people? But a figurative use can exist only where there is a literal use. So what can Wittgenstein have thought? I will return to this presently.

Russell's Eliminator and the Concept of Criteria

Let us review Wittgenstein's reasons for wanting behavioristic criteria. The primary reason is that he wanted to combat philosophical skepticism. This desire would not *by itself* recommend behavioristic criteria, for one could satisfy it in another way, by applying Ramsey's maxim so as to renounce Cartesian bodies and restore girls and boys, women and men to their rightful place. But that's what Wittgenstein *failed* to do. And having missed that opportunity, he was faced with the generalized form of Russell's Eliminator, which obliged him to reject dualism and look for an acceptable form of behaviorism. Accordingly, his way of dealing with skepticism regarding "other minds" was to find a way to map descriptions of the mental life of others onto (the *behavior* of) their Cartesian bodies. Doing so, however, required him to regard such ordinary words as *groaning* and *complaining* as words used in speaking of Cartesian bodies. Put differently, Wittgenstein's aim was to dismiss skepticism by showing that there is nothing to be skeptical *about.* The road to skepticism begins with dualism, which then encounters the thought that there is no way of inferring the existence of another's mental life from the behavior of his (Cartesian) body. And Wittgenstein is saying: no such inference is needed, because another's mental life is *not* something over and above his bodily behavior. Consider again the following passage from Wittgenstein's notes: "'But aren't you saying that all that happens is that he moans, and that there is nothing behind it?' I am saying that there is nothing *behind* the moaning" (NFL, p. 302). Here is Wittgenstein opposing not merely the dualist but also the dualism of the skeptic.

I said above that Wittgenstein thought that the nurse—and all the rest of us— employ behavioristic terminology in speaking of other people. I also said that this idea encounters the difficulty that a strictly behavioristic terminology wouldn't contain a word such as *groan*. Wittgenstein was not unaware of this difficulty. He saw quite clearly that the language we use doesn't *look* like behavioristic language. We say, for example, "He smiled," whereas language that looked behavioristic would be something like "The corners of his mouth turned up" or "The corners of its slit turned up." And we say, "He groaned," whereas behavioristic language would be something like "A wavering, low-pitched sound came from its slit." So Wittgenstein had a problem: how can it be that we are really describing behavior when our actual wording looks as non-behavioristic as possible?

Reconciling Reductionism and Ordinary Language

The passages from the *Investigations* that I've just been discussing were originally part of a longer discussion (RPP, I, §§284–292) in which Wittgenstein takes up this question and, among other things, writes: "If you describe a painting, do you describe the arrangement of paint strokes on the canvas—and *not* what someone looking at it *sees?*" (RPP, I, §287). His point is that the way to describe a painting *is* to describe, not paint strokes, but what someone sees. And it's the same, he's suggesting, with describing behavior. The fact that we don't employ *explicitly* behavioristic language doesn't mean that we aren't describing *behavior*. Think of the following, he suggests:

> I recount: "He made a dejected impression." I am asked, "What was it that made this impression on you?" I say: "I don't know."—Can it now [in light of this admission] be said that I described his behavior? Well, can one not say I have described his face if I say "His face changed to sadness"? Even though I cannot say what spatial alterations in the face made this impression? (Ibid.)

The implied answer to the latter question is: we *can* be said to describe a face even when we can't give a description of it in spatial terms. And this, in turn, gives us his answer—an affirmative answer—to the question whether we can be said to describe another's *behavior* when we are unable to provide an explicitly behavioristic description.[16]

At the beginning of this chapter I explained that my aim was to discover whether Wittgenstein's descriptions involving his concept of criteria were meant to leave us with no ontology or were meant, instead, to leave us with a suitably reductionist ontology. Rule #6 specifies that Wittgenstein's criteria, since they must pass muster with the philosophical skeptic, were meant to leave us with a reductionist ontology. I believe that I have now shown how Wittgenstein's criteria in the case of "other minds" satisfy Rule #6, despite the fact that, in giving examples, he uses words like *groaning* rather than terms that are explicitly behavioristic.

What about criteria in those cases in which we speak, not of people, but of things? Wittgenstein says that in these cases we take sense-impressions as our criteria. We should expect, then, to find Wittgenstein treating ordinary language as a phenomenalistic language in disguise. And this is what he does: he says that in speaking of chairs and planets and hands and feet we *are* speaking of sense-impressions.

Commenting on "It looks as though my hand were moving," Wittgenstein says: "We are handicapped in ordinary language by having to describe . . . a sensation by means of terms for physical objects . . . . We have to use a roundabout description of our sensations." He adds: "This of course does not mean that ordinary language is insufficient for our special purposes, but that it is . . . sometimes misleading" (BB, pp. 52). It is misleading, he means, because the word *hand* and hundreds of others like it appear to be something other than what they actually are, namely, roundabout descriptions of our sensations (i.e., sense-impressions). In notes that he made for his own use in 1938 we find him saying: "[Y]ou can say that I speak of sense impressions. Only realize that talk about sense impressions does not look the way you imagine. . . . I speak 'of sense impressions' by speaking of physical objects" (CE, Appendix B, pp. 435–437; my translation). He means that in speaking of a tree that one sees, one *is* speaking (in the only way one *can*) of sense-impressions. A decade later he was still insisting on this, saying: "We learn to describe objects, and thereby, in another sense, our sensations" (RPP, I, §1082). This comes to: although we use such (philosophically misleading) words as *hand* and *tree,* when we do so we are speaking (in a roundabout way) of our sensations. "Certainly it's clear," he says, "that the description of impressions has the form of the description of '*external*' objects" (RPP, I, §1092). Plainly, then, Wittgenstein held that ordinary language is a phenomenalistic language in disguise, and when he tells us that sense-impressions serve as our criteria for such a thing as there being a chair over there, his aim, once again, is to preserve his reductionist ontology.

Here again, then, we can say that Wittgenstein's criteria, although not described in an *explicitly* reductionist terminology, satisfy Rule #6: they are nothing that a skeptic would regard as unknowable.

The Linkage of Verification and Interpretation

One other rule is worth noting, a rule that helps to clarify what Wittgenstein hoped to achieve with his concept of criteria.

Rule #7: If we make Y our criterion for X, we thereby determine the meaning of "X"—or to put the matter slightly differently, a criterion for the truth of a proposition determines the sense of that proposition, so that a philosopher can discover *what proposition it is* by taking note of the criterion for its truth.

The first of these two, slightly different, formulations is supported by a passage in The Blue Book: "[T]o explain my criterion for another person's having toothache is to give a grammatical explanation about the word 'toothache' and, in this sense, an explanation concerning the meaning of the word 'toothache'" (p. 24). The second formulation is supported by many things Wittgenstein said—for example, "Asking . . . how a proposition can be verified is only a particular way of asking 'How d'you mean?'" (PI, §353). In lectures he said: "How far is giving the verification of a proposition a grammatical statement about it? So far as it is [such a statement], it can explain the meaning of its terms. Insofar as [that which verifies a given proposition] is a matter of experience, as when one names a symptom, the meaning is not explained" (WL35, p. 31). This shows us an important difference between symptoms and criteria: only the latter, which are not "a matter of experience," explain the meaning of a proposition (or its terms).

Wittgenstein also spoke of criteria as grounds "which are grammatically related to a proposition, and tell us *what proposition it is*" (Z, §437, emphasis added). Let us ask: why would we need something to tell us "what proposition it is" or what its meaning is? The answer comes in Wittgenstein's remark that "when we do philosophy, we are like savages, primitive people, who hear the expressions of civilized men, put a false interpretations on them, and then draw the queerest conclusions from it" (PI, §194). He means that, for example, realists put a false interpretation on the things we say about the mental states of other people, and then conclude that another man's toothache is something behind his moaning and that he moans *because of* his toothache. So what philosophers need is something to show them the *right* philosophical interpretation of various propositions. This is the point I discussed in chapter 2, where I pointed out that for Wittgenstein there is an essential linkage of verification and interpretation.

We can now say why criteria are of special relevance here. Wittgenstein believed (i) that his concept of criteria is useful for giving philosophically illuminating *descriptions* of certain things we commonly say, (ii) that once we see them described in terms of criteria we will realize that Rules #1 through #6 apply to these things we say, and (iii) that when we realize that those rules apply we will abandon our old (realist) interpretation of the words and phrases of ordinary language and accept an entirely different interpretation. This three-part answer is what Rule #7 comes to.[17]

This should remind us of the account Wittgenstein gave, in *Philosophical Remarks,* of his new philosophical method. Although his new method no longer involves the construction of an *explicitly* phenomenological language, it is a method, he tells us, that "amounts to constructing a phenomenological language" because this method gives us "an immediate representation of immediate experience" regardless of "what idiom it may be written or expressed in" (PR, p. 51). It is a method, he means, by which he will demonstrate that our ordinary language is a phenomenological language in disguise. One of the ways he undertook to demonstrate this was to use his concept of criteria for "describing" various things we say, thereby imposing on what we say the reductionist Rules #1 through #6.

At the front of this book I used as a motto Wittgenstein's remark about the need for philosophy to be complicated. But someone may think that I have now made it *too* complicated, that Wittgenstein *couldn't* have meant by "criterion" anything so complicated as my rules make it out to be. "How in the world," she may protest, "could Wittgenstein have expected a reader of the *Investigations* to gather his meaning from the little he says there about criteria?" Such a protest assumes, however, that Wittgenstein wanted to reach a large audience. I do not think he did. He spoke of his book as being "meant for only a small circle of people" (CV, p. 10) and also said that "if a book has been written for just a few readers that will be clear just from the fact that only a few people understand it. The book must automatically separate those who understand it from those who do not" (CV, p. 7).[18] Wittgenstein made it clear that he did not expect the *Investigations* to be widely understood: "It is not likely," he said, that this book will "bring light into one brain or another" (p. x).[19]

As for his concept of criteria, I suspect that he thought it pointless to give a systematic account of it because it would be understood, anyway, only by those who, by seeing what is needed, could invent the concept, in all its complexity, for themselves. But he evidently thought that few, if any, of his students were capable of this, and he said as much. He concluded his 1939 lectures with the remark: "The seed I'm most likely to sow is a certain jargon" (LFM, p. 293).

What Criteria Cannot Be

In chapter 3 I pointed out that one of the ways in which Wittgenstein has been misunderstood is the naive way in which philosophers have understood his claim that his method is "purely descriptive" (BB, pp. 18 and 125) and that philosophy "can only describe" the use of words (PI, §124). The mistake was to think that Wittgenstein aimed at giving descriptions that had no metaphysical ideas or assumptions built into them. This mistake extends to Wittgenstein's concept of criteria: it is generally taken to be a genuinely *descriptive* term, one that carries no metaphysical baggage. This misconception about Wittgenstein has, I believe, caused more mischief than any other.

The Fluctuation of Symptoms and Criteria

The first misconception I want to discuss arises from the fact that Wittgenstein several times spoke of a fluctuation of symptoms and criteria. What do the rules tabulated in chapter 8 tell us about this? Rule #2 states that if Y is our criterion for X, then X and Y are not two distinct things. From this it follows that if at one time Y were our criterion for X and at another time Z were our criterion for X, then at these different times X was first one thing and then something else. This may be obscured by the fact that Wittgenstein says (BB, p. 25) that doctors, at different times, have taken first one thing and then another as their criterion for angina. It would be natural, I think, to interpret this in the following way: the medical profession was investigating a given disease called "angina," and initially, before they knew much about it, they said that someone had angina if they had a severe inflammation of the throat, but eventually researchers learned enough to declare that someone has angina if they had a certain bacillus in their blood, at which point the initial criterion, inflammation of the throat, was relegated to the status of a symptom. We may, that is, understand in this way what Wittgenstein meant when he spoke of a *fluctuation* of symptoms and criteria. And if we do take him to be saying something like this, we will take him to be saying that there may, at different times, be different criteria for *one and the same thing*. There are decisive reasons, however, for thinking that this is not what Wittgenstein meant.

One reason is the fact that he distinguishes criteria from symptoms by saying that the former but not the latter give us the *meaning* of a word or phrase, which is to say that changing the criterion would entail a change of meaning, so that upon the adoption of a *new* criterion, "angina" will no longer *mean* what it used to mean.[1] Because of this view, he said: "Then [once the new criterion has been adopted] to say 'A man has angina if this bacillus is found in him' is a tautology or it is a loose way of stating the definition of 'angina'" (BB, pp. 24–25). This clearly implies that if the criterion were to "fluctuate" again, Wittgenstein would then offer a *new* tautology (or a *new* definition of "angina"). And this, in turn, implies that if there is a change of criteria, these *cannot* be different criteria for one and the same thing. So while we may retain *angina* (as a *word)* through several fluctuations of criteria, what we are talking *about* won't remain constant.

It may be thought that I am making too much of this point or that I am trading on a piece of careless wording by Wittgenstein. But to take that attitude is to miss the whole point of his introducing the term *criterion*. And his wording is so far from being careless that he elsewhere makes this idea entirely explicit: "Nothing is commoner than for the meaning [*die Bedeutung*] of an expression to oscillate, for a phenomenon to be regarded sometimes as a symptom, sometimes as a criterion, of a state of affairs" (Z, §438). In other words, the meaning of an expression will "oscillate"—not remain constant—when first one thing and then another is taken as a criterion.[2]

Unquestionably, then, Wittgenstein did not think that angina is some state or condition that remained constant throughout the various developments in medical research. Someone who thinks otherwise will be making the mistake I mentioned above—the mistake of thinking that Wittgenstein's concept of a criterion is a genuinely *descriptive* term, that it, like the words *imperative* and *interrogative* was introduced in order to describe something that a person could notice in our language. Someone who tries to think about Wittgenstein in this way will miss his entire *point* of his introducing the term *criterion*. He designed it precisely to meet his metaphysical requirements. It has no other rationale.

Albritton's Account of Criteria

A second thing we can deduce from the rules of chapter 8 is that if Y is the criterion for X, then Y is (in appropriate circumstances) what we *call* "X" or what we describe as "X," just as five spades (when dealt to a poker player) is what we *call* "a flush." (Instructor: "If you were holding these five cards, you would be holding what we call 'a flush.'") This cannot be said of evidence: smoke, while it may be evidence of a fire, is not what we *call*, or describe as, "fire." Rogers Albritton has pointed out that in The Blue Book and The Brown Book Wittgenstein often says or implies (and in the *Investigations* occasionally says or implies) that the phenomenon that is our criterion of X is itself the very thing we *call* "X," which means that the behavior which is our criterion for a man's having toothache is what we *call* "toothache."[3] (This, as we saw in chapter 8, was Kohler's view. He says that when another person gets excited, the agitated *behavior* we observe "*is* . . . what I call the man's excitement.") That Wittgenstein says or implies this is a striking fact, for it shows that he was engaged in a reductionist enterprise, that he was endorsing some sort of behaviorism. But Albritton fails to take this lesson from the numerous passages he cites. Instead, he does two other things. First, he chides Wittgenstein as follows: "But can what a man does or says be called his having a toothache, or referred to or described as that . . . under any circumstances, in a proper and literal sense of the words? No."[4] The second thing Albritton does is to say that Wittgenstein *distorts* what is properly his conception of criteria by implying that the phenomenon that is a criterion for X is *itself* what is called "X."[5] Wittgenstein, in Albritton's view, must have had in the back of his mind some other, more sensible, conception of criteria, for surely he *couldn't* have wanted to say that his neighbor's toothache just *is* his behavior (or: his behavior in these circumstances)! Such outright behaviorism, Albritton thought, is simply too absurd a view for Wittgenstein to have taken seriously.[6] And yet Albritton himself has pointed out a great many passages in which Wittgenstein says or implies the very thing that—allegedly—he couldn't have wanted to say. Let us see, then, whether Albritton presents us with a more reasonable interpretation of Wittgenstein.

Albritton is confident in specifying what Wittgenstein's proper conception of a criterion is. When Wittgenstein introduced that concept, says Albritton, his reason for doing so was the following: "A criterion for so-and-so's being the case was to be something by which one might *know* that it was the case," and moreover it is always a matter of convention that one thing is a criterion for another.[7] This much of what Albritton says is certainly correct, but what he says next is certainly not. He writes:

> What Wittgenstein calls a "criterion" of having a toothache is a phenomenon by which, under certain circumstances, one would be justified in saying that a man had a toothache or in saying, should one have occasion to do so, that one knew he had a toothache. . . .
>   . . . Suppose that a man sits rocking miserably back and forth, holding his jaw, every now and then cautiously pushing on a loose tooth on that side with certain kinds of grimaces and sharp intakes of breath, and so on, in my presence. Under a variety of circumstances I would not be justified by this behavior in saying that the man had a toothache. . . . As it happens, such circumstances are exceptional. A man who behaves in this manner, under normal circumstances, always or almost always does have a toothache. That is, a man who behaves in this manner, under circumstances that have no tendency to show that he is *not* so behaving because he has a toothache, always or almost always *is* so behaving because he has a toothache.[8]

Moreover, it is *this*, says Albritton, that Wittgenstein deems to be a *necessary* truth.[9] What should we think of this interpretation?

The first thing we can say is that it involves the following absurdity. On Albritton's interpretation a man's toothache and the phenomenon that is our criterion for his having a toothache are, considered in themselves, two distinct phenomena or states of affairs—no less so than they would be if the phenomenon that is the criterion were, instead, merely a symptom, that is, if it were, say, a reddish spot on a person's cheek. But how could it be a matter of logic, a convention, that if one thing occurs something else—some *other* state of affairs—occurs? Plainly, it couldn't. We can't sensibly say: "Let's make it our convention that when Y occurs, then this entirely distinct phenomenon X will occur." For this reason alone I would say that Albritton's interpretation cannot be right.10

But this is not his most serious error. I said above that Albritton is certainly right in saying that for Wittgenstein a criterion for so-and-so's being the case was to be something by which one might *know* that it was the case. But in order to make proper use of this obvious point, we need to answer two questions: (i) why would Wittgenstein be concerned with our knowing or not knowing that so-and-so is the case? and (ii) what particular hurdles did he think his philosophizing had to get us over if knowing something was to be possible?

Criteria and Skepticism

The first question is easy to answer: Wittgenstein wanted to find a reply to philosophical skepticism. The second question is less easily answered, but we can begin by taking note of something in Albritton's account of what is involved in knowing that another person has a toothache. He begins his account as follows: "Suppose that a man sits rocking miserably back and forth, holding his jaw, every now and then cautiously pushing on a loose tooth on that side with certain kinds of grimaces and sharp intakes of breath, and so on, in my presence." Let us ask: if one were concerned, as Wittgenstein was, to respond to the philosophical skeptic— and in particular, the skeptic within one's own breast,11 could one think that an *appropriate* response could begin in that manner? I am referring to the adverbs "miserably" and "cautiously" and to the verbs they modify: "rocking back and forth" and "pushing." I am also referring to the subject of those verbs, "a man." If we are wearing our skeptic's hat, are we going to accept all of this as a given? Of course not! One couldn't even be tempted by skepticism if one saw no problem in starting out with a description such as Albritton gives. The problem of other minds, after all, is not a problem about how we know that *this* man has a toothache or is angry. The problem is not about what we can know about other sentient beings, as if their existence were a given. It is about whether we can know whether there *are* other sentient beings. What creates the problem is the idea that even if there are other sentient humans, all that we can perceive of them are (Cartesian) bodies that move about in certain ways and make a variety of sounds. So if one has not, by invoking Ramsey's maxim, challenged *that* idea and yet hopes to overcome skepticism, one is faced with having to figure out how one could *start* with bodies and their movements and yet *come to know* that these are humans with various mental states.

Clearly, then, if we have failed to invoke Ramsey's maxim and yet begin our response to skepticism as Albritton does, with a *man* who is rocking *miserably* back and forth, the skeptic within us should leap up in protest, for to begin in *that* way is clearly question begging. It assumes the very thing that the skeptic finds questionable: that here we have a sentient being—and a miserable one at that![12] So, on Albritton's interpretation Wittgenstein must be convicted of begging the question. And yet this is the very thing Wittgenstein was most critical of in other philosophers:

> [P]hilosophers should not attempt to present the idealistic or solipsistic positions, for example, as absurd. . . . You must not try to avoid a philosophical problem by appealing to common sense; instead, present it as it arises with most power. You must allow yourself to be dragged into the mire, and get out of it. . . . One must not in philosophy attempt to short-circuit problems. (WL35, pp. 108–109)

He seems to have thought that philosophers influenced by Moore "short-circuit problems," and it seems to me entirely unlikely that, as Albritton's interpretation would have it, Wittgenstein was himself guilty of this.

How, then, would Wittgenstein have us proceed so as to "present [the problem] as it arises with most power"? Having failed to invoke Ramsey's maxim, he would have us begin with bodies and their movements. Next would come the thought that skepticism about other minds arises from an assumption about the very nature of the mental, that *if* there are other sentient beings, their mental states are something very different from bodily states or movements, so that in observing something about their bodies, we are still far from knowing anything about their minds.

That being so, Wittgenstein was left with three options: (i) surrender to skepticism, (ii) embrace some form of the argument from analogy, or (iii) challenge the skeptic's assumption regarding the nature of the mental. (I say that he was confined to these three options because he had overlooked the fourth, Ramsey's maxim.) We know that Wittgenstein did not surrender to skepticism. We also know (see chapter 7) that, on account of the generalized form of Russell's Eliminator, Wittgenstein thought that the argument from analogy is self-contradictory. We can infer, therefore, that he chose the third alternative, to challenge the skeptic's assumption about the nature of the mental. To do this, he would have to show that another person's toothache, for example, is *not* related to his behavior as something inner is related (e.g., causally) to something outer. (See the Corollary to Rules #1 and #2 in chapter 8.) Moreover, he would have to do this without short-circuiting the problem, that is, without losing sight of the fact that the *behavior* in question is that of a (Cartesian) body. So the task for which Wittgenstein designed his concept of criteria was that of showing how we can rightly speak of these "bodies" using words such as *toothache* and *fear*. One thing this concept could *not* do—and mustn't be *thought* to do, on pain of fudging the entire issue—is to convert Cartesian bodies into something capable of inner states. (Hence Wittgenstein's use of inverted commas in his remark: "An 'inner process' stands in need of outward criteria" (PI, §580).) Wittgenstein's criteria cannot give us something new, something that's not already there in a Cartesian body and its movements. Albritton, I believe, lost sight of this; Wittgenstein, I feel sure, did not.

In Search of the Real Wittgenstein

Wolfe Mays, who attended Wittgenstein's lectures during the early 1940s, reports the following:

> In his lectures Wittgenstein made valiant efforts . . . to show that psychological data could be externalized. He talked a good deal about the criteria for deciding whether a person was in pain or not. Suppose, he said, so and so was on the operating table and surgeons were sticking knives into him; if he showed no signs of reacting, could he therefore be said to be in pain or was he shamming? In these examples Wittgenstein sometimes tended to regard other people as if they were inanimate objects or automata, as when he said, "Suppose I cut off Mr. X's arm thus," at the same time striking his own left arm with the edge of his right hand. I sometimes felt that this way of looking at other people covered something more than a philosophical position. It is, of course, possible that Wittgenstein's engineering background made him attempt to externalize psychological states and also to look upon people as automata.[13]

What Mays seems not to have realized is that Wittgenstein's philosophical views obliged him to think of others—not, indeed, as automata—but as Cartesian bodies.[14]

I said above that Wittgenstein has been misunderstood partly because it has been assumed that when he spoke of philosophy being purely descriptive, he harbored no empiricist preconceptions about what constitutes a description. One of the ways this misunderstanding is manifested is in the assumption that his concept of a criterion carries no metaphysical baggage, that it was designed for describing something we can find by taking an unbiased look at what people actually say. This assumption often slips in unnoticed when commentators say that Wittgenstein's method is descriptive, for they fail to point out that Wittgenstein would accept as *suitable* descriptions only those of a very specialized sort. As I demonstrated in chapter 3, the descriptions Wittgenstein regarded as suitable are designed to leave us with an ontology of reductionist proportions. For this reason it is a mistake to think that Wittgenstein's philosophical method consists of giving descriptions like Albritton's—unphilosophical descriptions—of the use of philosophically perplexing words. Such a method would be not only question begging but most un-Wittgensteinian. Why is it, then, that Wittgenstein is so often misunderstood on this critical point?

The answer is that Wittgenstein came to be associated in the minds of many philosophers with G. E. Moore. It has been widely assumed that Wittgenstein's method is an extension or development of the style of philosophy that Moore had practiced for many years—or rather the sort of philosophy that some *thought* Moore had practiced. This admixture of Wittgenstein and the pseudo- Moore has been disastrous not only for our understanding of Moore and Wittgenstein but also for our understanding of philosophy itself. In the remaining chapters I will try to explain how this misunderstanding came about and how it might be undone.

Part III

PHILOSOPHY AND LANGUAGE

Standard Ordinary Language Philosophy

Wittgenstein is, without doubt, a very difficult philosopher, and those who have tried to understand him have gone about this in various ways. Some have picked out a few passages whose meaning seemed unproblematic and used them as a Rosetta stone for deciphering Wittgenstein's more obscure remarks. (A favorite seems to be the passage about bringing words back from their metaphysical to their everyday use, as though there could be no doubt about which uses Wittgenstein took to be metaphysical and which not.) Others have tried to locate Wittgenstein's philosophical position by employing a triangulation procedure, using as their coordinates G. E. Moore, common sense, and ordinary language.

Moore, Common Sense, and Ordinary Language

Although Wittgenstein said many things that should have discouraged this triangulation procedure, it has been—and still is—widely employed. For example, Hans Sluga, in his introduction to *The Cambridge Companion to Wittgenstein,* published just last year, tells us that in his post-*Tractatus* years Wittgenstein

> concerned himself mainly with the actual working of ordinary language. This brought him close to the tradition of British common-sense philosophy that G. E. Moore had revived. Wittgenstein thus became one of the godfathers of the ordinary language philosophy that was to flourish in England and particularly in Oxford in the 1950s.[1]

Years earlier G. A. Paul, one of Wittgenstein's students, began a piece on Wittgenstein by saying: "He follows Moore in the defence of Common Sense and in a regard for our ordinary language."[2] Gilbert Ryle, who also attended Wittgenstein's lectures, wrote:

> Like Moore, he explores the logic of all the things all of us say. . . . What had, since the early days of this century been the practice of G. E. Moore has received a

rationale from Wittgenstein; and I expect that when the curtain is lifted we shall also find that Wittgenstein's concrete methods have increased the power, scope and delicacy of the methods by which Moore has for so long explored in detail the internal logic of what we say."[3]

Alan White, in his excellent book on Moore, wrote: "Although Wittgenstein never acknowledged any debt to Moore, . . . it seems to me that the change in his views [after 1929] is in a Moorean direction, though it goes much beyond." He explains that Wittgenstein's view "that the meaning of an expression is to be found by considering its use" is "anticipated in [Moore's] appeal to ordinary language," and adds on a later page that "Wittgenstein agrees with Moore in defending ordinary language."[4] Finally, K. T. Fann writes: "Moore's . . . persistent defence of common sense [is] also conspicuously present in Wittgenstein's later work."[5]

I could quote similar comments from many other philosophers, but I think I needn't: the association of Wittgenstein with Moore, "common sense," and "ordinary language" is firmly fixed in the minds of a great many philosophers.[6] Moreover, what is meant by "ordinary language" and "common sense" is taken by these philosophers to require no explanation, apparently because they think of Moore as having clarified these matters. In this way Moore has been relied on as a guide to Wittgenstein's thinking. It became standard practice, I mean, for commentators who employ this triangulation procedure to assume that Wittgenstein would never settle for any of those views, such as phenomenalism and behaviorism, that Moore declared to be at odds with common sense and the ordinary use of words.

A clear instance of this (discussed in the preceding chapter) is Albritton's way of explicating Wittgenstein's concept of criteria: he dismisses what Wittgenstein actually says and then substitutes his own, nonbehavioristic, account of criteria. In agreement with this, Hacker declares that Wittgenstein's account of criteria—or "the criterial relation"—"enables Wittgenstein to refute behaviorism on the one hand, and idealism, phenomenalism, and solipsism on the other."[7] More recently Hans Sluga has written that Wittgenstein "has often been taken to be an advocate of a logical behaviorism, but nowhere does he deny the existence of inner states. What he says is merely that our understanding of someone's pain is connected to the existence of natural and linguistic expressions of pain."[8] Had Wittgenstein advocated logical behaviorism, that would have put him in conflict with Moore's dualistic account of common sense, and so, it is reasoned, he did *not* advocate that view, did not deny the existence of inner states.[9] This is a wonderful example of how a preconceived idea can distort one's perception of things, for there is nothing Wittgenstein was more critical of than the notion of "inner states."[10]

Another example of interpreting Wittgenstein in conformity with Moore's notion of common sense is the assumption that he was opposed to phenomenalism. For example, we find George Pitcher summing up Wittgenstein's view of philosophy as follows:

Philosophy begins, then, in puzzlement. . . . No doubt some philosophers are never cured of their maladies and remain as deeply puzzled by sense perception, free will, and the rest at the end of their careers as they were at the beginning. But more often, a philosopher seeks to free himself from this deplorable condition by developing a theory or system to deal with the puzzles. He may, for example, become a phenomenalist and maintain that physical objects are families of sense-data. . . . These philosophical theories inevitably conflict with common sense, and indeed with what the philosopher himself believes in his unreflective moments. Wittgenstein considers such "cures" to be worse than the original disease.[11]

This reading of Wittgenstein is shared by Rogers Albritton, whom I have already quoted (chapter 9, note 6) expressing his conviction that Wittgenstein "couldn't possibly not notice that phenomenalism is a metaphysical theory, and wouldn't be caught dead in its grip." But can anyone find a passage in Wittgenstein's writings or lectures in which he dismisses phenomenalism? No! Although he eventually abandoned his early (analytic) version of phenomenalism, that only led him to develop a new version of it. Yet even A. J. Ayer, who should have known better, said that Wittgenstein and Moore "both accept [the idea] that there can be no doubt of the existence of the physical world of common sense."[12]

Wittgenstein's Opinion of Moore

Using the aforementioned triangulation procedure for locating Wittgenstein's philosophical positions is open to a number of criticisms. For one thing, it conflicts with many things that he himself said about Moore. For example, when asked by Oets Bouwsma about the talents needed for philosophizing, he answered, in part, that Moore is "barren" and "has no talent for disentangling things."[13] He is also reported to have said: "Moore?—he shows you how far a man can go who has absolutely no intelligence whatever."[14] When one of his least able students, M. O'C. Drury, told Wittgenstein that Moore had been critical of a paper he had read at the Moral Science Club, Wittgenstein said to him: "Surely you were able to stand up to Moore?"—as if Moore were no match, philosophically, for this rather naive student.[15] And to Malcolm, Wittgenstein remarked that "he did not believe that Moore would *recognize* a *correct* solution [to a philosophical problem] if he were presented with one."[16]

We can be more specific about Wittgenstein's objections to Moore's philosophizing. In lectures he said: "If I had to say what is the main mistake made by philosophers of the present generation, including Moore, I would say that it is that when language is looked at, what is looked at is a form of words and not the use made of the form of words" (LC, p. 2). What happens when Moore and others look at language in that way? "When we do philosophy," says Wittgenstein, "we are like savages, primitive people, who hear the expressions of civilized men, put a false interpretation on them, and then draw the queerest conclusions from it" (PI, §194). This is how Wittgenstein viewed Moore and Moorean realism. His criticism is not that the forms of words Moore noticed aren't really part of ordinary language; it's that they are the *misleading* part. Where Moore thought he'd found evidence of the plain man's view—the commonsense view—of the world, Wittgenstein saw phrases whose forms invite misinterpretation—Moore's realist interpretation. In consequence, he could dismiss Moore by saying that "the common-sense philosopher . . . *n.b.* is not the common-sense man, who is as far from realism as from idealism" (BB, p. 48). Moore, of course, is the commonsense philosopher, and here Wittgenstein implies both that Moore is a realist and that that is what sets him apart from the commonsense man. Wittgenstein goes on to say that "the trouble with the realist is always that he does not solve but skip[s] the difficulties which his adversaries see. . . . The realist answer, for us, just brings out the difficulty" (BB, pp. 48–49). As Wittgenstein saw it, Moore's attempts at philosophizing were hopelessly confused.

During the years 1930–33 Moore attended Wittgenstein's lectures, which Karl Britton later recalled as follows: "We felt that Wittgenstein addressed himself chiefly to Moore, although Moore seldom intervened and often seemed to be very disapproving. Sometimes the lecturer appealed to him, but my recollection is that Moore's replies were very discouraging."[17] We find this discord also in Moore's own remarks. In 1942 he wrote: "He [Wittgenstein] made me think that what is required for the solution of philosophical problems which baffle me, is a method quite different from any I have ever used—a method which he uses successfully, but which I have never been able to understand clearly enough to use it myself."[18]

In chapter 9 I quoted a passage from one of Wittgenstein's lectures in which he seems to have been admonishing those of his students who had been influenced by Moore. He said that one must not "present the idealistic or solipsistic positions, for example, as absurd" and "must not try to avoid a philosophical problem by appealing to common sense." Rather, "you must allow yourself to be dragged into the mire, and get out of it. . . . One must not in philosophy attempt to short-circuit problems" (WL35, pp. 108–109). Wittgenstein was clearly warning his students not to emulate Moore.

These and other passages strongly suggest that there is something seriously wrong with using the aforementioned triangulation procedure. How, then, could the views of Moore and Wittgenstein have become confused with one another?

A Source of Misunderstanding

An answer is suggested by something Wittgenstein said about those who attended his lectures. Referring to the general remarks he occasionally made about the nature of philosophy as his "hints," he said:

> I could leave out all the hints and just treat special [specific?] problems. It is only a psychological fact [i.e., nothing to do with the nature of philosophy itself] that people only understand what I am driving at when they begin to understand my general remarks, my hints, and cannot imagine what I am talking about when they hear me dealing with some special difficulty.[19]

In other words, his students understood him when he said that philosophical problems are to be dealt with by paying attention to language, not by seeking new information, but they failed to understand him when he offered his (reductionist) solutions to particular problems. But to see why they misunderstood him in the particular way that they did, confusing him with Moore, we need to add that many of his students were already great admirers of Moore and when they gravitated to Wittgenstein, they wanted to find affinities between the two philosophers they admired. Consequently, when they heard Wittgenstein say that philosophy was concerned with language, they tried to practice philosophy in the manner they imagined Wittgenstein had prescribed and imagined that their quasi-Moorean results would have met with Wittgenstein's approval. They thought that by giving Moore's conclusions a linguistic turn, they would get Wittgensteinian results.

This was not at all pleasing to Wittgenstein. Von Wright reports that "Wittgenstein repudiated the results of his own influence. . . . He was of the opinion—justified, I believe—that his ideas were usually misunderstood and distorted even by those who professed to be his disciples. He doubted that he would be better understood in the future."[20] The same dissatisfaction has been reported by others.[21]

Wittgenstein may have had more than one reason for being disappointed in his followers, but we can discern one of his reasons in his admonition that one should not treat solipsism and idealism as absurd and shouldn't short-circuit problems by appealing to common sense. He no doubt found it necessary to admonish his students in this way because they attempted to combine his idea that philosophy is a linguistic affair with what they took to be a great virtue in Moore: his sturdy and blunt opposition to philosophers who attack "common sense." To combine these they had only to claim that the philosophers Moore opposed were really attacking ordinary language, not anyone's *beliefs,* and that Moore, without realizing it, was defending, not our beliefs, but our language. This amalgam of Moore and Wittgenstein is what came to be called "ordinary language philosophy."

The Illegitimate Birth of Ordinary Language Philosophy

It was Norman Malcolm who first proposed this amalgamation. In an influential article he argued that the importance of Moore's philosophy lies in the fact that he

> takes his stand upon ordinary language and defends it against every attack, against every paradox. The philosophizing of most of the more important philosophers has consisted in their more or less subtly repudiating ordinary language. Moore's philosophizing has consisted mostly in his refuting the repudiators of ordinary language. . . . Moore's great historical role consists in the fact that he has been perhaps the first philosopher to sense that any philosophical statement which violates ordinary language is false, and consistently to defend ordinary language against its philosophical detractors.[22]

What did this defense of ordinary language amount to, as Malcolm understood it? As regards skepticism, he says,

> Moore is right. What his reply does is to give us a *paradigm* of absolute certainty. . . . What his reply does is to appeal to our language-sense; to make us feel how queer and wrong it would be to say, when we sat in a room seeing and touching chairs, that we *believed* there were chairs but did not know it for certain, or that it was only highly probable that there were chairs. . . . By reminding us of how we ordinarily use the expressions "know for certain" and "high probability,"

> Moore's reply constitutes a refutation of the philosophical statement that we can
> never have certain knowledge of material-thing statements.[23]

Malcolm goes on to say that there are only two ways in which a person may be
wrong when he makes an empirical statement: he may be making a mistake as to
what the empirical facts are, or he may be using the wrong words to describe those
facts. Now the skeptic who says that we can see only sense-data, never material
things, and that therefore we can't know whether material things exist, "does not
disagree with the ordinary man about any question of empirical fact," and therefore he must be regarded as taking exception (in a disguised way) to what ordinarily we would *say*. But for that very reason this philosopher is in a most peculiar
situation:

> He will agree that the facts of the situation are what we should ordinarily describe
> by the expression "seeing a cat in the tree." Nevertheless, he says that the man
> does not *really* see a cat; he sees only some sense-data of a cat. Now if it gives the
> philosopher pleasure to always substitute "I see some sense-data of my wife" for
> the expression "I see my wife," etc., then he is at liberty thus to express himself,
> *provided* he warns people beforehand so that they will understand him. But when
> he says that the man does not *really* see a cat, he commits a great absurdity; for he
> implies that a person can use an expression to describe a certain state of affairs,
> which is the expression ordinarily used to describe just such a state of affairs, and
> yet be using incorrect language.[24]

According to Malcolm, then, the skeptic's peculiar situation is this: he must allow
both that "see a cat" is an ordinary, frequently used expression *and* that, nevertheless, whenever that expression is used the use of it produces a false statement.

This would not, Malcolm allows, be an inconceivable state of affairs if "see a
cat" were an expression like "ghost," whose meaning "can be explained to [peo-
ple] in terms of the meanings of words which they already know."[25] But the situation is otherwise in the case of expressions that cannot be thus explained:

> In the case of all expressions the meaning of which must be *shown* and cannot be
> explained, as can the meaning of "ghost," it follows that, from the fact that they
> are ordinary expressions in the language, that there have been *many* situations
> of the kind which they describe; otherwise so many people could not have learned
> the correct use of the expressions. Whenever a philosophical paradox asserts,
> therefore, with regard to such an expression, that always when the expression is
> used the use of it produces a false statement, then to prove that the expression is
> an *ordinary* expression is completely to refute the paradox.[26]

But this, says Malcolm, is exactly what Moore, without quite realizing it, has been
doing in his refutation of philosophers' conclusions.

In a later article Malcolm slightly amended the foregoing argument, saying:
"Moore did not have to offer a *paradigm* . . . as I once thought. He only had to
remind his listeners and readers that the sentence . . . has a correct use and,
therefore, *can* express a true statement."[27] But this didn't alter Malcolm's view of
Moore's importance. "I believe," he said,

> that in order to grasp Wittgenstein's idea that a philosophical problem is essen-
> tially a confusion in our thinking, and that philosophical work cannot interfere

with the actual use of language . . . , one must understand what is right in Moore's defence of ordinary language. The latter was an advance in philosophy because it brought us nearer to a true understanding of philosophy itself.[28]

Despite the many signs that Wittgenstein strongly disapproved of Moore's philosophical views, Malcolm and a few like-minded philosophers proceeded to spread the idea that the way to understanding Wittgenstein is through Moore. As Bouwsma expressed it, "Like Moses, Moore took us to the promised land, had a glimpse of it, but never enjoyed it himself."[29] Thus, Moore's defense of common sense came to be thought of as leading us toward Wittgenstein and a fully developed ordinary language philosophy. This is how Wittgenstein came to be heralded as (in Sluga's words) "one of the godfathers of . . . ordinary language philosophy."

Varieties of Ordinary Language Philosophy

What do philosophers mean when they say such things about Wittgenstein? It has become commonplace to speak of ordinary language philosophy as though this were a readily identifiable school of thought, but this betokens a failure to discern fundamental differences among the philosophers who are lumped together under this label, some of whom do and some of whom do not have affinities to Moore. There are, in fact, three very different approaches to philosophical problems that might be thought of as ordinary language philosophy.

These three philosophical methods could be called "Standard," "Metaphysical," and "Investigative," and in later chapters I will discuss the differences between them. These differences are interesting in themselves, but the real harm in glossing over them is that the three methods are not equally subject to criticism. In fact, Standard Ordinary Language Philosophy—the type associated with Moore (or with Malcolm's pseudo-Moore)—can be attacked and dismissed very easily, with the result that when the aforementioned differences are ignored, the other two methods get dismissed without due consideration. In the remainder of this chapter I will discuss Standard Ordinary Language Philosophy, which turns out to mean different things to different philosophers, depending on their ideas about language.

A Preliminary Definition of Standard Ordinary Language Philosophy

Standard Ordinary Language Philosophy consists, in part, in the claim that (as Malcolm puts it) "any philosophical statement which violates ordinary language is false." In practice it involves asking whether something a philosopher says sounds funny, has the ring of oddity, when it is compared with the way people talk at the grocery store. If it does—if the philosopher says, for example, that we can't see a tree or feel an eel, we can be sure that he's gone wrong *somewhere*. This is a point Malcolm emphasized, saying that "the philosophical positions that Moore opposes can, therefore, be seen to be false *in advance* of an examination of the arguments adduced in support of them."[30] So although a philosopher may be "unable to detect anything wrong in his reasoning," he will have to concede to Moore "that *something* was wrong in it."[31]

We can say, then, that Standard Ordinary Language Philosophy involves at least the following two elements. It involves the claim that (a) any philosophical statement that "violates ordinary language" is false, that is, it is false *because* it "violates ordinary language." It also involves the claim, implicit in the foregoing, that (b) we needn't begin by considering a philosopher's arguments to see whether they prove something remarkable, for if the conclusion he reaches "violates ordinary language," we can be sure that *something* is wrong with his argument. It is the idea, in other words, that by appealing to ordinary language we can make a *direct* assault on philosophers' conclusions.[32]

In addition to (a) and (b) there is a third feature of Standard Ordinary Language Philosophy, but just what this feature is is a matter of considerable controversy. Because of its association with Moore, this method of comparing philosophical claims with ordinary language tends to impart to the phrase "ordinary language" a particular meaning, namely, "a language that carries the metaphysical baggage of Moore's realism." But there is not universal agreement about this. Although critics of Standard Ordinary Language Philosophy insist that "ordinary language" does have this meaning, its defenders have not always concurred. To appreciate the significance of this disagreement, we must understand this view of language.

A Pivotal Issue: Is Ordinary Language a Conceptual Scheme?

Moore thought of ordinary language in the following way: people who are not philosophers are constantly saying things that have philosophical implications, things that imply what Moore called "the common sense view of the world." For example, Moore, who was himself a mind-body dualist, held that many of the things we all say imply that humans have both minds and bodies. Thus, his account of the commonsense view of the world includes the following:

> We certainly believe that there are in the Universe enormous numbers of material objects . . . [and] we believe that men, besides having bodies, also have *minds*. . . . We all commonly believe . . . that acts of consciousness are quite definitely *attached*, in a particular way, to some material objects, and quite definitely not attached to others.

He adds that "we all constantly talk as if we believed" these things, meaning that we say various things that *imply* these general philosophical views.

The idea that our language carries philosophical baggage is not peculiar to Moore. It was—and perhaps still is—a commonly held view of ordinary language.[33] Russell was affirming it when he declared that "it is undeniable that our every-day interpretations of perceptive experience, and even all our every-day words, embody theories."[34] Russell was speaking, not of scientific theories, but of what Moore called "the common sense view of the world."

Some philosophers who have agreed with Moore and Russell that our language embodies philosophical theories have disagreed with them about the details of those theories. (Whereas Russell and Moore held that the plain man's language shows him to be a mind-body dualist, others—for instance, Wolfgang Kohler—have maintained that the plain man is a behaviorist.) For the moment I am not concerned with such disagreements; I am interested only in the idea that our language embodies some philosophical view or other.

I will refer to that idea henceforth as the idea that our language is a *conceptual scheme,* by which I mean the following. It is the idea that many of the things we commonly say have philosophical implications, implications held to be true by some philosophers and false by others. Thomas Reid was clearly taking such a view of language when, in criticizing Hume, he wrote:

> The mind that perceives, the object perceived, and the *operation* of perceiving that object, are distinct things, and are distinguished in the structure of all languages. In this sentence "I see, or perceive, the moon", *I* is the person or *mind*, the active verb *see* denotes the operation of the mind, and the [noun] *moon* denotes the object. What we have said of perceiving is equally applicable to most operations of the mind. Such operations are, in all languages, expressed by active transitive verbs; and we know that, in all languages, such verbs require a thing or person, which is the agent, and a noun following in an oblique case, which is the object. Whence it is evident that all mankind, both those who contrived language and those who use it with understanding, have distinguished these three things as different—to wit, the operations of the mind, which are expressed by active verbs; the mind itself which is the nominative to those verbs; and the object, which is, in the oblique case, governed by them.
>
> It would have been unnecessary to explain so obvious a distinction if some systems of philosophy had not confounded it. Mr. Hume's system, in particular, confounds all distinction between the operations of the mind and their objects.[35]

For reasons that I will explain in chapter 13, Reid cannot rightly be classified as a Standard Ordinary Language Philosopher, but he did hold that ordinary language is a conceptual scheme.

A Telling Criticism of Standard Ordinary Language Philosophy

I said above that, because of its association with Moore, ordinary language philosophy is very often assumed to incorporate not only (a) and (b) but also the idea that (c) our language is a conceptual scheme. When it is understood in this way, Standard Ordinary Language Philosophy becomes very easy to criticize. C. D. Broad formulated the objection succinctly as follows: "In philosophy it is . . . silly to be a slave to common speech. . . . When we remember that it represents the analysis made unconsciously for practical ends by our prehistoric ancestors we shall not be inclined to treat it as an oracle."[36] This criticism was to be repeated many times by many philosophers.[37]

What do the practitioners of Standard Ordinary Language Philosophy say in response to this criticism? This question is not easily answered because most of these philosophers have, unfortunately, given little or no thought to this issue, or they have failed to make their views perfectly clear. And when their critics have confronted them with this issue, they have not responded convincingly. Almost by default, then, they have given encouragement to the idea that our language embodies a conceptual scheme, which in turn leaves them vulnerable to Broad's criticism.[38] Is their plight hopeless, then, or can they be rescued?

The issue can be sharpened somewhat by considering a more precise definition of "conceptual scheme." If this task is left to the critics of ordinary language philosophy, they might offer the following:

> *Definition*: To say that our language is a conceptual scheme is to say that the following five theses are true. (1) Ordinary language, by virtue of the philosophical categories embodied in its standard forms, is a map of the ontological terrain.[39] (2) Ideally, our language would be (and is often trusted by philosophers as though it were) a good and reliable map. (3) Yet many philosophical arguments, namely, those whose conclusions clash in some way with ordinary language, purport to demonstrate that ordinary language is a poor map, that it contains distortions or outright misrepresentations of reality. (4) We could dismiss those arguments out of hand if we had reason to believe that our ancestors were infallible metaphysicians and had constructed our language in accordance with their metaphysical insights, but, while it's conceivable that among the world's very different languages there is a philosophically ideal language, that is, one that is a flawless ontological map, philosophers must never proceed on the mere assumption that their own is such a language. (5) In order to determine whether our language (or some feature of it) *is* a flawless ontological map, it is necessary to engage in philosophical inquiries that are not unduly influenced by the way we commonly talk about things. For example, when investigating Berkeley's claim that to be is to be perceived, we must not appeal to the fact that we say such things as "The pot boiled over while no one was watching" and "The jewels are presently locked in my safe." (N.B.: theses 4 and 5 are only slightly different ways of making the point about philosophical method that C. D. Broad was making in the passage I quoted above.)

This, as I said, is the way in which critics of ordinary language philosophy might define "conceptual scheme," and this should make it apparent why philosophers who practice ordinary language philosophy cannot remain indifferent about this, for in doing so they allow their critics to dismiss them as irrelevant. Indeed, when Standard Ordinary Language Philosophy is defined so as to include (c), which is defined by (1)–(5), it is clearly self-contradictory. (This is so because (a) and (b) are contradicted by theses (4) and (5): the latter two theses *denounce* appeals to ordinary language, whereas the former two *commend* such appeals.) Obviously, then, a defender of ordinary language philosophy cannot share the critics' view of these matters. And yet, as I said above, very few of these philosophers have discussed—or, I suspect, even thought about—these matters.[40]

A Kantian Defense of Ordinary Language Philosophy

Hubert Schwyzer is an exception. He has proposed what amounts to a Kantian defense of ordinary language philosophy. His defense challenges something that is simply assumed in the foregoing definition of "conceptual scheme," namely, that ontology and language are two, quite separable things, in the sense that the metaphysical categories of a language may or may not correspond to how things are in the world.

Thesis (1) of the foregoing definition states that "ordinary language, by virtue of the philosophical categories embodied in its standard forms, is a map of the ontological terrain." Schwyzer, although he might want to alter this wording a bit, accepts this thesis as part of ordinary language philosophy.[41] He says that "the appeal, in philosophy, to how we speak is meant, by those who practice it, to tell us something about how things really are."[42] But he also recognizes that philosophers who, with that intention, appeal to what we say need to justify what they are doing.

> But if the appeal to the use of language can tell us about the nature of things—not only that sensations are private, and so on, but also, apparently, that belief is a disposition rather than an occurrence, that a cause is something more than what regularly precedes something else, and so on, we must ask: How is this possible? How *can* how we speak tell us how things really are? Those who refuse even to consider this question invite the attacks of Russell and other traditional philosophers.
>
> But it seems to me that there are only two even potentially plausible answers to the question. How we speak about things can tell us how things are only if *either* how we speak is a function of how things are, *or*, conversely, how things are is a function of how we speak. . . . If the ordinary language philosopher [rejects these answers] then I fail to see how it can be claimed that his appeal to the use of language has any bearing on philosophical inquiry into the nature of things.[43]

Schwyzer's own view, which he also attributes to Wittgenstein, is the second of these alternatives, namely, that how things are is a function of how we speak. He writes:

> [U]nderlying, or bound up with Wittgenstein's way of philosophizing, as the very rationale of his appeal to the use of language, is a certain metaphysical orientation, a certain position about the nature of thought and reality, and of the relation between them. It is part of the position which Kant thought of as his "Copernican Revolution", the view, bluntly, that the nature of reality conforms to the nature of thought, not the other way around. I believe that this view pervades Wittgenstein's later work, and that it is already present in his repudiation of what he calls "Augustine's picture of the essence of language", the "picture" according to which language is a system of signs or names for things. . . . Wittgenstein's response to Augustine is, I maintain, itself a version of Kant's Copernican Revolution. Briefly: the meaning of words (for things), the meaning of our discourse about things, is not determined by the nature of the things the words are for, the nature of the things we talk about. Rather, it is the other way around: the nature of the things our words are for, the nature of the things we talk about (be they slabs, colours, numbers, understanding, pain, expectation) is determined by the use of language

with regard to them, by what it makes sense to say about them, by their "grammar". . . . How we speak and think, e.g., about colours, is not accounted for by what colours are, by our knowledge independently of how we speak and think of what they are; rather the "language-game" of colours dictates *what,* in our ontology, *a colour is.*[44]

Clearly, if Schwyzer were asked why one should think that the world is the way our language represents it as being, he would reply that the very asking of this question betrays the mistaken idea that the nature of things is independent of language.[45]

Schwyzer, then, would amend the foregoing definition of "conceptual scheme" in the following ways. He would accept (1), but would eliminate the map metaphor so that it reads: "Ordinary language, by virtue of the philosophical categories embodied in its standard forms, contains a philosophy." He would then amend (2) to read: "Our language is of necessity a flawless guide to metaphysics because how things are is a function of the way we speak of them." And he would eliminate theses (3), (4), and (5).

I suspect that philosophers like Broad, who criticize ordinary language philosophy, will reject Schwyzer's defense of it and will thus continue to heap scorn upon that style of philosophizing. I also suspect that many of the philosophers who practice some form of ordinary language philosophy will be dissatisfied with Schwyzer's Kantian defense. If they do so, however, they must recognize that until they produce some other defense their critics will dismiss them as irrelevant. What sort of defense might they offer?

Is A Non-Kantian Defense Possible?

At least some of them, I believe, would want to reject an idea that is shared by critics like Broad and by Schwyzer's Kantian defense, the idea that ordinary language is a conceptual scheme, that our language embodies a particular philosophical point of view. If they could justify the rejection of this idea, ordinary language philosophers could dismiss critics like Broad. But any justification they offer must be consistent with the rest of their philosophical practice, and there is a reason, as I will presently show, why a philosopher who, like Malcolm, advocates Standard Ordinary Language Philosophy is in no position to defend ordinary language philosophy against Broad's criticism. That reason will emerge if we first consider Malcolm's claim that Moore was an early practitioner—or at least a near proponent—of Standard Ordinary Language Philosophy.

By "Standard Ordinary Language Philosophy" I do not now mean the self-contradictory position that includes the definition (1)–(5). I mean, rather, the sort of philosophical procedure advocated by Malcolm, the procedure that treats it as reasonable to attack a philosopher's conclusion while ignoring his premises and to do so on the grounds that his conclusion "violates ordinary language." This philosophical method can be illustrated by the following passage in which Malcolm attacks Descartes' claim that animals are incapable of thinking.

In real life we commonly employ the verb "think" in respect to animals. We say, "Towser thinks he is going to be fed." . . . A million examples could be produced in which it would be a correct way of speaking to say, of an animal, something of the form "He thinks that *p*." Clearly there is an error in Descartes' contention that animals do not think.[46]

This passage illustrates Malcolm's general position that in many cases a philosophical claim can, regardless of the arguments put forth on its behalf, be seen to be false simply from the fact that it "violates" ordinary language.[47] And it is this sort of reasoning that I am concerned with when I ask whether Moore was an early proponent of "Standard Ordinary Language Philosophy." So my definition of that phrase includes (a) and (b), but it also, implicitly, treats the idea that language is a conceptual scheme as a nonissue, as an idea we can simply ignore. But for that very reason it cannot be right, as I will show, to think that Moore was receptive to—and was an early proponent of—Standard Ordinary Language Philosophy.

When some of his admirers insisted that he was actually recommending to philosophers that they abide by (and not "violate") the ordinary use of words, Moore replied: "If this is all I was doing I was certainly making a huge mistake, for I certainly did not think it was all. And I do not think so now."[48] It is easy to see why Moore would regard Standard Ordinary Language Philosophy as a mistake. He undoubtedly thought that if someone attempted to dismiss a philosophical claim as untrue and gave as his *grounds* for dismissing it the fact that it conflicts with (or "violates") ordinary language, he would be guilty of begging the question—the question whether the commonsense views embodied in ordinary language are true.

We find Moore taking this position when he explained that a philosopher of the sort he opposes—a skeptic, for example—"would be very likely to say that, though he knows that such language is often used, yet he is *not* aware that it ever describes what could be the case: that, on the contrary, it always asserts that something is the case, which could not possibly be the case."[49] Moore is here acknowledging that the philosophers he opposes hold that ordinary language embodies a conceptual scheme, so that a given form of words might have a conventional use and yet, on account of the conceptual scheme embodied in it, be unusable for saying something true. Clearly, in replying to such a philosopher it is pointless to insist, as Malcolm does, that a given expression has a conventional use, for his opponent is not denying *that*.[50]

Moore would, I am sure, have allowed that in defending the beliefs of common sense he was *also*—but indirectly—defending ordinary language (with its conceptual scheme), but he would have insisted that his *way* of defending both was by declaring that he *knows* that this or that element of the commonsense view of the world is true.[51] In other words, his *justification* for disputing certain views was simply that he *knows* that the commonsense views they conflict with are true.[52] In the next chapter I will consider why Moore argued in this fashion and whether it constitutes a sound way of philosophizing, but for the moment I am content to conclude that Moore was not in sympathy with Standard Ordinary Language Philosophy. He did not accept (a) and (b), and the reason he did not accept them is that he thought that ordinary language embodies a (realist) conceptual scheme, whose adequacy is in dispute among philosophers.

I can now explain why Malcolm is in no position to defend ordinary language philosophy against critics such a Broad. There is, of course, no doubt that Malcolm was an advocate of Standard Ordinary Language Philosophy, for he explicitly said that he subscribed to parts (a) and (b). But unlike Moore he did not take seriously the idea that our language is a conceptual scheme. This comes out most clearly in his claim that when a nonphilosopher makes a statement of the sort in question here, such as "I see a cat in that tree," he can be wrong in only *two* ways: he may be mistaken as to the empirical facts or he may be using the wrong words to describe those facts. In saying this, Malcolm is implicitly denying that there is a third way this person could be wrong, namely, by using a form of words that embodies an unsuitable conceptual scheme.

This is not a point that Malcolm explicitly defended. I suspect that he would have said, if asked, that he didn't *need* a reason for dismissing the idea that ordinary language is a conceptual scheme, that it's enough that he's never seen a good reason for accepting that idea. This, I believe, is the stance Malcolm assumed: he thought of himself as holding no philosophical views of his own and as addressing philosophical problems from without, from some neutral position. But this is not sufficient as a defense of Standard Ordinary Language Philosophy, for it leaves his arguments open to the charge that they beg the question. The reason for this is as follows.

The philosophical arguments that Malcolm says we needn't consult before rejecting their conclusions include those that have been taken to show—to *demonstrate*—that ordinary language is a conceptual scheme. Recall here that the first of the five theses defining this view of language is: "Ordinary language, by virtue of the philosophical categories embodied in its standard forms, is a map of the ontological terrain." That view of language doesn't leap into philosophers' heads for no reason. It arises, rather, from various pieces of philosophical thinking. As Dudley Shapere has put it, "[T]he entire philosophical tradition from Thales on . . . has nearly always been conceived, at least tacitly, as the replacement of ordinary ways of looking at the world—and of talking about it—with a new and more precise one."[53] Moreover, philosophers have not regarded this "as an assumption made in advance of their thinking" but have regarded it instead "as a conclusion drawn from a detailed analysis of ordinary ways of looking at things and talking about them."[54]

Alternative Conceptual Schemes

An example would be the dispute between realists and idealists over whether things such as chairs and pots can exist unperceived. Because we commonly say such things as "The pot boiled over while no one was watching" and "The patient, while left unattended, went into convulsions and died," it is alleged that ordinary language conceptualizes the world in a certain way, in a way that puts our language at odds with Berkeley's phenomenalism. Once philosophical arguments of this kind have been set loose in the land, they can't be simply ignored. Why? Because they purport to demonstrate that ordinary language is just one conceptual scheme among several. A. J. Ayer, for example, maintains that Berkeley "opted for a radically different way of interpreting experiences, in which [Moore's] realistic assumption [about certain things existing unperceived] had no place." And this, said Ayer, goes to show that "whether or not there is anything wrong with our ordinary method of interpreting experience, *the possibility of there being other workable methods is not excluded.*"[55] One can disagree with Ayer on this point, but if we are going to dismiss his way of viewing "ordinary language," we must be able to give an adequate reason.[56]

I am confident that such a reason can be given. I am confident, that is, that it *needn't* be a mistake for a philosopher to settle an issue by calling attention to ordinary language—to what we all say. In chapters 14 and 15 I will explain this in detail, but I can here provide a sketch of what this alternative would look like.

A Different Kind of Ordinary Language Philosophy

The sort of objection raised by Broad and others rests on the idea that ordinary language is a conceptual scheme, but this idea, as I said, does not leap into philosophers' minds for no reason. This idea comes to us as the result of various pieces of philosophical reasoning—Descartes' dream argument, the arguments from illusion, and the like. But there is no need for such pieces of reasoning to remain forever unchallenged. There may, therefore, be a way to successfully dispute the idea that our language embodies a conceptual scheme—by challenging the premises (or presuppositions) of any argument that fosters the idea that our language is a conceptual scheme. If one undertook to investigate their premises instead of attacking their conclusions, one would be perfectly entitled to proceed by reminding oneself of the ordinary use of the relevant or operative words. This procedure would beg no questions because in this case such reminders are addressed to the *roots* of philosophical problems. If we introduce such reminders at a point *before* the idea of a conceptual scheme gets a toe hold, we may be able to show that that idea arises only from error, not insight. It should be noted, however, that, while this approach may be consistent with some other variety of ordinary language philosophy (see chapters 14 and 15 below), it is clearly *not* consistent with Malcolm's procedure of taking direct aim at philosophers' conclusions.

Before leaving this investigation of Standard Ordinary Language Philosophy I want to return briefly to the idea that Wittgenstein practiced or endorsed this style of philosophy.[57] If this was his method, then his reasoning was defective. He would, I mean, be guilty of begging the question if he thought it appropriate to dismiss skepticism about other minds by saying: "Just look at what we normally say: we say, 'You could tell from his groaning that he was in a lot of pain.'" This way of rebuffing the skeptic would, of course, be a clear-cut case of Standard Ordinary Language Philosophy, but as Wittgenstein's use of the concept of criteria makes clear (see chapters 8 and 9 above), his treatment of philosophical issues was entirely different from that of Standard Ordinary Language Philosophy. I am not denying that he practiced ordinary language philosophy of one sort or another, but it remains to be seen what sort it was. I will take this up in chapters 12 and 13.

I began this chapter by quoting a number of philosophers who either say or imply that Wittgenstein, because of his similarity to Moore, was an ordinary language philosopher. The style of philosophy they had in mind, an amalgam of Wittgenstein and Moore, I dubbed "Standard Ordinary Language Philosophy." And I have now shown, I believe, that Standard Ordinary Language Philosophy is neither viable nor Wittgensteinian.[58] Its most striking feature is its use in making direct assaults on philosophers' conclusions, and this, in an obvious way, is a derivation from Moore's blunt opposition to the conclusions of skeptics, idealists, and others. Moore has been admired for this approach, and some who admired it may think that, although the linguistic version some philosophers made of it is indefensible, Moore's original version is worthy of emulation. I will investigate this in the next chapter.

Moore's Method

G. E. Moore's various attempts to defend common sense against philosophical skepticism and prove the existence of an external world[1] have left many
philosophers puzzled. I am not aware of anyone who thinks that Moore was entirely successful in this endeavor. Yet there is something seductive about Moore's
way of replying to the skeptic, and one can easily come to think, as Malcolm did,
that even if it is not entirely satisfactory, there is nevertheless something right—
and important—in his procedure. In this chapter, then, I mean to inquire into the
seductiveness of Moore's procedure and decide whether some part or aspect of it
can be successfully defended.

Translating into the Concrete

A striking feature of Moore's refutations of skepticism regarding the external
world is that he seems not to have thought it essential to begin by examining the
arguments that have traditionally led to such skepticism. Although he did, from
time to time, turn his attention to those arguments, his attitude in this matter
seems to have remained that which he summed up in the following remarks about
the views of skeptical philosophers:

> [I]t seems to me a sufficient refutation of such views as these, simply to point to
> cases in which we do know such things [as the skeptic denies we can know]. This,
> after all, you know, really is a finger: there is no doubt about it: I know it, you all
> know it. And I think we may safely challenge any philosopher to bring forward
> any argument in favor either of the proposition that we do not know it, or of the
> proposition that it is not true, which does not rest upon some premise which is,
> beyond comparison, less certain than is the proposition which it is designed to at-
> tack. The questions whether we do ever know such things as these, and whether
> there are any material objects, seem to me, therefore, to be questions which there

is no need to take seriously: they are questions which it is quite easy to answer, with certainty, in the affirmative.[2]

Moore's view, then, is that one can be entirely confident in advance of examining any such skeptical argument that it contains some defect.

His confidence on this point was born of the conviction that the skeptic's conclusion is vulnerable to a direct attack. How does Moore go about this? In the passage quoted above Moore does not reply to the conclusion that one can't know whether there's an external world by simply saying, "On the contrary, I do know there's an external world." Rather, he says that we can "simply point to cases in which we do know such things"—such things as the skeptic denies we can know. To arrive at "cases" that will serve his purpose, he employed a technique he called "translating into the concrete,"[3] a technique by which he transformed highly general philosophical claims into "concrete" instances or cases. Thus, the skeptic's conclusion that we have no knowledge of an external world is transformed into some such concrete claim as that one cannot know whether this is a finger or that Moore cannot know whether he has hands. This, then, enabled Moore to make his reply by saying, for example, "But this is a finger, and we all know that it is" or "But I do have two hands; this is something I *know* to be so."

This technique of translating into the concrete is one that Moore used in dealing with a variety of philosophical issues, and one of the justifications he gave for its use was that it serves to diminish the plausibility a philosophical claim may have when it is stated in a highly general form. "So long as [the philosophical view in question] is merely presented in vague phrases," said Moore, "it does in fact sound very plausible. But as soon as you realize what it means in particular instances . . . it seems to me to lose all its plausibility."[4] It could hardly be doubted that this is the effect Moore meant to achieve by translating into concrete instances the skeptic's conclusion about our knowledge of the external world. For so long as we are confronted with the question "Is there an external world?" it may seem plausible for the skeptic to say, "No one can know," whereas if we put to ourselves the question "Do I have hands?" one may feel impelled to answer, "Of course I do! How could I ever—*seriously*—doubt such a thing?!" Thus, whereas it would have seemed merely perverse had Moore flown in the face of the skeptic's argument by replying, "But there *is* an external world. I *know* there is," it seems not at all perverse, but highly impressive, when he replies by insisting that he knows that he has hands. He seems to bring us back to reality, like someone who dismisses foolish speculations with the admonition, "Stop talking nonsense and get down to cases!"

Yet, impressive though this may be, I have misgivings about it. I cannot help but feel that Moore is somehow dealing unfairly with the skeptic when he translates into the concrete. I want, therefore, to examine this move carefully, and I will do so in two stages. I will begin by trying to make clear exactly what is at issue between Moore and the skeptic, and here my concern will be to show that both Moore and the skeptic understand the issue to be a metaphysical one. I will then go on to consider what is achieved by Moore's translating into the concrete.

Moore's Metaphysical Concerns

It is easy to forget, while reading Moore's essays, that his concern with skepticism was a metaphysical one. This is easily forgotten because Moore keeps our attention riveted, for the most part, on his own "concrete cases," such as "This is a finger" or "I am dressed and not absolutely naked." But we will have misunderstood Moore's aims if we take him to have been, at any point, wholly or chiefly concerned with no broader issue than whether, for example, he was wearing clothes. His real interest, of course, was not in any such question at all. Rather, his real interest here was that which he described as follows in his 1910–11 lectures:

> [T]he most important and interesting thing which philosophers have tried to do is no less than this; namely: To give a general description of the whole Universe, mentioning all of the most important kinds of things which we *know* to be in it, considering how far it is likely that there are in it important kinds of things which we do not absolutely *know* to be in it, and also considering the most important ways in which these various kinds of things are related to one another.[5]

Moore goes on to say that providing such an account of the Universe is "the first and most important problem of philosophy." Now it could hardly be doubted that it was this problem to which Moore was addressing himself in formulating his defense of common sense and in giving his proof of an external world. That is to say, Moore was concerned with metaphysical issues, with what there is. There are numerous indications that this was his concern, and I will mention four of these.

First, Moore was concerned to defend common sense and to give a proof of an external world because other philosophers had advanced arguments, such as those in Descartes's First Meditation, which purport to cast doubt on the existence of an external world of material objects. Or to put the matter in another way, Moore was concerned to reply to that form of skepticism which, as he himself explains it, "asserts that we simply do not know at all whether there are any material objects in the Universe at all. It admits that there may be such objects; but it says that none of us knows that there are any."[6] In what follows I will occasionally refer to this as "Cartesian skepticism," in order to emphasize that the skepticism in question holds that, for all we know, there may be no external world of material objects. Such skepticism is quite different from that of phenomenalists who, although proposing no doubts about an "external world," hold that propositions about hands and chairs, because they imply things about future sense-data, can never be known to be true. The latter is a purely epistemological skepticism, whereas the former, which was of great interest to Moore, has plainly metaphysical implications. It tells us that we cannot know what kind of Universe we inhabit. The phenomenalist is certain that the Universe he inhabits is a purely phenomenal one. The Cartesian skeptic says that one can't know this, for there may be material as well as phenomenal objects. Moore insists that both are wrong: the Universe contains material objects, and we know this for a fact.

Second, as is implicitly conceded by Moore in a passage quoted above, he regarded it as a genuine question, albeit an easily answered one, whether there are any material objects in the Universe. That he so regarded the question is due, or partly due, I think, to something Arthur Murphy was pointing out when he remarked that "Moore rejects the skeptical conclusion, but he seems, at least at times, to have retained the assumption from which it was naturally derived."[7] Murphy was calling attention to a shared premise of the sort that Ramsey's maxim urges us to challenge. He was alluding to the fact that Moore did not reject the representative theory of perception, with its notion that what we directly perceive are sense impressions (or sense-data). And I take it that Murphy was suggesting, although he did not explicitly say so, that so long as Moore was prepared to accept this part of the skeptic's own view, he was in no position to claim to know things the skeptic denies he can know. Moore, of course, was not ready to agree with this; he thought it possible to reconcile the representative theory of perception with having knowledge of the external world. But he did acknowledge that that theory is vulnerable to a "serious objection," namely, that it makes it "difficult [when looking at coins] to answer the questions: How can I ever come to know that these sensibles [i.e., sense-data] have a 'source' at all? And how do I know that these sources are circular?"[8] His only answer to this "serious objection" was that our knowledge of the external world is "based on an analogical or inductive argument," so that one crucial point on which he differed from the skeptic, he said, is that "I am inclined to think that what is 'based on' an analogical or inductive argument, in the sense in which my knowledge or belief that this is a pencil is so, may nevertheless be certain knowledge and *not* merely more or less probable belief."[9]

I will not here enter into the question whether Moore could in this way reconcile the representative theory of perception with our having knowledge of an external world. (I do not think he could.) I want only to point out that Moore, along with the Cartesian skeptic, understood the question about our knowledge of an external world to be a question about whether we have knowledge of things that transcend experience. In other words, in answering the question "Is there an external world?" Moore understood himself to be answering some such question as "Is there anything, such as a pair of coins or a pair of hands, on the far side of sense-data?"

My reason for emphasizing this is that it is usually forgotten or neglected in discussions of Moore. For example, Wittgenstein seems to have been either forgetting or neglecting this aspect of Moore's thinking when, in *On Certainty* he suggested that Moore's saying that he knew he had hands was "nonsense" because Moore's saying this lacked a suitable context, a context in which there was, in fact, something to be known.[10] Had Wittgenstein been mindful of what Moore *meant* to be claiming knowledge of, he would not, I believe, have thought that such a criticism was the relevant one to make. For as Moore understood the matter, there *was* something to be known here, namely, whether one's sense-data have a "source" (or a "source" of the kind one takes them to have).

Third, an important feature of Cartesian skepticism is that it conjures into existence a body of hitherto unheard-of "propositions"—metaphysical propositions that it attaches to the remarks and comments we make in our ordinary, nonphilosophical discourses. It does this by alleging that many of the things we ordinarily say can be false in a way that never occurs to us in the ordinary affairs of life. For example, if a child were to say to its mother, "I've washed my hands," this, according to the skeptic, can be false not only in the way we all recognize (as when the child is telling a falsehood and still has unwashed hands), but also in the following way: if there is no external world of material objects, so that the one who says (or "says") that he has washed his hands is a disembodied being, then what he has said (or "said") is false, not because his hands remain unwashed, but because he has no body and so has no hands at all, neither washed nor unwashed hands. Accordingly, the skeptic maintains that when, ordinarily, one says (or "says") "I've washed my hands," this implies the further proposition, "At least two human hands exist" or, more generally, "Material objects exist." Similarly, if someone says, "I'm taking a bath," this, according to the skeptic, implies the further proposition "I have a body." Now these allegedly implied "propositions" are not among the things we ordinarily have occasion to say. Indeed, one cannot even begin to understand them apart from an understanding of Cartesian skepticism. They are plainly metaphysical propositions. But it is propositions *of this sort*— propositions allegedly implied by what one might say outside philosophy—whose truth the skeptic is chiefly concerned to deny we can know.

To understand Moore, it is essential to recognize that he was in complete agreement with this metaphysical view of language—that he thought of language as a conceptual scheme. Thus, although he keeps our attention focused, for the most part, on his "concrete cases," we are meant to understand that these have metaphysical implications. Moore makes this explicit in his essay "Certainty," which begins with his making (what he calls) seven "assertions," such as "I am standing up" and "I have clothes on," all of which, he tells us, were "propositions which implied the existence of *an external world*—that is to say, of a world *external to my mind,*" so that

> if I did know anyone of them to be true, when I asserted it, the existence of an external world was at that time absolutely certain. If, on the other hand, as some philosophers have maintained, the existence of an external world is never absolutely certain, then it follows that I cannot have known any one of these seven propositions to be true.[11]

Accordingly, when we find Moore telling us that he knows, for example, that he has hands or has clothes on, we must bear in mind that on his view these knowledge claims have built into them, by their implications, the further metaphysical knowledge claim that he knows that there are material objects on the far side of sense-data. This is why Moore could not be content with thinking that a wartime casualty who wanted to know whether he still had hands would need only to probe the bandages or peer beneath them—why, that is, Moore thought it necessary to employ (as he put it) "an analogical or inductive argument."

Fourth, when Moore undertakes to identify what he calls "the common sense view of the world," he does so—in part, at least—by means of metaphysical propositions of the kind mentioned above. When, in "A Defence of Common Sense," he begins his list of "truisms" by saying "There exists at present a living human body, which is *my* body," Moore surely did not think of this as something a plain man would ever say, but he did undoubtedly think of it as both a metaphysical proposition (one that would contradict "Moore is a disembodied being") and as a proposition that would be *implied* if he were to say to his wife, "I'm taking a bath," or "I've washed my hands." And there are other of his truisms that apparently fall into this category, as when he goes on to say that his body "has existed continuously" since it was born and that it has always been "at various distances" from other things "having shape and size in three dimensions."[12] These truisms, too, are to be thought of, not as things a plain man would ever say, but as metaphysical propositions that are implied by things we all say.

Thus, what Moore calls "the Common Sense view of the world" is—in part, at least—a plainly metaphysical view, and Moore, in defending it, meant to be defending that metaphysical view. His defense of common sense, in other words, belongs to that project which, in a passage quoted above, he described as giving "a general description of the *whole* Universe."

I have now mentioned four ways in which Moore, despite his focusing our attention on his "concrete" cases, can be seen to be concerned with metaphysics. There may be additional indications of this in his writings, but I believe that these four are sufficient to make the point inescapable.

Cartesian Skepticism

The question to which we must eventually address ourselves is how Moore could have thought that he knew something the skeptic denies one can know. Before turning to this question, however, it may be useful to make explicit several features of Cartesian skepticism that are often neglected by its opponents.

1. The skeptic's conclusion, as Moore expresses it in a passage quoted earlier, is that "we simply do not know at all whether there are any material objects in the Universe at all." And because this is the skeptic's conclusion, anyone who would undertake to challenge this conclusion would be begging the question if his manner of challenging it somehow took it for granted—as something the *skeptic* would grant—that he has a body and a normal compliment of bodily sense: eyes, ears, etc.

An essential feature of Cartesian skepticism is the sweeping nature of the grounds it adduces for philosophical doubt, namely, its claim that one can never recognize whether one is actually seeing such things as rocks and trees or (as in a dream) only seeming to see such things. This being the strategy of the skeptic's argument, it precludes our replying to the skeptic in anything like the way one might answer the sort of skepticism one occasionally encounters in daily life. If, in a case of the latter sort, someone scoffingly said to me, "You didn't know that that gun was loaded," I could sometimes rightly reply, "But I did know it was loaded. I was there and *saw* it being loaded." If, on the other hand, the skeptic, elaborating his position, were to say that one can never know such a thing as that a gun is loaded, one could not rebuff his skepticism in the same way ("I was there and saw . . ."), for he would, quite rightly, protest that such an answer begs the whole question by merely assuming, not only that one was on the scene with a full compliment of bodily senses, but also that one can successfully distinguish seeing a material object from *seeming* to see a material object. Accordingly, anyone wanting to dispute the skeptic's conclusion in a plausible fashion must avoid depicting that conclusion as though it were vulnerable to anything like an ordinary rebuff.

2. In trying to understand Cartesian skepticism about the external world, it would be a mistake to think of it as though it could be the sum of a vast number of "isolated" doubts about the existence of such particular things as the pencil I am holding or the desk at which I am writing. And yet it is easy to make such a mistake. Indeed, such as interpretation might be suggested by Descartes's own words. For as part of his dream argument he says, "Well, suppose I am dreaming, and these particulars, that I open my eyes, shake my head, put out my hand, are incorrect; suppose even that I have no such hand, no such body," and further on he writes: "I will consider myself as having no hands, no eyes, no flesh, no blood, no senses, but just having the false belief that I have all these things."[13] One might think that one could extrapolate from these remarks and say that one of the things that Descartes's argument purports to call into question is whether Descartes has any hands. But is this true? I want to suggest that it is not.

First of all, Descartes raises no doubt especially about his hands. He did not, for example, harbor a suspicion that there was a ghoulish surgeon on the loose who was going about in the night severing people's hands and replacing them with scarcely detectable imitations. Moreover, if ever one were to entertain such a doubt, a doubt about whether he or someone else has lost his hands through amputation or accident, there are certain things that could *not* be in doubt—for example, that the person in question has arms or at least a head and torso. Consider what it would be like, after all, to have such a doubt. Apparently it is, or was, not uncommon for the beggars of India to kidnap children, cut off their hands, and put them back on the street with bandaged stumps, so that the child, now a pitiful spectacle, would be a more effective beggar. If I happen to have heard of this dreadful practice, and a friend of mine who is with me on the streets of Calcutta remarks, pointing to a bandaged child, "Oh, that poor child! What can be wrong with her hands?" I might reply, "I wonder if she even has any hands." And I might then go on to tell about the kidnapping and mutilation of children. Here, then, is a case in which I could be said to be in doubt about whether someone has hands, but obviously my doubt could not be expanded to include whether the child has arms, a torso, a head. After all, it is only because I see the child's bandaged arms that I had a doubt in the first place. There might, of course, be a different sort of case, one in which I hear conflicting stories about some accident victim, one story being that he lost his hands in the accident, the other being that he was entirely incinerated in the accident. In that case, I may have various doubts about what happened to this person, but if I were to read a newspaper account of the accident which stated, "The victim was entirely incinerated in the accident and was left without hands," I could only think that this was some sort of mistake or misprint.

From this we can see that if we were to say that the Cartesian skeptic doubts whether he (or whether Moore) has hands, we would be implying that the skeptic is prepared to concede that he (or Moore) has arms or at least a head and torso.

But the Cartesian skeptic is not, of course, willing to concede such a thing. It would therefore be extremely misleading to say that Descartes doubted whether he had hands. His skepticism regarding the external world will be properly understood only if we understand that it cannot be divided up into subsidiary doubts which themselves suggest that the skeptic concedes the existence of most of our familiar world. While it is true that the skeptic may, if pressed, say that one cannot know whether there is a tree growing in front of his house, it would be a mistake to infer from this that his skepticism is comprised, in part, of a doubt about the vegetation in his own front yard, as though he did not gainsay the real estate but only claimed ignorance of what was growing there.

If, then, one is properly to reply to Cartesian skepticism, one must avoid representing the skeptic as though he harbored such isolated doubts as those mentioned above.

3. As can be seen from the previous point, there is a problem about how the skeptic's conclusion is to be thought of as related to (or impinging on) what we say and think outside philosophy. Consider now a further aspect of this problem.

The skeptic, like everyone else, regularly engages in ordinary conversations and is occasionally faced with answering such questions as "Did you know the gun was loaded?" and "Did you know you left the door unlocked?"—questions which we so understand that a person will, in some circumstances, be lying if he says, "No, I didn't know that." Now how is the skeptic to think of his skepticism in relation to such questions as they arise in ordinary, nonphilosophical discourse? Is he going to endorse a negative answer to all such questions, regardless of the circumstances? In other words, does the skeptic hold that one should invariably reply in the negative to such a question as "Did you know the gun was loaded?" on the grounds that one can never know whether there exist any material objects?

Skeptics have not, I think, made clear their solution to this problem. But one solution would seem to be the following. It would be a mistake to interject one's philosophical skepticism into the discourse of the plain man (assuming there are such people). And the reason it would be a mistake is this. If the one who asks, "Did you know the gun was loaded?" does not mean to be asking a philosophical question, a question which probes philosophical issues, but means only to be asking a question within the framework of the commonsense view of the world, it would create a highly misleading answer in some instances if one were to say, "No, I didn't know that," while thinking to oneself that of course one *couldn't* know such a thing because the existence of an external world is unknowable. So if one is going to answer the question at all, one must answer it in the spirit in which it is asked. And the same goes for such other questions, asked by the plain man, as "Could you be mistaken about the color of her eyes?" and "Do you know where he's living now?" When such questions are put to one without philosophic intent, the skeptic, like anyone else, must answer them, if he answers at all, with a view to what the inquirer meant to ask. And in general one must not interject one's philosophical skepticism into ordinary discourse, for doing so would not only create misunderstandings of an ordinary sort but would also misrepresent the nature of philosophical skepticism. Cartesian skepticism calls into question the assumptions underlying ordinary discourse and therefore attacks it, not in a piecemeal fashion (e.g., whether one has hands or feet), but as a whole. The decision facing the skeptic is whether to engage in ordinary discourse at all or to give it up altogether. And if he chooses the former alternative, then he must talk like everyone else. As Russell once remarked,[14] he would, if he were "a true philosopher," speak only about sense-data, but "life is too short," he said, for the long-winded sentences this would require, and so he speaks as nonphilosophers speak. Perhaps the skeptic will add that when he goes along with the plain man by answering affirmatively such a question as "Did you know the gun was loaded?" he is doing something that resembles in certain (but not all) respects what many adults do when small children ask them whether Santa Claus brought the presents, that is, he is saying something he does not believe but which is, under the circumstances, the conventionally expected (or acceptable) answer.

Some such account, it seems to me, is one the skeptic might give of the way in which Cartesian skepticism impinges on what we say outside philosophy.[15] It finds fault with "ordinary language" as a whole and is not to be thought of as finding faults *within* our ordinary discourses.

This point can be put differently as follows. The Cartesian skeptic can readily allow that within ordinary discourse there is a distinction to be observed between circumstances in which one could sensibly raise a question or express a doubt about or plead ignorance of such a thing as whether one has hands (or feet, etc.) and circumstances in which one could *not* sensibly do so. (For example, a wounded soldier who feared that his hands may have to be amputated, and who, upon reviving from anesthesia in the field hospital, had not yet probed the bandages, might ask the nurse, "Do I still have my hands?" or might groggily reply, if asked, that he didn't know (or wasn't sure) whether the doctors had saved his hands. But some days later, when his bandages have been removed and he is washing his hands, he could not sensibly, or rationally, say such a thing.) That there is such a distinction to be recognized within ordinary discourse is a point the skeptic can readily acknowledge. He can allow, that is, that the plain man, except in highly unusual circumstances, would have to be insane to raise questions or have doubts about whether he has hands.

This, I take it, is something like the point Descartes was making when, prior to introducing his dream argument, he observed:

> But although the senses may sometimes deceive us about some minute or remote objects, yet there are many other facts as to which doubt is plainly impossible, although these are gathered from the same source [the senses]: e.g. that I am here sitting by the fire, wearing a winter cloak, holding this paper in my hands, and so on. Again, these hands, and my whole body—how can their existence be denied? Unless indeed I likened myself to some lunatics, whose brains are so upset by persistent melancholy vapours that they firmly assert . . . that they are clad in purple when really they are naked; or that they have a head of pottery, or are pumpkins, or are made of glass; but then they are madmen, and I should appear no less mad if I took them as a precedent for my own case.[16]

Having given himself this caution, Descartes goes on immediately to formulate his skeptical argument, and this fact should suggest to us that there must be some relevant difference between the conclusion of that argument and the ravings of a madman, despite any seeming similarities. And one difference, surely, is that the skeptic, while treating as dubious (what he takes to be) the metaphysical assumptions of "ordinary language," is not thereby bound to conduct his nonphilosophical conversations differently from any other rational man. It therefore behooves one who would persuade us to reject the skeptic's conclusion to avoid, in his persuasions, any suggestion that the skeptic's conclusion is (or resembles) the sort of lunacy from which Descartes sought to distinguish his project.

With these three points in mind, let us turn to the question of how Moore could have thought that he knew something that the skeptic denies one can know.

Moore's Treatment of Skepticism

As I remarked earlier, it would have seemed merely perverse had Moore, in attacking the skeptic's conclusion, flatly replied, "But there *are* material objects on the far side of sense-data. I *know* there are!" Yet, although he was aiming to make such a claim (i.e., that he *knows* there are material objects), he did *not* think he was being perverse when (translating into the concrete) he said, "I know I have hands," etc. Not only did these "concrete" asseverations not seem perverse; they seemed—to Moore, at least—to be the *right* sort of thing to say to the skeptic.

To see why this seemed reasonable to Moore, we must bear in mind that he understood the matter at hand to be this: either I do know that there are material objects on the far side of sense-data or (as the skeptic claims) I don't know this. For Moore the truth lay in one or the other of these alternatives. Now when one begins from an assumption of this sort, there are two quite different ways in which one may attempt to establish in which alternative the truth lies. One way is to argue *for* one of the alternatives; the other is to argue against (or to otherwise discredit) one of the alternatives. Perhaps Descartes could be thought of as proceeding in the former way when, in the Sixth Meditation, he argues that God is no deceiver and that therefore the world is as we judge it to be when we make reasonable judgments. Moore did not argue in this way. He made no attempt to *prove*, that is, offered no premises from which it would follow, that he knows that, for example, this is a finger or that he has hands. It would therefore seem reasonable to suppose that he had adopted the second of the aforementioned methods, that of disproving or discrediting one of the two alternatives, namely, the skeptic's conclusion. This is borne out when he says, in a passage quoted earlier, "This, after all, you know, really is a finger: there is no doubt about it: I know it, and you all know it." Asserting this, Moore tells us nothing that would establish or convince us that he does know it, and yet he is, in a subtle way, aiming to discredit the other alternative, namely, the skeptic's claim that no one does know it. And he has achieved this discrediting by translating into the concrete. As was pointed out earlier, Moore declared that this technique robbed his opponents' skeptical claims of their plausibility. I think we can safely say that this was Moore's *only* way of taking issue with the skeptic, so that if this technique should prove to be unsound, Moore must give the skeptic a pass.

That Moore's method consists of depicting skepticism as absurd becomes obvious in his "Proof of an External World," where, having said that he has two hands and that this is something he knows to be so, he went on to say:

> How absurd it would be to suggest that I did not know it, but only believed it, and that perhaps it was not the case. You might as well suggest that I do not know that I am standing up and talking—that perhaps after all I am not, and that it's not quite certain that I am.[17]

His way of trying to discredit the skeptic's alternative, then, it to brand that alternative as being obviously *absurd*.

Even more revealing of this aspect of Moore's method is a passage in his essay "Certainty." He begins the essay by making (what he calls) "seven assertions," one of which is: "I have clothes on and am not absolutely naked." He continues:

> And I do not think that I can be justly accused of dogmatism or over-confidence for having asserted these things positively in the way that I did. In the case of some kinds of assertions, and under some circumstances, a man can justly be accused of dogmatism for asserting something positively. But in the case of assertions such as I made, made under the circumstances under which I made them, the charge would be absurd. On the contrary, I should have been guilty of absurdity if, under the circumstances, I had *not* spoken positively about these things, if I spoke of them at all. Suppose that now, . . . instead of saying "I have got some clothes on," I were to say "I think I've got some clothes on, but it's just possible that I haven't." Would it not sound rather ridiculous for me now, under these circumstances, to say "I *think* I've got some clothes on" or even to say "I not only think I have, I know that it is very likely indeed that I have, but I can't be quite sure"? For some persons, under some circumstances, it might not be at all absurd to express themselves thus doubtfully. . . . But for me, now, in full possession of my senses, it would be quite ridiculous to express myself in this way, because the circumstances are such as to make it quite obvious that I don't merely think that I have [clothes on], but know that I have.[18]

Here it is entirely clear that Moore's method is to secure our agreement that he does know, not by *proving* that he knows, but by depicting as ridiculous any suggestion to the contrary. The effect of his translating into the concrete, then, is to make the skeptic's position appear ridiculous, absurd, even irrational.[19] But is this fair to the skeptic?

Being Fair to the Skeptic

Let us ask: is the skeptic really prepared to say (or committed to saying) those things Moore calls absurd or ridiculous? Is he, for instance, prepared to say, "Moore, you don't know that you have hands" or committed to saying, when situated as Moore was, "It is possible that I have no clothes on"? The question is ambiguous, and ambiguous in a way that mirrors an ambiguity in Moore's own method. For we need to distinguish the question "Is the skeptic prepared to say (or committed to saying) such things in the course of philosophical discussions?" from the very different question "Is the skeptic prepared to say (or committed to saying) such things in the course of ordinary, nonphilosophical discourse?" The answer to the first of these questions is plainly "Yes," while the answer to the second, as I pointed out in the previous section, is "No," for Cartesian skepticism is to be thought of as attacking "ordinary language" *as a whole* and not in a piecemeal fashion. It would therefore be misleading to say, without qualification, that the skeptic is prepared to say (or is committed to saying) "I don't know whether I have hands."

It would also be misleading, and for much the same reason, to claim, without qualification, that it would be absurd (ridiculous, irrational) for a person who has no ordinary grounds for doubt, to express those doubts that Moore was concerned with (about having hands, etc.). For again we need to distinguish between: (i) "It would be absurd (ridiculous, irrational) for someone having no ordinary grounds for doubt to express such doubts in ordinary, nonphilosophical discourse," and (ii) "It would be absurd (ridiculous, irrational) for a Cartesian skeptic, who has no ordinary grounds for doubt, to express such doubts in the course of expounding his philosophical skepticism." If we take Moore to be saying (i), then everyone, *including the skeptic,* can agree with him, for if someone, not meaning to philosophize, were to say "I don't know for certain whether . . ." in circumstances in which there are no ordinary grounds for a rational man to have doubts, we *would* take the person to be a lunatic[20] or to be saying something ridiculous to get a laugh. On the other hand, if Moore is saying (ii), in other words, that it would be absurd for the skeptic to say, in the course of philosophizing, that he (or Moore) doesn't know he has hands or has clothes on, then what Moore is saying is surely false. Skeptics have been saying such things for centuries, and although others of us may take issue with their reasoning, no one who was following the course of the skeptic's reasoning has thought that these philosophers, when drawing their skeptical conclusion, were (or sounded like) lunatics. And the reason for this is that their skeptical conclusion, understood in its philosophical context, does not sound like a doubt for which the skeptic ought to have, yet lacks, ordinary grounds for doubt. The fact that Moore heard a ring of absurdity in the skeptic's conclusion is due to the fact that, quite unwittingly, he has, by translating into the concrete, *misrepresented* the skeptic, and has thereby made it appear that the skeptic ought to have, but lacks, ordinary grounds for doubt.

This misrepresentation comes about in ways that are not easily recognized or described. I believe, however, that we can identify how it comes about if we focus on the following aspect of several passages quoted above. In the passage from "Proof of an External World" Moore tells us that it would be absurd "to suggest" that he didn't know he had hands, and yet he says nothing about who is to be thought of as making this suggestion or why he makes it. Similarly, in the passage from "Certainty" Moore asks us to "suppose" that he himself had spoken doubtfully about whether he had clothes on and says that his so speaking would have been "ridiculous." Yet he fails to tell us, in this passage, what we are to suppose his reason to have been for speaking thus doubtfully. In both passages, then, he invites us to consider someone's saying something, something he brands "absurd" or "ridiculous," but in neither passage does he provide any details as to *why* the person whom we are to consider saying these things *says* them. Or rather, he doesn't do so explicitly. Nevertheless, there is something about both passages which, in a covert way, suggests these further details. For although Moore is taking issue with skepticism, so that what he here presents as absurd or ridiculous is a skeptic and what skeptics say, yet his translating into the concrete somehow creates (I don't say *deliberately*) the opposite impression, the impression that the imagined person is not a philosopher engaged in philosophical discussion but rather someone speaking without philosophic intent, someone engaged in ordinary discourse. How does his translating into the concrete (covertly) create this impression?

It does so, I believe, in the following ways. First, since Moore does not *say* that the person speaking is speaking with philosophic intent, and since he does not (as Moore presents him to us) speak in the (less "concrete") phraseology we are accustomed to hear from Cartesian skeptics, there is nothing to suggest that the person *is* speaking as a philosopher. Second, the person we are invited to consider would seem (because of the lines Moore gives him to speak) to be expressing an isolated doubt, as we do in ordinary thought or discourse, that is, a doubt *only* about Moore's hands or *only* about his state of dress, and not a doubt about the whole of the external world. It therefore looks as though this person ought to have grounds that are appropriate for doubting precisely that Moore *has hands* (or *is dressed),* and such grounds would, of course, be ordinary (not philosophical) grounds. Third, since the doubt (or seeming doubt) that we are asked to contemplate is apparently about whether Moore is dressed *or naked* (and in the other case, whether Moore has hands *or has lost them through amputation or accident),*[21] the suggestion is that the person we are invited to consider is not to be thought of as being skeptical about having a body (or about Moore's having a body). But this, in turn, suggests that the person we are invited to consider is *not* speaking in the role of a Cartesian skeptic. And finally, since the person we are being invited to consider seems to have no doubt about having a body, we are inclined (since Moore does not warn us against doing so) to picture him as having no doubt that he is on the scene with a full compliment of properly functioning bodily senses. (Recall here Moore's saying, in the passage from "Certainty," ". . . for me, now, in full possession of my senses.") And this, too, leads us to think of him as being someone other than the skeptic, as being someone who does *not*, as he speaks (dubiously) about the matter at hand, have in mind any philosophical grounds for doubt.

All of this, and perhaps more of the same, is suggested to us by Moore's trans lating into the concrete. This, then, explains why Moore found that by transla the skeptic's conclusion into the concrete he had robbed it of all plausibilit what he has in fact done is this: he has covertly scuttled the skeptic and th tic's conclusion and has given us (and himself) something quite different template, namely, the picture of someone with neither ordinary grounds nor philosophical grounds for skepticism who, nevertheless, goes ab that (or speaking as though) he is in doubt or finds various things d is, assuredly, an altogether ridiculous picture, but hardly a picture th barrass the skeptic.

To put the matter in another way, the "expression of doubt" into the mouth of this imagined person cannot be *both* an instar skepticism ("what it means in particular instances") and at th thing said in ordinary, nonphilosophical discourse. And yet Moore needs to have it both ways. For were he to allow that the "expression of doubt" is *not* to be thought of as an instance of the skeptic's skepticism, then anything that might be said about it will be irrelevant to rebutting such skepticism, while if the "expression of doubt" *is* to be thought of as an instance of the skeptic's skepticism (and therefore *not* something said in ordinary discourse), then it cannot be thought of as being (cannot be heard to be) absurd, ridiculous, irrational. Or conversely, insofar as it is to be thought of as being (or heard to be) absurd (ridiculous, irrational), we must think of it as something said in ordinary discourse, since philosophers' talk does not, in its context, sound that way, but in that case it is not something said with philosophic intent and so is not an expression of the skeptic's skepticism. So Moore needs to have what he cannot have: he needs to have it both ways. So the fact that he *thought* he had succeeded in confuting the skeptic can only lead us to conclude that he was (unwittingly) equivocating in his thoughts between these two incompatible alternatives.

Moore's Mistake

We now have, I think, the explanation of how Moore, despite holding the representative theory of perception, could have thought he knew things the skeptic insists one cannot know. Moore thought this because he began by thinking: "Either I know such things or (as the skeptic claims) I do not," and because he then thought, as a result of his translating into the concrete, that he had detected an absurdity in (what he takes to be) the skeptic's claim or conclusion. This, as we have just seen, was a mistake, but Moore, having made that mistake, concluded that it was only reasonable that he should say, as a reply to the skeptic: "I know this is a ~ger; I know I have hands; I know I am dressed." But just as Moore must have ~quivocating in his thoughts about what it would be ridiculous or absurd to ɔ he must have been equivocating in his thoughts about the nature of ˺ge claims. For if they are to be taken (as Moore would have us take ˹ᵗᶦⁿᵍ the skeptic, then Moore cannot rightly hope to secure our by saying: "Anyone who contradicts my knowledge claims ˼dity and deserving of ridicule." Moore could not secure ˹ause if his knowledge claims do contradict the skep- ˹oore, we would be saying what the skeptic says, be ridiculous: we would sound, not like lu-

Moore and the skeptic are in agree-
ᵃl scheme, that the things we actually
lications. But Moore, by translating
ɔ to think that what the skeptic treats
ᴵ world but only whether his hands are
ᵈ or undressed, and so on. And when the
of in this way, the skeptic can be made to
˼tions" represents him as harboring, in a lan-

guage *without* a conceptual scheme, doubts of a sort that would make sense only if our language were a conceptual scheme. But Moore cannot have it both ways. He cannot engage the skeptic unless he allows that our language is a conceptual scheme, but if he does allow that, his "translations" will do no damage to the skeptic; they will have no power to make the skeptic appear irrational or ridiculous. Conversely, if he insists that his translations rob skepticism of its plausibility, the philosophical skeptic can rightly reply: "Not *my* skepticism!"

Conclusion

Moore's translating into the concrete has been taken to be a harmless, and even a valuable, philosophical technique, and yet in the present case it has served only to mislead and confuse. And the confusion extends considerably beyond Moore's own work, for the confusion has, as I indicated in the preceding chapter, been extended by Malcolm and others into much of what has, for half a century, passed for "ordinary language philosophy." Whether it can be rescued from that fate will be discussed in chapters 14 and 15.

Wittgenstein and the Metaphysical Use of Words

I have argued that Wittgenstein, far from being the ordinary language philosopher that he has been taken to be, was as deeply engaged in metaphysics as Russell and Moore. Why, then, did he say that what he does is "to bring words back from their metaphysical to their everyday use" (PI, §116)? Doesn't this show that his aim was to steer *away* from the metaphysical use of words—and, hence, from metaphysics?

Bringing Words Back from Their Metaphysical Use

The answer to that question depends entirely on what one takes to be the metaphysical use of words. As I remarked in chapter 10, there has been a strong inclination to suppose that Moore went a long way toward drawing the line between the metaphysical and the everyday use of words, and philosophers inspired by Moore's work are disposed to view ordinary language in terms of Moore's realism. As I have tried to show, however, Wittgenstein held exactly the opposite view, namely, that a realist interpretation of ordinary language leads one straight into a calamitous skepticism, where even language becomes impossible (see chapter 2), and that the proper interpretation of ordinary language will allow our everyday assertions to pass muster with the skeptic.

This, of course, requires our language to be a phenomenalistic language, so that bringing a word back to its *everyday* use means showing that, appearances not withstanding, the word belongs to a (covert) phenomenalistic language. The metaphysical use, then, from which our words must be rescued is any use that is incompatible with belonging to a (covert) phenomenalistic language.

So when Wittgenstein tell us that what *he* does is to bring words back from their metaphysical to their everyday use, he is telling us that he is defending a phenomenalistic interpretation of English (or German, etc.). In this chapter I want to show how this works by investigating what Wittgenstein says about one of the words that he explicitly mentions in PI, §116, the word *Sein,* which Anscombe has translated as "being." I have no quarrel with this translation, except that it is likely to throw readers off the track. The other possible translation, "existence," would have pointed more surely in the right direction, to the question whether things—tables and chairs—can *exist* unperceived. This is a question Wittgenstein discussed or alluded to quite often, and so far as I can determine the philosophical use of the word *existence* in this context is the only use he ever explicitly spoke of as a "metaphysical use." This, then, is a good test case for deciding how we are to understand Wittgenstein's claim to be bringing words back from their metaphysical to their everyday use.

A Revealing Example

In chapter 2 I quoted Wittgenstein's remark that it is "misleading" to say that in ordinary language we speak of chairs, etc. and that in a phenomenalistic language we would speak of "perceptual objects." This is misleading, he said, because "there is nothing in the one language which cannot also be said in the other, only it will be said differently. We are talking about the same things in each case." A philosopher like Moore would be sure to object to this and might reply as follows: "In ordinary language we say such things as 'The pot boiled over while no one was watching' and 'The diamonds are locked in my safe' but one could not say such things in a phenomenalistic language. For a phenomenalistic language would be characterized, in part, by the fact that one couldn't speak of things existing or happening while no one perceives them."

How might Wittgenstein have responded to this? The answer, as I pointed out in chapter 3, will be apparent if we recall that Wittgenstein held Berkeley is high esteem, for Berkeley had a ready answer. He said that when we talk about a pot in that way, using the indicative mood, we really *mean* something else, something that can be elucidated in the subjunctive mood: we only mean that if we *had* been in the kitchen, we *would* have seen the pot boiling over. And if someone were to protest, saying, "No, we mean, for example, that at 2:00 p.m. no one was in the kitchen, and *at that very time* the pot was boiling over," Berkeley would reply, "Yes, I understand; you mean that if you *had been* in the kitchen at 2:00 p.m. you would have seen the pot boiling over." Berkeley's own example was a slightly different one, involving the word *exist*. He writes:

> The table I write on I say exists, that is, I see and feel it: and if I were out of my study I should say it existed; meaning thereby that if I was in my study I might perceive it, or that some other spirit actually does perceive it. (*Principles*, I, 3)

What Berkeley has done here is a perfect illustration of Wittgenstein's substitution method. He is claiming that instead of saying "That table still exists," we could do away with the indicative mood and say "If I were in my study, I would see a table." And as I pointed out in chapter 3, Wittgenstein endorsed this analysis, saying that "we can actually *transform* a statement about a pencil into a statement about appearances of a pencil—even when no one is there: 'If someone *were* there, he would see . . . etc.'" (LSD, p. 28).

Our question was this: how would Wittgenstein respond to a realist like Moore who opposed his claim that whatever can be said in our ordinary language could also be said in a phenomenological language? The answer, as we can now see, is that he would counter the realist's objections with "transformations" like the one just given. And he would no doubt justify this by saying that his transformation preserves that which in our language engages with experience while eliminating a wheel that is idling, namely, the indicative mood.

Dealing with the Realist's Objection

This will become more apparent if we notice that there is a further parallel between Berkeley and Wittgenstein as regards this issue. Having presented his counterfactual analysis of "exist," Berkeley anticipates that someone who has not grasped his point might pose an objection:

> [I]t will be objected that from the foregoing principles it follows [that] things are every moment annihilated and created anew. The objects of sense exist only when they are perceived: the trees therefore are in the garden, or the chairs in the parlour, no longer than while there is somebody by to perceive them. Upon shutting my eyes all the furniture in the room is reduced to nothing, and barely upon opening them it is again created. (*Principles*, I, §45)

In reply to this objection—which I will call "the realist's objection"—Berkeley refers his reader back to the passage in which he explains that if he were out of his study he would say his table exists, *meaning* thereby that if he were in his study he would perceive it. His point is that no one would raise the realist's objection if they were mindful of the actual *meaning* of the word *exist*. Put differently, Berkeley's point is that whoever poses the above objection has been misled by our using "exist" in the indicative mood—misled into thinking that in the sentences in question "exist" has what we may call an occurrent sense, rather than the sense Berkeley elucidates with a subjunctive sentence.

Wittgenstein, as it happens, also responded to the realist's objection. He stated the objection as follows: "If I turn away the stove is gone. (Things do not exist during the intervals between perceptions.)" and then replied:

> If "existence" is taken in the empirical (not in the metaphysical) sense, this statement [i.e., the *indicative* form "Things do not exist during the intervals between perceptions"] is a wheel turning idly. Our language is in order, once we have understood its syntax [e.g., understood that "exists" requires Berkeley's counterfactual analysis] and recognized the wheels that turn idly. (WVC, p. 48)

In the present case, the "wheel turning idly," in other words, that *does not engage with experience,* is the use of "exist" in the indicative mood. Berkeley, as we have seen, replies to the realist's objection by alluding to his earlier remarks about the meaning of "exist," thereby implying that no one would try to raise that objection if they understood the actual meaning of "exist," which Wittgenstein calls "the empirical sense." So Wittgenstein is declaring that the occurrent sense of "exist" is the metaphysical sense. And following Berkeley he is saying that the ordinary sense, the empirical sense, and the nonoccurrent sense of "exist" are one and the same. That is Wittgenstein's claim.

His claims in this passage about "exist"—about its "empirical" and "metaphysical" uses—are reflected, I suggest, in his listing the word *exist (Sein)* among those of which he says: "Our job is to bring words back from their metaphysical to their everyday use" (PI, §116). His inclusion of the word *exist* strongly suggests that he thought of it as his job to show that realists like Moore are giving the word *exist* a metaphysical use and are thus *mis*using it.

Moore's Protest

I suggested that a realist, such as Moore, would dispute Wittgenstein's claim that anything we say in our ordinary language could also be said in an explicitly phenomenological language. And I further suggested that the realist would point out that we speak of things as existing at times when they are not perceived, which one could *not* do in a phenomenological language. But Wittgenstein, as we can now see, would dispute this, and he would do so by invoking his distinction between what we actually *mean* and what our grammar *suggests* we mean. What we actually mean, he would say, is compatible with phenomenalism. But are realists obliged to accept this answer?

In his 1914 essay "The Status of Sense Data," Moore stated his opposition to phenomenalism by insisted that Berkeley's counterfactual analysis of "exist" fails to capture the "natural sense" of the word. He also put his objection by saying that on Berkeley's view of the matter, when we say such a thing as "There are some jewels locked in this safe," what we say can be true only if it is understood in an "outrageously Pickwickian sense." And this, said Moore, "seems to me to constitute the very great objection to it."[1]

Unfortunately, Moore was not very adept at supporting this objection. He could only say that he had a "strong propensity to believe" that *what* he knows when he knows that something, such as a coin in a safe, existed while unperceived, is that it existed in the occurrent sense, not in Berkeley's Pickwickian sense.[2] Let us consider, then, what Wittgenstein might have said in reply, and in particular let us try to figure out *why* Wittgenstein might have thought that the everyday use of "exist" is that explained by Berkeley.

The place to begin is by reminding ourselves that sometimes the dispute between realists and idealists is carried on by idealists saying that tables and chair do not exist in the intervals between perceptions and realist insisting that they do exist at such times. Both parties treat the issue as a factual one, and yet it is clear that neither is proposing to settle the dispute by an empirical investigation. It is also clear that both parties are using the word *exist* in what Moore called its "natural sense," that is, the occurrent sense. With this in mind, let us also notice the following.

An attorney might say to his clients: "Your uncle's will, which you all thought had been destroyed in the fire, still exists. It is locked in the safe at my office." If a client then expressed a doubt about this, the attorney might say, "Come, I will show you," whereupon he opens the safe and produces the will. Now, if it can, in this way, be established that the attorney spoke the truth, why is it that the dispute between realists and idealists cannot be similarly settled? Could the insoluble character of their dispute have anything to do with the word *exist?* The attorney, clearly enough, is using words—including the word *exists*—in an ordinary way. It is equally clear that the metaphysicians, whose dispute cannot be settled empirically, are using "exist" in the occurrent sense. Shouldn't we infer, then, from the insoluble character of the philosophical dispute both (i) that the occurrent sense is *not* the ordinary sense and (ii) that the insoluble character of the dispute between realists and idealists is the result of their using "exist" without its ordinary, nonoccurrent meaning?

I can imagine Wittgenstein saying that if realists and idealists were using the word *exist* with its ordinary meaning, they wouldn't be embroiled in an *insoluble* dispute, for when "exist" is used in its ordinary sense, the question whether something that isn't now perceived still exists can be answered by empirical means, as the attorney did.

This is the position Wittgenstein takes in The Blue Book, where he says that sometimes "an assertion which the metaphysician makes . . . can also be used to state a fact of experience. . . . [W]hen he says 'this tree doesn't exist when nobody looks at it', this might [but does not] mean: 'this tree vanishes when we turn our backs to it'" (pp. 56–57). Presumably, Wittgenstein meant that "The tree doesn't exist when nobody looks at it" would be used to state 'a fact of experience' if it meant that, having turned our backs to the tree, we discover, on turning back around, that the tree is nowhere to be found. This comes out more clearly in *Philosophical Remarks,* where he writes:

> If, for instance, you ask, 'Does the box still exist when I'm not looking at it?', the only right answer would be 'Of course, unless someone has taken it away or destroyed it'. Naturally, a philosopher [whose question uses "exist" in the occurrent sense] would be dissatisfied with this answer, but it would quite rightly reduce his way of formulating the question *ad absurdum.* (PR, p. 88)

I take it that Wittgenstein is saying that there is an ordinary way of asking whether a box that is not in view still exists and that this ordinary question can be answered because the answer—whether it be negative or affirmative—will state "a fact of experience." A negative answer will mean that the box has been destroyed, for example, smashed up for kindling wood ("Look here. These splinters are all that's left of it"). An affirmative answer will mean that the box has *not* been destroyed ("Here, you see, is the box; nothing's happened to it"). What I am suggesting, then, is that Wittgenstein's view of the metaphysical dispute is this: if Moore and the idealist were using language in the ordinary way, their disagreement could be settled by experience, so the fact that it *cannot* be settled that way shows that they are *not* using language in an ordinary way, and in particular they are misusing the word *exist* by using it in the occurrent sense.

So Wittgenstein would conclude both (a) that the occurrent sense of "exist," which Moore called the natural sense, must, since it figures in the insoluble metaphysical dispute, be a nonstandard—or metaphysical—use, and (b) that the attorney's usage, which is our ordinary usage, gives "exist" a nonoccurrent meaning, namely, that elucidated by Berkeley.

This, I suggest, is how we are to understand Wittgenstein's distinction, in the above-quoted passage, between the empirical and the metaphysical sense of "exist" or "existence." Then, having introduced this distinction, Wittgenstein made his point by saying, "Our language is in order once we have understood its syntax and recognized the wheels that turn idly." In this instance, understanding its syntax means coming to see that "exist" requires (in the relevant instances) Berkeley's counterfactual analysis. And the wheel that turns idly here, that is, that does not engage with experience, is the metaphysical use of "exist." (Wittgenstein: "The confusions which occupy us arise when language is like an engine idling, not when it is doing work" (PI, §132).)

The Invisible White Rabbit

To illustrate his point Wittgenstein elsewhere considers someone saying, "There is a white rabbit on my sofa which cannot be seen because whenever anyone looks at it, it vanishes." Here "There is" is being used in an occurrent sense, and Wittgenstein comments (WL32, p. 111) that since this (indicative mood) statement admits of "no falsification or verification," that is, since it does not in any way engage with experience, it is "merely senseless (an idle running wheel)." This, according to Wittgenstein, is why Moore's use of "exist" is also senseless, for Moore, using "exist" in an occurrent sense, wants to say that his hand continues to exist at those very times when no one perceives it. Let us ask: is it fair of Wittgenstein to compare Moore's claim with his own white rabbit example?

The comparison is not fair, although one can see why Wittgenstein would have thought otherwise. Moore insists that he *believes* that things like documents and hands exist unperceived, and yet he seems not to regard his belief as verifiable. He does not, that is, undertake to prove that he's right by doing anything like what the attorney in my example did. (Whereas the attorney established that the document still exists by producing it from his safe, Moore did not, for example, put his hand into his pocket and then undertake to prove that it continued to exist while out of sight by drawing forth his hand and displaying it triumphantly.) Wittgenstein, no doubt, thought that Moore's failure to act like the attorney made him like someone saying there's a rabbit on the sofa so long as no one is looking. But this is not true. For it is not Moore but the idealist who renders irrelevant any such hand-in-the-pocket demonstration. The idealist is thinking as follows. When I tell you that my headache is gone and then, two hours later, say that my headache has come back again, it will not make sense, except as a joke, to ask me, "Where do you think it was in the meantime?" Any talk about the headache in the interim is going to be nonsensical. And that is how the idealist thinks it is with a hand that is out of sight for an interval: to say that it *existed* during the interval makes no more sense than asking where my headache was in the interim. This, as Moore well understood, is *why* he can't answer the idealist by, for example, putting his hand in his pocket and then withdrawing it and saying, "There, you see, it *didn't* cease to exist while in my pocket." The fact that this sort of reply was not available to Moore was not *his* fault, so to speak, but the idealist's. And that is why Moore's case is not at all like someone saying *both* that there is a white rabbit on his sofa and that it's there only when no one sees it. Unlike Moore, someone who said *this* would be the person who is *both* (a) asserting the existence of something at a given time and (b) rendering his assertion unverifiable.

What creates the problem in Moore's case is not that, by using "exist" in an occurrent sense, he misuses the word and makes the problem insoluble. Moore is using the word with the same occurrent meaning as did the attorney in my example. And therefore Moore is *right* to protest that Berkeley's proposed nonoccurrent sense is Pickwickian. (And, of course, Wittgenstein was wrong to claim that *he* was bringing "exist" back from its metaphysical to its everyday use.) What Moore failed to consider is that things like documents or chairs meet their ends in quite particular ways: they may be consumed by flames, may rot away, may be devoured by insects, and so on. And when we say that something does or does not still exist, we mean that it did or did not meet its end in one of these possible ways. But when idealists say that chairs, etc. do not (or cannot) exist unperceived, they do not mean that when I turn out the light at night, the chair that was in the corner of my room is instantly devoured by insects or immediately rots away. Rather, they are saying: a chair is nothing but sense-impressions, and therefore, since sense-impressions can exist only so long as someone has (or perceives) them, chairs, too, can exist only while they are perceived. Clearly, there is only one way to take issue with idealists, and that is *not* by a hand-in-the-pocket demonstration of the sort mentioned above. The only way is to show that the word *chair* is not used in the way idealists think it is.[3] Once *that* is established, there will no longer be a problem about whether chairs depend for their existence on being perceived. I mean, we won't need to go on saying, with Moore, that we *believe* that such things exist unperceived.

I have discussed this example at length in order to illustrate my point that when Wittgenstein proposed to bring a word back from its metaphysical to its everyday use, he decided which use was the everyday one, not by paying attention to what people actually say, but by considering what sort of use is consistent with his own metaphysical views.

The Misperception of Wittgenstein

There are several reasons why philosophers have failed to see that this was Wittgenstein's procedure. One reason is that empiricism still has some influence on our thinking, and philosophers in whom this influence is strongest are prevented from recognizing that Wittgenstein's pronouncements about language were the product, not of any attention to language, but of his own empiricist assumptions. (These philosophers seem to think that empiricism, or a certain strain of empiricism, differs from other philosophical views in being commonsensical and in harmony with "ordinary language."[4]) For other philosophers the problem is that Wittgenstein's aphoristic style allows them to see in his writings what they want to, and many of them have taken him to be a sort of Moorean defender of ordinary language.

Despite these difficulties it should be possible to see that on a number of issues Wittgenstein took positions that would seem plausible only to someone who subscribed to phenomenalism or behaviorism or some other reductionist view. I will mention three such cases, all of which I have discussed at length elsewhere. First, the epistemological problems that Wittgenstein grappled with in *On Certainty* are, for the most part, problems he was obliged to deal with for one reason only: because phenomenalism *creates* those problems.[5] Second, his wrestling with the "private language" problem was a direct consequence of his reductionist views about memory and the past.[6] Finally, the most obvious instance of Wittgenstein's resort to a reductionist solution is his treatment of religion, for he explicitly maintained the thoroughly implausible view that religious believers are not to be thought of as necessarily harboring beliefs about the world over and above their secular beliefs.[7]

Wittgenstein and Ordinary Language

In the *Tractatus* Wittgenstein said that philosophical problems arise because "the logic of our language is misunderstood" (p. 3). It follows that the way to escape from philosophical problems is to redress such misunderstandings. And the way to do that, it would seem, is to pay close attention to language in some appropriate way. In the *Investigations,* where he continued to think of philosophical problems as requiring close attention to language, Wittgenstein said:

> One cannot guess how a word functions. One has to *look at* its use and learn from that.
>
> But the difficulty is to remove the prejudice which stands in the way of doing this. It is not a *stupid* prejudice. (§340)

It was easy for others to assume that Wittgenstein had followed his own advice, that he had overcome his own prejudices and taken a good look at the use of those words that are philosophically troublesome. If I am right, he did nothing of the sort. Naturally, he *believed* he was following his own advice. He was sure that he could tell which use of a word is metaphysical and which everyday, so that he could find his way back from the one to the other. And his sureness, his enormous self-confidence, inspired devotion, even blind devotion.[8] But it was a case of the blind leading the blind. What he took to be an ordinary use of words was, instead, a metaphysical use that satisfied his metaphysical requirements.

Does this mean that Wittgenstein was not an ordinary language philosopher? It means that he wasn't what he has most often been taken to be. But he did invoke ordinary language, and he did so, moreover, in a manner that has a precedent in earlier philosophers. Berkeley gave quite a good account of this style of philosophy, and one can find intimations of it as far back at least as Augustine. It is a style one might call "Metaphysical Ordinary Language Philosophy."

Metaphysical Ordinary Language Philosophy

I have suggested that there are three very different approaches to philosophical problems that might be thought of as "ordinary language philosophy," and I have proposed to call them "Standard," "Metaphysical," and "Investigative." I do not mean to suggest by this division that every ordinary language philosopher fits neatly into one or another of these categories, for it is not uncommon for a philosopher to employ one of these methods at one time (or when dealing with one problem) and to employ another at another time (or when dealing with some other problem). This is not because they recognize that they are doing something different from time to time but because they fail to see how different these methods are.

In chapter 10 I discussed one type of ordinary language philosophy—the type I have called "Standard"—and argued that it is a question-begging strategy. In the present chapter I will discuss the oldest of the three types, Metaphysical Ordinary Language Philosophy.

When Philosophy and Language Collide

To understand this sort of ordinary language philosophy, we must begin from the fact that over the centuries philosophers have often recognized that their own philosophical theories conflict in some way with what people say in the common affairs of life. But these conflicts are not like those in which old wives' tales collide with science, where science shows that people have been saying something untrue. Rather, philosophers find themselves in conflict with certain features of the language in which we normally express ourselves.

What is the significance of such conflicts? Do they show that one's philosophizing has gone awry or that our language is somehow defective? One might think that philosophers would long ago have come to agreement about these ancient conflicts. In fact, however, no such unanimity exists, and the three types of ordinary language philosophy are, to some extent, different ways of thinking about and dealing with these conflicts. Standard Ordinary Language Philosophy, as we have seen, treats such conflicts as proof that philosophizing has gone awry.

Metaphysical Ordinary Language Philosophy takes a different approach. Philosophers of this school, when they notice a conflict between some theory they hold and ordinary language, declare that the conflict is more apparent than real. They say that their theory, although it conflicts with a literal interpretation of the plain man's words, is not in conflict with the plain man's actual *meaning*, which is determined by the practical application of those words. They say that when they propose a philosophical theory that conflicts with the plain man's words, they are not impugning ordinary language because those words, despite the appearance of conflict, serve us nicely in our practical affairs.

Philosophers who deal in this way with such conflicts have found that it serves their interests in several ways. They have found, for example, that it provides them with a way to defend their pet theory against its critics, for when it is pointed out that their theory sounds absurd when measured against many things we commonly *say*, they can reply that their critics are guilty of attending only to the plain man's words and not to the *use* of those words. In addition, some of these philosophers have used it to turn the tables on their critics. Instead of defending their own views, they say to their critics: "Your philosophical views differ from mine because you've been taken in by the misleading forms of words in our language."

Augustine

An early example is found in Augustine's *Confessions* where, in Book XI, he writes:

> What is now plain is that neither future nor past things are in existence, and that it is not correct to say there are three periods of time: past, present, and future. Perhaps it would be proper to say there are three periods of time: the present of things past, the present of things present, the present of things future. For, these three are in the soul and I do not see them elsewhere: the present of things past is memory; the present of things present is immediate vision; the present of things future is expectation.

Augustine is saying here that although we misleadingly speak of remembering past wars or past worries, we are speaking only of present recollections. This would seem to put him in conflict with the fact that, in our ordinary use of words, we do not express everything in the present tense, that we also make statements in the past and future tenses. Augustine goes on to say, however, that when he declares "that it is not correct to say there are three periods of time: past, present, and future," he is not criticizing what we commonly say, for "there are few things which we express properly; more frequent are those that we express improperly, though making our intentions understood." This comes to: what we say when using the past and future tenses is misleadingly expressed, but that does not matter because in practice we succeed, despite the misleading character of our words, in making ourselves understood.

This is what puts Augustine in the class of those who hold that, although their philosophical theories appear to conflict with what we all commonly say, there is in fact no such conflict because we do not *mean* what our words *suggest* we are saying. So Augustine has inoculated himself against a critic who might say to him: "You were born many years ago, so the events of your childhood are not something present, as your theory of time makes it out to be; those events occurred in the past." Augustine's reply would be: "You are right in thinking that in practice I use the past tense to refer to my childhood, that is, that I might now say I *stole* an apple when I was a boy, but this form of words is misleading, for it wrongly suggests that that event is not now present to me."

Leibniz

Leibniz is another example of a philosopher who disarms his critics in this way. Writing to Christian Huygens about his own philosophy, Leibniz remarked, "I try to accommodate myself to common usage wherever I can."[1] What did this come to in Leibniz's actual practice? Not always the same thing. In his lengthy debate with Samuel Clarke concerning whether space and time are merely "something relative," Leibniz skillfully defended his position by appealing to ordinary language.[2] In other instances, however, he managed to reconcile his philosophy with "common usage" only by declaring that the plain man's words do not mean what they appear to mean. His theory of preestablished harmony regarding human actions is a case in point.

It was Leibniz's view that (many) human actions consist of two distinct parts: something happens in one's soul (e.g., a man decides to go to the library) and also something bodily happens (his legs move). Or: he wants to look out the window and his head turns. But events in the soul cannot affect the body, according to Leibniz, and so he devised his theory of preestablished harmony to explain how the two parts of a human action are coordinated. God, he said, has prearranged a harmony between the events in people's souls and the movements of their bodies, and this is how it's possible for me to walk to the library. (If God had not established this harmony, I might decide to go to the library and then nothing further would happen—my legs would remain motionless.)

Understandably, some people found Leibniz's theory quite peculiar. One of them, Simon Foucher, undertook to criticize it by insisting that on Leibniz's view a person no more actually *moves* his foot than does a dreamer who, while remaining motionless, *dreams* that he moves his foot, in other words, in each case there occurs the mental part of an action—the desire to go somewhere, but in neither case does the desire *itself* produce locomotion. That is, since Leibniz holds that there is no connection between mind and body, when a man's foot moves, that's not something the man does; it happens only because God has arranged a sort of coincidence. Therefore, said Foucher, it is a consequence of Leibniz's view that we oughtn't to express ourselves in the *ordinary* way by saying "I tapped my foot" or "I walked to the library," but should say instead, "In harmony with my desires my foot moved" or "In harmony with my desires my body proceeded to the library."[3]

Foucher took this consequence to be perfectly absurd and so thought he had made a telling point against Leibniz's theory. Leibniz, however, refused to concede that his theory entailed this absurd consequence. While it is true, on his theory, that our minds do not, in a strict sense, act on our bodies, it does not follow, he insisted, that we oughtn't to say "I tapped my foot" or "I walked to the library." For, "provided we rightly understand them," said Leibniz, even Copernicans "speak truly of the rising of the sun," and "in the same way I hold that it is most true that substances act upon one another, provided we understand that one is the cause of changes in the other in consequence of the laws of harmony."[4] Leibniz's argument is this: although the Copernican theory declares that the sun does not circle the earth, no one thinks that that theory implies that we should stop saying that the sun rose at seven this morning, and in similar fashion we shouldn't think that his theory of preestablished harmony requires a change in the way we speak of human actions. Our ordinary form of expression is perfectly all right, he is saying, but philosophers must be careful not to misconstrue it, as Foucher did in thinking the plain man means that we directly (without God's harmonizing) produce the motions of our bodies.

It is this sort of thing, when practiced in a systematic way, that I am calling "Metaphysical Ordinary Language Philosophy." Its essential features are these: philosophers of this school form philosophical theories while paying no heed to words or language and, having done so, then argue that their theories, although they appear to conflict, do not *really* conflict with what we all say in the common affairs of life. And to remove the appearance of conflict, they adopt a use theory of meaning, which says, "Don't look at the forms of words in the plain man's speech; look, instead, at his *use* of those words, at how they serve practical purposes."[5]

Berkeley

Neither Augustine nor Leibniz gave a systematic account of this style of philosophizing. The first to do so seems to have been Berkeley. This came about because he advances a theory of causation that resembles Leibniz's preestablished harmony. According to his theory, when I extend my hands toward the fire to warm them, it is not the fire that warms them but rather, at the right moment, God "excites in me a sensation of warmth." More generally, his theory is that all the objects of our perception are perfectly "inert," which appears to conflict with the fact that we say that the fire *warmed* my hands, that the big fire in the hearth *made* the room too hot, and so on. Berkeley, having recognized that his theory appears to conflict with many of the things we commonly say, entertained the following objection to it:

[I]t will . . . be demanded [of me] whether it does not seem absurd [for a philosopher] to take away natural causes, and to ascribe everything to the immediate operation of spirits? We must no longer say upon these principles that fire heats, or that water cools, but [must say instead] that a spirit heats [the room], and so forth. Would not a man be deservedly laughed at, who should talk after this manner?

In reply Berkeley concedes that a man who talked in that manner would be deserving of ridicule, but he denies that his theory requires that we talk in this absurd way. For, he says,

> in such things we ought to think with the learned, and speak with the vulgar. They who . . . are convinced of the truth of the Copernican system do nevertheless say "the sun rises," "the sun sets," or "comes to the meridian"; and if they affected a contrary style in common talk it would without doubt appear very ridiculous. A little reflection on what is said will make it manifest that the common use of language would receive no manner of alteration or disturbance from the admission of our tenets [regarding causation].
>
> In the ordinary affairs of life, any phrases may be retained, so long as they excite in us proper sentiments, or dispositions to act in such a manner as is necessary for our well-being, how false soever they may be if taken in a strict and speculative sense.[6]

Notice that this last sentence contains the germ of Wittgenstein's idea that we should look upon a "sentence as an instrument and its sense as its employment" (PI, §421). This needs exploring.

Berkeley says that there are forms of expression in our language that will mislead us if we take them at face value, if we take them in a "strict sense." But how else, we might ask, *can* we take (what at least appear to be) causal verbs in our language, as when someone orders us to "warm up the room with a big fire"? Berkeley's answer would be that sentences of this sort serve us well because "they excite in us proper sentiments or dispositions to act." If someone says to me, "Warm up the room with a fire in the hearth," he only wants me to build and light a fire. He doesn't additionally want me to think that the fire has in it an "active principle" for raising the room temperature. If I build a fire and then God (not the fire) does the rest, he will have the result he wanted. And if he compliments me by saying "The fire warmed the room quickly," I can rightly feel complimented, for after I lit the fire, the room did warm quickly—and not because warm air entered the room through an open widow. So despite the fact that our form of expression unfortunately lends itself to philosophical misunderstanding—to the idea that one thing we observe (the fire) actually *causes* something else we observe (the rise in temperature), it is nevertheless eminently practical, and that is all that's required of the words and phrases of ordinary language. If they perform their office, there can be no reason to object to them.

This is Berkeley's answer to a philosopher who would ridicule his metaphysics by saying that it conflicts with what we say in the common affairs of life. Appropriating Wittgenstein's terminology (PI, §664), we may say that what conflicts with his metaphysics, as Berkeley sees it, is only the "surface grammar" of our language, not its "depth grammar," its use in human activities.

This, it must be added, is a particular application of Berkeley's more general point about language, namely, that

> the communicating of ideas marked by words is not the chief and only end of language, as is commonly supposed. There are other ends, as the raising of some passion, the exciting to or deterring from an action, the putting the mind in some particular disposition; to which the former [i.e., putting an image in one's hearer's

mind] is in many cases barely subservient, and sometimes entirely omitted, when these [i.e., passions, actions, etc.] can be obtained without it, as I think does not unfrequently happen in the familiar use of language. . . . If anyone shall join ever so little reflection of his own to what has been said, I believe that it will evidently appear to him that general names are often used in propriety of language without the speaker's designing them for marks of ideas in his own, which he would have them raise in the mind of the hearer.[7]

Berkeley is here rejecting Locke's account of the "chief and only end of language"[8] and is replacing it with a use theory of meaning. This is what enables him to say, in the preceding passage, that "in the ordinary affairs of life, any phrases may be retained, so long as they excite in us proper sentiments, or dispositions to act in such a manner as is necessary for our well-being, how false soever they may be if taken in a strict and speculative sense."[9] If such misleading phrases have a use in human activities, they are not defective and in need of reform, for they serve their purpose.

This is, I believe, the earliest attempt to work out a systematic account of Metaphysical Ordinary Language Philosophy. Its principal characteristics are that (i) it is resorted to as a means of reconciling a philosopher's pet theory with the fact that it seems to conflict with things we commonly say, and (ii) to achieve this reconciliation it declares that the appearance of conflict is owing to the fact (a) that we misinterpret certain ordinary words and phrases and (b) that we make this mistake because we fail to realize that the meaning of words and phrases, that is, their philosophically relevant interpretation, is fixed by their *use*.

Reid

Another philosopher in whom these ideas can be found is Thomas Reid. Although he appears at times to appeal to ordinary language in a way suggestive of Standard Ordinary Language Philosophy (see the passage quoted from Reid in chapter 10), his actual views about language and philosophy are rather more complex. We can discern an important feature of them by considering a passage in which Reid addresses the fact that we commonly say things that conflict—or *seem* to conflict— with his own mind-body dualism. He writes:

There is another question relating to phraseology which this subject suggests. A man says he feels pain in a particular part of his body; in his toe, for instance. Now reason assures us that pain, being a sensation, can only be in the sentient being, as its subject—that is, in the mind. And though philosophers have disputed much about the place of the mind, yet none of them ever placed it in the toe. What shall we say, then, in this case? Do our senses really deceive us, and make us believe a thing which our reason determines to be impossible? I answer, *first*, That, when a man says he has pain in his toe, he is perfectly understood, both by himself and those who hear him. This is all that he intends. He really feels what he and all men call a pain in the toe, and therefore there is no deception in the matter. Whether, therefore, there be any impropriety in the phrase or not, is of no consequence in common life. It answers all the ends of speech, both to the speaker and the hearers.

In all languages there are phrases which have a distinct meaning; while, at the same time, there may be something in the structure of them that disagrees with the analogy of grammar or with the principles of philosophy. And the reason is, because language is not made either by grammarians or philosophers. Thus, we speak of feeling pain as if pain was something distinct from the feeling of it. We speak of pain coming and going, and removing from one place to another. Such phrases are meant by those who use them in a sense that is neither obscure nor false. But the philosopher puts them into his alembic, reduces them to their first principles, draws out of them a sense that was never meant, and so imagines that he has discovered an error of the vulgar.

I observe, *second,* That, when we consider the sensation of pain by itself, without any respect to its cause, we cannot say with propriety that the toe is either the place or the subject of it. But it ought to be remembered that, when we speak of pain in the toe, the sensation is combined in our thought with the cause of it, which really is in the toe. The cause and effect are combined in one complex notion, and the same name serves for both. It is the business of the philosopher to analyse this complex notion, and to give different names to its different ingredients. He gives the name *pain* to the sensation only, and the name *disorder* to the unknown cause of it. Then it is evident that the disorder only is in the toe, and that it would be an error to think that the pain is in it. But we ought not to ascribe this error to the vulgar, who never made the distinction, and who, under the name pain, comprehend both the sensation and its cause.[10]

It is not hard to see where Reid's reasoning goes wrong. He sets up the wrong contrast when he writes, "A man says he feels pain in a particular part of his body; in his toe, for instance," but "reason assures us that pain, being a sensation, can only be in the sentient being, as its subject—that is, in the mind." Here is what Reid will claim to be no more than an apparent conflict, but in support of this claim he declares that when we speak of a pain in the toe or the elbow, we are using "pain" in such a way that its meaning includes the physical cause of pain as well as the sensation. This is not true, of course, for I can say that there's a pain in my foot although I don't know *what* the cause is (it might be in my toe, in case I have a broken blood vessel, or not in my toe, in case there's a pebble in my shoe). And in order to say that my head hurts, I needn't first decide whether the cause is in my head, as with a migraine headache, or not in my head, as happens when I'm wearing a tight-fitting hat. So when we say, "There is a sharp pain in my foot," we are, contrary to Reid, giving the location of the pain, qua sensation. But if Reid were to concede this, he would think that our manner of speaking is indefensible, for he is sure that a pain, qua sensation, can be nowhere but in the mind. But this is his mistake. A doctor may ask an accident victim, "Where is your greatest pain: in your neck or your back?" That is a question we understand and can answer. And our asking and answering questions of *that* sort gives us the only meaning we attach to locutions regarding "the location of pain," such as "sharp pain in my chest."

It would, however, be possible to introduce a new meaning, one that is of philosophical interest only. For we can call attention to a difference between pointing to "where the pain is" and pointing to something like a splinter in our thumb. If one is asked "Where do you hurt?" or "Where is the pain?" one can point without paying attention to whether one's finger is aimed directly at some place on one's body, and sometimes, as in the case of a phantom limb, one will *not* be aiming at some part of one's body. By contrast, if you want someone to remove a splinter from your thumb and are asked, "Where is the splinter?" it is necessary, when you point, to pay attention to the splinter's location in your body, that is, to look for it or feel for it with a finger. If, in response to that question, you pointed to a place in midair, the person you are speaking to couldn't take that as any sort of answer. You would not have shown or said where the splinter was, and you might be told, reproachfully, "You're not *pointing* to anything."[11] But if an amputee complained of a sharp pain and, when asked, said, "Right here," pointing (perhaps unwittingly) into thin air, we would understand. We would not say, reproachfully, "You're not *pointing* to anything!"

On account of this difference someone might introduce a distinction between location in regard to bodily sensations and location in regard to something like a splinter or a blister, and it might be natural to do so by saying that splinters and blisters have bodily location and sensations do not. But if we did say this, we would not be suggesting that people should not say, "There is a pain in my toe" or "My head hurts." The new distinction would have no bearing on the doctor's question "Where do you hurt?" or "Where is your greatest pain?" And it doesn't give us a new way of answering when the dentist asks, "Is the toothache in an upper or a lower tooth?" We aren't going to say, "Neither; the toothache is in my mind."

Consider now Reid's reasoning in the passage quoted above. He says that reason assures us that a pain can only be in a mind and that some philosophers, being aware to this, insist that for this very reason ordinary language is defective since we talk as though aches and pains could be somewhere in the body. Reid clearly agrees with these philosophers that *if*, in such cases, we were speaking of pain qua sensation, this *would* be in error, that when speaking of "the sensation of pain by itself," one must, if one gives its location, say that it's in the mind. But unlike those other philosophers, Reid was unwilling to accuse the plain man of an error, and since he was not about to abandon dualism and the idea that sensations (along with thoughts, feelings, etc.) are denizens of the mind, he sought to reconcile his theory with ordinary language by saying that "pain in the toe" is a misleading form of words, that it does not, as it seems to, place a *sensation* in a toe. So those who disagree with him are guilty, he says, of distilling out of these words "a sense that was never meant."

But how did Reid decide what is or is not meant by these ordinary phrases? Clearly, he did not do so by paying close attention to language. Rather, his mind was made up by his antecedent allegiance to dualism, to the idea that pains, being mental phenomena, can no more be in one's toe than in a stone. His observations about language, instead of being philosophically unbiased, were dictated by his dualism. So the passage under discussion reveals Reid's adherence to the two main elements of Metaphysical Ordinary Language Philosophy, which are that (i) philosophers resort to it in order to reconcile their pet theory with something we commonly say when the two seem to conflict, and (ii) to achieve this reconciliation, philosophers say that the appearance of conflict arises only from the fact that ordinary language contains misleading forms of words and that the apparent conflict disappears when those forms of words are properly interpreted.

The Characteristics of Metaphysical Ordinary Language Philosophy

Let us now think more generally about philosophers who regard (i) and (ii) as important truths about language and philosophy. It seems clear that they would want to distinguish between the real and the apparent meanings of our ordinary words and phrases, perhaps locating the apparent meaning in linguistic structure and the real meaning in the *use* of words. This is the position taken by the philosophers quoted earlier in this chapter. Reid, for example, says: "In all languages there are phrases which have a distinct meaning; while, at the same time, there may be something in the structure of them that disagrees with . . . the principles of philosophy." Augustine says that "there are few things which we express properly; more frequent are those that we express improperly, though making our intentions understood." And Berkeley says that despite the fact that such phrases will prove to be false if they are "taken in a strict sense," they may be retained "in the ordinary affairs of life . . . so long as they excite in us proper sentiments, or dispositions to act in such a manner as is necessary for our well-being." This is Metaphysical Ordinary Language Philosophy. It is also Wittgenstein's position.

Wittgenstein

It should be clear from what we have seen that Wittgenstein exhibits the defining characteristics of Metaphysical Ordinary Language Philosophy. First of all, in order to reconcile his empiricism with ordinary language at just those points where there appears to be a conflict between them, he claims to be aligning himself with the ordinary use of a word—the word *exist,* for example. Second, to achieve this reconciliation, he says that the appearance of conflict arises only from the fact that ordinary language contains misleading forms of words and that if we will ignore those grammatical forms and pay attention to the *use* of words, we will see how those forms of words ought to be interpreted, and the appearance of conflict will vanish.

"Language," said Wittgenstein, "sets everyone the same traps; it is an immense network of easily accessible wrong turnings" (CV, p. 18). "We are up against trouble caused by our way of expression" (BB, p. 48). So we must be on guard against "the confusion our language creates" (PR, p. 153). "Philosophy is a battle against the bewitchment of our intelligence by means of language" (PI, §109). Even so, there is no good philosophical reason to call for the reform of ordinary language, for "the confusions which occupy [philosophers] arise when language is like an engine idling, not when it is doing work" (PI, §132). If philosophers are to overcome their problems, they must pay attention to the *use* of words, to their role in human activities, for in most cases "the meaning of a word is its use in the language" (§43).

It would be inappropriate to speak as though Metaphysical Ordinary Language Philosophy were a school of thought, as though its aims were clear and were shared by a recognized group or by philosophers who recognized in each other a shared conception. It would be more appropriate to say that Wittgenstein stands alone as the apostle of this sort of philosophizing. Although Berkeley came close to enunciating its principles, it remained for Wittgenstein to define philosophy in terms of them. But what he thus defined remained an enigma to others. While there were those who fancied themselves as his followers, they were evidently a disappointment to him. ("It cannot be said that Wittgenstein was happy about the effect of his work. Rightly or wrongly, he appeared to believe that philosophical questions were very much harder than, in his view, many philosophers thought."[12]) Although Wittgenstein did not care about broadcasting his views or gaining acceptance, at some point he seems to have abandoned all hope of communicating his ideas: "Nearly all my writings are private conversations with myself. Things that I say to myself tête-à-tête" (CV, p. 77).[13]

The Futility of Metaphysical Ordinary Language Philosophy

There is an obvious difficulty with Metaphysical Ordinary Language Philosophy. It is a strategy available to philosophers of almost any persuasion—to dualists as well as behaviorists, to materialists as well as idealists, and so on. It is practiced by philosophers who begin from preconceived philosophical theories, which they never test against the actual use of words because when a conflict arises, they immediately place the blame, not on their theory, but on some feature of our language, which they denounce as misleading. Consequently, several of these "ordinary language philosophers" can hold conflicting philosophical theories—as Reid and Wittgenstein do in regard to the self or ego. Each will claim to be right and the others wrong, but their disagreements can never be resolved because they pay no attention to language until it is too late, until they have adopted a theory and a biased view of language.

This, it seems to me, is what we find in so much of the "linguistic philosophy" of recent decades, including the work done by philosophers who regard Wittgenstein as their champion. Among those claiming to be on the side of ordinary language we find, mainly, empiricists, but also some Kantians and, owing to Moore's influence, a number of dualists.[14] And when it comes to philosophy of religion, one can find almost anything—anything from empiricists to Kierkegaardians.[15] It is hardly to be wondered at, then, that a growing company of philosophers view this scene with considerable exasperation and regard "ordinary language philosophy" as something contemptible. This verdict would be justified, perhaps, except that there is another, very different type of ordinary language philosophy, one that suffers from none of the deficiencies of the other two types.

Investigative Ordinary Language Philosophy

As I remarked in chapter 10, there is a danger, when thinking about ordinary language philosophy, of ignoring some fundamental differences. The most important of these is the difference between the Investigative variety of ordinary language philosophy and the Standard and Metaphysical varieties, which I have already discussed. I attach such significance to this because I believe that the Investigative variety may be the only sort of philosophy that will ever produce viable results. Why, then, has it gone unnoticed—or unheralded—for so long? The reason, apparently, is that word has gotten around that ordinary language philosophy is a failure. How did that happen?

The Universal Dismisser

When it is assumed that there are no important differences among ordinary language philosophers, it is also assumed that a criticism that succeeds against one succeeds against all. The criticism that has been deemed most successful in this way—the Universal Dismisser, as we might call it—is the criticism discussed in chapter 10. According to this criticism, ordinary language philosophers proceed on the naive assumption that English is an ideal language, that its vocabulary and grammar reflect the actual metaphysical structure of the world. This assumption is unwarranted, say the critics, because there are other natural languages having very different vocabularies and grammars and we could invent still other languages that differ even more widely. Accordingly, these critics insist that before we can decide on the merits of our native tongue we must somehow discover what the world, in its metaphysical aspect, is like, for until we learn the truth about metaphysical matters we have no basis for judging how well (or badly) any given language matches up with the world.[1] Therefore, it is said, every philosopher who appeals to ordinary language is guilty of putting the cart before the horse and can be safely ignored by the rest of the profession. This is the Universal Dismisser.

This criticism, since it rests of the assumption that our language is a conceptual scheme, can be regarded as naive. Even so, it cannot be denied that so far as Standard Ordinary Language Philosophy is concerned, the Universal Dismisser performs the service of exposing its question-begging character. The same criticism cannot, however, be leveled against Metaphysical Ordinary Language Philosophy, as practiced by Wittgenstein, Berkeley, and others, for these philosophers arrive at their views without first appealing to ordinary language. This is often overlooked in Wittgenstein's case. It is assumed that if the Universal Dismisser is a sound refutation of Malcolm's style of philosophizing, it must bring down Wittgenstein as well. This misunderstanding has arisen, I suppose, because Malcolm and other Standard Ordinary Language philosophers have repeatedly declared Wittgenstein to be their champion. The result is that the one argument—the Universal Dismisser—is thought of as discrediting all of ordinary language philosophy. Stuart Hampshire, for example, concludes that "the mere plotting of the ordinary use of words . . . is a necessary check upon philosophy, . . . it is not philosophy itself."[2]

Fodor and Katz arrive at the same sweeping conclusion. They remark that if a philosopher is to draw philosophical conclusions from observations about the English language, he requires for such reasoning, "a further assumption, namely that English is a philosophically privileged language."[3] But this assumption, they say, will no longer seem plausible once we realize that there are natural languages that differ greatly from English.[4] From this they conclude that it is a fallacy—they call it "the natural language fallacy"—to draw philosophical conclusions

> just by appealing to the way speakers in fact talk. This takes doing philosophy.
> . . . The general philosophical importance of this fallacy is this: once the natural
> language fallacy has been recognized, it becomes necessary to raise seriously the
> question of the utility of appealing to what we ordinarily say as a means of resolv-
> ing philosophical disagreements.[5]

Here again is the Universal Dismisser. Fodor and Katz, like Hampshire, regard the one argument as sufficient for discrediting all of ordinary language philosophy. Evidently there is considerable agreement about this, for ordinary language philosophy has clearly fallen into disfavor.

A New Beginning

In response to this development, Frank Ebersole has said:

> Many people are going around saying that ordinary language philosophy has had
> its day. . . . I do not for a moment believe that this is true: I think that ordinary
> language philosophy was never given more than a most cursory consideration.
> And, far from learning a lesson from it, most philosophers merely used it to mildly
> reshape some of their preconceived misconceptions.[6]

I believe that I have, in the preceding chapters, shown that this appraisal is justified. For the Standard variety of ordinary language philosophy is a question-begging style of reasoning and practitioners of the Metaphysical variety fail to consult language until it is too late, until their philosophical views have jelled. But

such failures have not dissuaded Ebersole from declaring that his own philosophizing belongs "in the niche of 'ordinary language philosophy.'" He explains: "I
believe that the only way in which we can clear up [philosophical] problems is to
look carefully at examples in which such words as 'know,' 'true,' 'means,' 'explains,' and others are used."[7]

What we need to consider, then, is that it may be possible to practice ordinary
language philosophy in a way that has not been generally recognized. In fact,
Ebersole himself says that his approach "is almost without precedent" and even
that it is "queer."[8] Evidently, Ebersole's version of ordinary language philosophy is
in some way unique, in which case it may not be vulnerable to the Universal Dismisser. In the remainder of this chapter I will try to indicate what this alternative
method—which I will call "Investigative Ordinary Language Philosophy"—must
be like, and how it differs from other versions of ordinary language philosophy.

Some Differences

Some of the differences can be described quite easily. First, it differs from Standard
Ordinary Language Philosophy in that it does not undertake to *refute* the views of
other philosophers. (It attempts, rather, to understand a philosophical idea and
gives up on it only when every attempt one can think of has fizzled. Ebersole's essays generally take the form, "I want to try to understand this idea," and then he
tries to give that idea a run for its money.) Second, it differs from Metaphysical
Ordinary Language Philosophy in that it does not initially settle on some tempting
philosophical theory and then try to ratchet ordinary language into such a shape
that it will no longer seem to clash with that theory. Berkeley permitted himself to
"think with the learned" while he at the same time adopted a use theory of meaning, which allowed him to "speak with the vulgar." It allowed him, that is, to read
into what we, the vulgar, say whatever is most congenial to his own preconceived
views, with the result that those views remain untested and unscathed. This is
Metaphysical Ordinary Language Philosophy, and those who practice it will see
in what we say only what suits their purpose. Much will go unnoticed; much may
be badly distorted. Such defects are avoided by Investigative Ordinary Language
Philosophy.

There are other, more important differences than the two I have just mentioned. I am not quite sure how to rank the others, but one very important difference is that Investigative Ordinary Language Philosophy does not regard anything
from past philosophy as being safely assumable, not even such hallowed notions
as sense-impression, concept, proposition, and the like. Wittgenstein once remarked: "One keeps forgetting to go right down to the foundations. One doesn't
put the question marks *deep* enough down" (CV, p.62). This could not be said of
Investigative Ordinary Language Philosophy. It takes an absolutely fresh start at
thinking about philosophical problems, so that the most deeply ingrained philosophical ideas can be challenged.

This is especially important when it comes to the ideas philosophers have had
about language, about words and meaning. Philosophers are prone to think of

language as being, so to speak, a chalkboard phenomena. But while we can, for certain purposes, as in grammar exercises, write a sentence on a chalkboard, that's not how, for the most part, we encounter language in our lives. An isolated sentence on a chalkboard is not like a person's saying something, for the latter includes not only the speaker, with his intent and awareness, but also the context or occasion for the speaker's speaking, and the person or persons addressed, whom the speaker will think of as bringing to the situation their grasp of the language (or the lack of it), their awareness of certain facts (or the lack thereof), and so on. This, and not an isolated sentence, is what we encounter in the real world. Once we are aware of this, we see how implausible it is to think of language in certain ways. For example, in the *Tractatus* Wittgenstein spoke as follows: "If all true elementary propositions are listed, the world is completely described" (4.26). The idea here is that there is a fixed totality of propositions. And as for the propositions themselves, Wittgenstein says: "Like Frege and Russell I construe a proposition as a function of the expressions contained in it" (TLP, 3.318). This is perhaps the most typical way in which philosophers think of language, especially when they are thinking about logic. They take it for granted that we go about with a head full of concepts and that we think and speak with propositions compounded of these concepts.

This view of language has consequences far beyond the philosophy of language. It affects the way in which philosophers think about such other topics as knowledge, perception, memory, human actions, and so on. When we take it for granted that there are concepts of knowing, seeing, remembering, and so on, and also assume that people think and speak with propositions compounded of such concepts, these assumptions prevent us from locating the relevant facts—the relevant details—about knowing, seeing, remembering, and so on. We may, for instance, take one or another example of seeing something as a paradigm and then either ignore other, very different, examples or take notice of other examples merely in order to fit them into the pattern of our chosen paradigm.

To avoid such mistakes, practitioners of Investigative Ordinary Language Philosophy lay aside the chalkboard view of language and work with detailed examples, examples consisting of stories or bits of dialogue, in which it is clear who is speaking to whom, to what purpose, and with what awareness or knowledge. In describing his own work, Ebersole says that he proceeds "as much as possible by inventing and thinking of examples. The examples I mean . . . are bits of stories, involving scenes and situations in which a person will properly and sensibly say something or think something."[9] By doing this, Ebersole enables us to see that we do not carry with us, from one set of circumstances to another, a concept of knowing or seeing or remembering which we exercise in these different situations. We come to see that the details of the various examples, the minutiae of the situations in which we say things, determine not only what we would naturally and straightforwardly say but determine also the *sense* of what we say, determine what it comes to to say *this* in *this* situation. And in a more general way we come to see that in talking, in saying things, we are not—as we are prone to imagine—availing ourselves of a ready-made stock of words and their meanings, from which to compound "propositions." (Even Wittgenstein's notion of family resemblances comes in for criticism.[10]) And so we come to see, too, that in a sense there is no such thing as "ordinary language"—at least not if "ordinary language" is assumed to have a "logic," a set of sense-determining rules which we learn and then employ. Or, as I might also put it, we come to see that the chief ambitions of logic and philosophy of language have been misguided.

It may be thought that this concern with examples is not altogether original. After all, Wittgenstein said in The Blue Book:

> The idea that in order to get clear about the meaning of a general term one had to find the common element in all its applications has shackled philosophical investigations; for it has not only led to no results, but also made the philosopher dismiss as irrelevant the concrete cases, which alone could have helped him to understand the usage of the general term. When Socrates asks the question "What is knowledge?" he does not even regard it as a *preliminary* answer to enumerate cases of knowledge. (BB, pp. 19–20)

And in the *Investigations* Wittgenstein said: "A main cause of philosophical disease—a one-sided diet: one nourishes one's thinking with only one kind of example" (§593). And yet if one goes looking for examples in his writings and lectures, one finds very few of them, and the few one finds are often too sketchy to be helpful.[11] Worse yet, instead of using examples as a check on his theorizing, Wittgenstein most often imposes his theories upon his examples. This is what Investigative Ordinary Language Philosophy aims to avoid.

Escaping the Universal Dismisser

How, then, does this sort of philosophizing escape the Universal Dismisser? If it appeals to examples of what people commonly say, is it not just as guilty as Standard Ordinary Language Philosophy of begging the question—the question, that is, of whether the conceptual scheme of ordinary language is a flawless map of the ontological terrain?

The important point to bear in mind here is that the philosophical method espoused by Malcolm claims to be able to refute philosophers' conclusions without first considering their arguments. Those conclusions can be rejected out of hand, according to Malcolm, because they "violate" ordinary language. What makes this question begging is that the philosophical arguments Malcolm says we needn't consider include those that seem to demonstrate that ordinary language is not only a conceptual scheme but also one that is philosophically deficient. That view of language gains its plausibility from various pieces of philosophical reasoning, and once such reasoning has become a central fixture of philosophy, it can't be simply ignored. But Malcolm does just that, and that is why his method is question begging and an easy target for the Universal Dismisser.

Is there, then, some other way for ordinary language philosophers to proceed? To see what alternatives there might be, we need to notice that those who brandish the Universal Dismisser make two assumptions. One assumption is that our language is a conceptual scheme, that it is a map—possibly a very poor map—of the ontological terrain. The second assumption is that we can't philosophize without taking sides in metaphysical issues. Could these assumptions be challenged?

The second assumption can be easily disputed: Our philosophizing does not always originate in some ontological issue. Sometimes we simply get into a muddle about the use of some word or phrase. In such cases the very thing we need is what the Universal Dismisser dismisses: we need to be reminded of how the relevant words or phrases are actually used. There is nothing else that would remove our problem, and nothing more is needed. So a philosopher who practices ordinary language philosophy in cases of *this* sort cannot be charged with begging the question. He or she is, in fact, doing the only thing that's appropriate.

But what about the other cases, those that seem to get us embroiled in ontological questions? To see whether ordinary language philosophy has a role to play in such cases, we must investigate the assumption that our language is a conceptual scheme. In doing this, as I've said, we must be careful to avoid begging questions. Since we clearly can't proceed by making a direct attack—in Malcolm's fashion—on the conclusions of philosophical arguments, we will have to get behind those conclusions somehow. But how is one to do this?

It is not difficult to depict an idealized version of this. It will involve retracing one's steps through a labyrinth of philosophical argumentation, through long chains of argument, arguments built on other arguments. This is often how it is in philosophy: the views currently in favor are the descendants of earlier views whose implications are only now being worked out, and those, in turn, are the descendants of still earlier views, and so on. Finding one's way in all of this is not easy, but it's clear how one must begin: by practicing the art of backtracking—an art, incidentally, in which Ramsey's maxim is an invaluable aid. If one is unrelenting in this and finds the beginning of each story, where new philosophical ideas are hatched, one will have found the point at which it will beg no questions to ask oneself: "Do these ideas arise simply from a failure to appreciate how these words are used?"

How does one find these incipient moments in philosophy? How will we know that we have done enough backtracking? I doubt that there is an answer to that question if we think of slogging our way through the history of philosophy. While we can—and no doubt should—pay some attention to the thinkers of yesterday and yesteryear, there will come a point at which we are on our own, at which we can say, "*I* got this philosophical idea by thinking that . . ." This is the sort of moment we are looking for.[12] If we now attempt to explain that idea to ourselves and discover, while paying attention to the actual use of the relevant word, that all our attempts fizzle, it can't be said that our admission of failure is the result of our begging some question. In the next chapter I will try to illustrate this point.

But what, in all of this, becomes of the idea that our language is a conceptual scheme? Could someone object to the kind of philosophizing I have just described by saying: "You have simply assumed that our language is not a conceptual scheme"? No, Investigative Ordinary Language Philosophy makes no such assumption. What is true is only this: it takes nothing from past philosophy as being safely assumable, and so does not assume that our language *is* a conceptual scheme. But making a fresh start in this way presupposes nothing about what we may find. If the idea that language is a conceptual scheme should somehow prove to be justified, that would not disqualify any aspect of Investigative Ordinary Language Philosophy. But, since the idea that language is a conceptual scheme is itself a philosophical theory, we must not accept it before conducting a thorough examination.[13]

Ordinary language philosophy is sometimes criticized on the grounds that its actual results have proved to be of little or no value. For example, A. C. Grayling, in a discussion of Wittgenstein, writes that "careful attention to our uses of language, for example our employment of expressions containing the terms 'good', 'true' and 'know', have [sic] not resolved our difficulties over goodness, truth and knowledge."[14] Grayling cites no examples of such philosophizing, but I doubt that he had Ebersole's work in mind or that he even knows of it. In fact, since he makes this comment as a criticism specifically of Wittgenstein, it is likely that what he counts as paying "careful attention" to the use of philosophically perplexing words is something closer to Metaphysical Ordinary Language Philosophy than to the work I have called "Investigative." In that case, of course, Grayling may have been right to disparage the particular results that he had in mind, but also he had no grounds for his wholesale dismissal of philosophers paying "careful attention to our uses of language."

Some Exceptions

I do not want to claim that philosophical problems are all alike and can be successfully dealt with by paying close attention to the way words are actually used. There are, I believe, some exceptional cases. In some, including problems in moral philosophy, paying close attention to language is extremely helpful, but it may not be enough. And in one case, philosophy of religion, we stand to gain little or nothing, I believe, by paying attention to the way in which words are actually used. Consider first the matter of moral philosophy.

There is an important difference between this branch of philosophy and most of the others. When discussing epistemological problems, for example, we are concerned with terms such as *see, looks, seems, appears, know,* and *believe,* and we can reasonably count on our students and colleagues to use these terms, in their non-philosophical activities, just as we do. So if we propose properly detailed examples, these are not going to be challenged as being tendentious or otherwise unacceptable. But the situation is otherwise when it comes to moral philosophy, for even well-educated people may, in their practical dealings, harbor all manner of biases and prejudices, may be ideologues or fanatics, may be thoroughly callous, thoughtless, or insensitive individuals. These are, in themselves, moral shortcomings, and they are not easily dealt with in a lecture hall or philosophy conference. More importantly, they cannot be dealt with by close attention to the use of words. Arthur Murphy said something important in this regard. He said that moral advice is intended for those who are morally serious individuals, and it is folly to think that philosophers can invent abstract arguments in moral philosophy that will stay the hand of, for example, a hit man for organized crime. It would be similar folly to suppose that by means of such arguments one could transform a cynical and callous person into a thoughtful and caring one. So if such people advance bad arguments—nihilistic arguments, for example—in moral philosophy, it is folly to hope that one could win them over, could bring them to recognize their prejudice, callousness, or whatever, for their attitudes were not adopted for rational reasons.

Iris Murdoch has said that since morality is concerned with making progress in our capacity for insight and understanding, "We cannot be as democratic about it as some philosophers would like to think. We do not simply, through being rational, and knowing ordinary language, 'know' the meaning of all necessary words."[15] Murdoch is surely right about this, but that does not mean that *no one* can profit from a careful discussion of detailed examples of the sort relevant to moral philosophy. It does mean, however, that in this area one should not expect the complete agreement that one may hope for in epistemology.[16]

In philosophy of religion the situation is somewhat different. Although there may be some—rather peripheral—problems in this area that can be dealt with by reminders about the ordinary use of words (of religious terminology), it would be a great mistake to think that we can solve philosophical problems about religion by paying close attention to the ordinary use of words such as *God, miracle, sin, evil, salvation, resurrection, heaven, hell,* and other terms that figure prominently in what religious believers say. Wittgenstein, unfortunately, fostered the view I mean to oppose: by placing Christianity in a person's conceptual world, where it cannot come into conflict with reality, he made certain that it contains nothing that is intellectually suspect.[17] On this view, the most that a philosopher can do is to take notice of and issue reminders about the use of religious terms. Accordingly, what religious believers say in sermons, prayers, the recitation of creeds, etc., must, if sufficiently orthodox, be immune to philosophical criticism. This gave rise, among his followers, to the idea that there is such a thing as "religious language," that is, words used in a uniquely religious manner. Some philosophers have viewed this as one of Wittgenstein's great contributions. But for the devout believer it has the unnerving consequence of telling him that those supernatural beings and events which he has taken to be at the heart of his faith are logical fictions, that they have a place in a person's conceptual world but cannot, except through confusion, be thought to have a place in reality.

Is there some other, more appropriate way of thinking about religious belief? This is an area that has been too little explored. But this much seems to me obvious and should be admitted on all sides: Evans-Pritchard, after his conversion to Catholicism, was right in saying that religious beliefs are *metaphysical* beliefs—are, as he put it, beliefs involving "terms which have a metaphysical reference."[18] They are metaphysical in at least the following sense: one cannot accept religious beliefs without accepting certain stories that are told about events of a supra-sensible sort, such as stories about the creation of the world and the creation of human beings. (Think of the idea that every fetus has been ensouled by God.) It is precisely because people, when using religious terms, mean to be speaking of supernatural beings or events that they create philosophical puzzlement, for there are no other words that the plain man uses in this way. How, then, are philosophical problems in this area to be dealt with?

One must, I believe, begin by asking whether we *understand* religious beliefs. Wittgenstein would have said that although we readily form *pictures* of these alleged metaphysical beings and events, we have no idea of how to *apply* such pictures (see PI, §§422–427 and p. 184). He was right, of course: we don't know how to apply such pictures. Can we say what it would be like, for example, to be faced with a Day of Judgment? How are we to distinguish between a true and just god presiding over a Day of Judgment and a lesser (but still enormously impressive) being presiding? How is a mere human to recognize the difference? To say that we will eventually face a Day of Judgment is not at all like saying that eventually we will meet with an extraordinarily delightful (or ghastly) event. (We'd know that a prediction of *that* sort had come true.) It is no use here appealing to faith and saying that we would trust that it is the one and only true God presiding and recounting our sins. For the question is not "Who is presiding?" (as if we were asking whether it is the chairperson or the vice chairperson) but rather, "What, if anything, can it *mean* to say (or believe) that it is God (none other) presiding or that it is the creator of the universe who is presiding?" Plainly, an appeal to "what we all say" will provide no answer. Nor is the problem solved by pious appeals to Scripture—to "God's Word," for it is precisely these *words* that are in question. They look and sound like words, but when we try to make something of them, they, like other metaphysical terms, turn to dust. So in the end one is forced to admit that we don't know what we are talking about when we use religious terms.

Investigating Appearances

How does Investigative Ordinary Language Philosophy work? What does it look like? It shouldn't be necessary to address these questions, because philosophy practiced in this manner, by Ebersole and a few others, has been around for nearly half a century. But for reasons I have tried to explain (such as widespread acceptance of the Universal Dismisser) it has been neglected, and only a handful of philosophers have tried to conduct their thinking in this manner. In view of its unfamiliarity, then, I will present here, as a small sample, a piece that I wrote (for the most part) forty years ago.

Sense-data and the Real Table

In *The Problems of Philosophy* Russell produces an argument about perception that many people have found persuasive. It is a simple argument, and that is part of its appeal. Not only is it brief, but it invokes such obvious and elementary facts that a person might easily think that no one could possibly find fault with it. But this simple beginning leads to momentous consequences, the most obvious of which Russell spells out as follows:

> [T]he real table, if there is one, is not the same as what we immediately experience by sight or touch or hearing. The real table, if there is one, is not *immediately* known to us at all, but must be an inference from what is immediately known. Hence, two very difficult questions at once arise; namely, (1) Is there a real table at all? (2) If so, what sort of object can it be?[1]

In chapter 11 we saw how Moore wrestled with the first of these "very difficult questions," and the failure of his answer may persuade us that the question is very difficult indeed. But there is another way of approaching the matter. One can suspect that the question "Is there a real table at all?"—which Moore and the skeptic take seriously but answer differently—is a question neither would ask if they hadn't already taken a wrong turn. For the question does not arise except on the assumption that it has been shown that we do not (or cannot) see things of the sort we say we see. Evidently, then, Moore and the skeptic share this assumption. So we have here an occasion for trying out Ramsey's maxim, to see whether there is some other way of dealing with the issue which (as Ramsey put it) "has not yet been thought of, which we can only discover by rejecting something assumed as obvious by both disputants."

Russell's argument is as follows. Everyone would agree, he says, that the table on which he writes is brown and oblong, but there is an error, he claims, in our thinking this, an error that can be demonstrated as follows. The parts of the table that reflect the light look much brighter than the other parts, and some parts look white because of reflected light. So if one moves one's head while looking at the table, the table will *look* different. Similarly, if several people are looking at the table, it will not look quite the same to any two of them, for they all see it from different points of view. Moreover, even from one point of view the table will look different by daylight and by artificial light. All of this, says Russell, is something that a painter must learn: He must "learn the habit of seeing things as they appear." And the same goes for the shape of the table, for "as we all have to learn if we try to draw, a given thing looks different in shape from every different point of view." Thus far Russell's reasoning seems to consist merely of some reminders of homely and indisputable facts. But it suddenly takes the following unexpected turn:

> It is evident from what we have found, that there is no colour which pre-eminently appears to be *the* colour of the table, or even of any particular part of the table— it appears to be of different colours from different points of view, and there is no reason for regarding some of these as more really its colour than others. . . . and therefore, to avoid favoritism, we are compelled to deny that, in itself, the table has any one particular colour.[2]

This is not quite the whole of Russell's argument, but it is the most important part of it, and it is this part that I want now to consider.

Consider first Russell's conclusion: the table has no one particular color. Do we understand this? The words are all familiar; they are simple English words. But what could it mean to say that something has no one particular color? One could say this of a chameleon, I suppose. If someone who knew nothing about chameleons were to ask us "What color are chameleons?" we might very naturally reply, "Chameleons have no one particular color." And we would then explain that chameleons frequently change color to blend in with their surroundings. But is Russell saying that this is what tables are like? Is he saying that they regularly change color, so that one cannot give a straightforward answer to the question "What color is your table?" If so, he would of course be quite wrong. Anyone who knows anything about tables knows that they are not chameleonlike.

Russell is not, of course, saying that tables are like chameleons. He is saying, not that they regularly *change* color, but that they *look* now one color and now another. But does this help us to understand his conclusion that the table has no one particular color?

Let us try another comparison. Is Russell saying that tables are like the irides-cent fabric that is sometimes used for the linings of coats? The warp and woof threads of this fabric are of different colors, so that when you turn it now one way and now another, the fabric looks first one color and then another. The fabric, of course, does not change color, as a chameleon does. Suppose, then, that a woman has just bought a dress, and you ask her, "What color is your new dress?" If her dress is made of iridescent taffeta, she cannot answer your question in a simple, di-rect way. Perhaps she will begin by saying, "It's iridescent blue and green taffeta," and then, if you don't understand that answer, she might go on to explain: "It is no one particular color; the threads running one way are blue and those running the other way are green, so that when you turn it one way it looks blue and when you turn it another way it looks green."

Here, then, is a case in which we would understand its being said that some-thing has "no one particular color," not because it changes color but because of the way it looks. We would, therefore, understand Russell if he were telling us that tables are all like a piece of iridescent taffeta. We would also, in that case, know that he was telling us something that isn't true. In fact, I have *never* come across a table that was like iridescent fabric.

What are we to conclude? Should we conclude that Russell is saying some-thing plainly false? Should we suspect that someone led him to *believe* that tables are made of iridescent materials and that he never looked at tables closely enough to see that this wasn't true? That is hardly plausible. He knows, as we do, that very few, if any, tables are like iridescent fabric. And in any case Russell tells us at the outset that he is talking about his own table and that *everyone would agree* that it's *brown*. Here Russell is telling us, by implication: no one thinks my table is iridescent. How, then, could Russell's reasoning have led him to talk about his table as one can—quite properly—talk about a piece of iridescent taffeta?

The answer is to be found in the way he reasons about colors and shapes. He begins by remarking on how tables look in various lights and from various angles, and he reminds us that artists and aspiring artists must take notice of this. Yet he concludes with remarks that seem to have (or are meant to have) some bearing on the question "What color is the table?"—a question that would not be of special interest to artists. People who paint tables or refinish them will be concerned with the actual color of the tables they are working on—concerned, for example, with the uniformity of the color, but then they have no such interest as the artist has in how the table *looks* from here or there. There is, then, something odd in Russell's juxtaposing these matters as he does. Let us think about this.

Russell says that the table looks different in color from different points of view, and in connection with this he mentions that this is something an artist must learn. He also says that the table looks different in shape from different points of view and that anyone wanting to draw must learn this. Plainly, then, Russell has in mind—or has partly in mind—the sort of thing an art instructor might say to her students or that one might say to a child who is learning to draw or paint. So let us review the sorts of things people say in those situations.

An art instructor might say to a student: "You haven't got this color right; you need more shading along this side of the vase. Remember, things look different from different points of view, depending on where the light is coming from." She might also say: "Look at the table. Does it look uniformly brown to you? No. You need to put some highlights into your painting. You do that with white paint."

Consider also the case of a child learning to draw. Children typically begin drawing such things as tables without any sense of perspective, so that a square table is drawn simply as a square figure. In helping a child, then, one might say to him: "If you look at a table from different places, you will notice that it doesn't look the same from each place. If you stand next to it, looking down on it, it may look square. But if you back away or squat down, the sides will look shorter than the end that's closest to you."

These are ways we talk in connection with painting and drawing. We say such things to help people get the proper shading and perspective into their pictures. The important thing to notice about this is that when, in these contexts, we speak of how a table or a vase looks, this is not connected with an interest in finding out what color or shape something is.

We do, of course, often use the word *looks* in connection with this latter interest. Consider, for instance, the case of someone rummaging through the dim recesses of a used furniture shop in hopes of finding a black oval coffee table for her new apartment. Perhaps she pulls a table out from behind an overstuffed chair and then says, "Oh, it's dark green. Back there in the corner it looked black." After a bit more rummaging she calls a clerk over and says: "That little table up there on the shelf looks like what I want. From here, anyway, it looks oval, but I can't see it very well," and then she asks the clerk to bring the table down where she can get a good look at it. In cases such as these our remarks that the table "looked black" and "looks oval" are connected with an interest in the color and shape of the table. This is one way these cases differ from those mentioned above. Consider now some additional ways in which the two sorts of cases differ.

When you say to a child who is learning to draw: "The sides of the table will look shorter if you back away from the table or squat down," you don't choose to speak this way ("will look shorter") because you have some reason to be hesitant about saying what the table is actually like. It's not that you're in doubt about the length of the sides. You aren't being cautious; you have no thought of a possible mistake in the offing. Indeed, in order to teach the child what he needs to learn, both you and the child must know to begin with what the shape of the table is that he's trying to draw. Suppose, for example, that part of your teaching consists of your sketching the square table for him using foreshortened lines and acute and obtuse angles. You show this to the child and say, "This is how it looks from here." Now the child, if he's to learn the lesson properly, has to know that you are drawing a square table, for otherwise he might, upon seeing your drawing, say: "That's a funny table. I've never seen a table like *that* before!" In a case such as this, then, in remarking to the child how the table looks from one angle or another, the whole procedure presupposes that there be no doubt as to the shape of the table.

Similarly, when an art instructor remarks to a student who is trying to paint a vase that it "looks different" in color under different lighting conditions or when the light source is moved, she is not announcing some difficulty in discovering what color the vase actually is. When she uses "looks" in this way, she isn't taking the kind of pains that one takes when trying to discover the color or shape of something. She does not, for example, tell the student to get a better light. Nor does she suggest that they move closer to the vase for a better look at it. The context is not one in which someone has asked, "What color is it?" Indeed, the student, in order to learn what's being taught, must already have a pretty good idea of the vases's actual color. If, for example, the instructor says, "Make it darker on this side," the student mustn't be thinking that the vase *itself* is darker on one side, for that would be to miss the instructor's point.

Although Russell alludes to situations in which students are taught about getting the proper perspective and highlights and the like into their paintings and drawings, he does not take note of the point I have just been making about these situations. And having ignored this point, he fails to notice another difference between these situations and those in which, being uncertain about the color or shape of something, we use "looks." The difference is the following.

In the instructional cases there is no investigation being conducted for the purpose of answering such questions as "What color is it?" or "Is it round or oval?" In such cases, then, there is no such thing as *coming to the end* of an investigation. There is no inquiry to be *completed*. Accordingly, one can in such cases go on using "looks" (in "looks shorter," "looks darker," etc.) *despite* knowing all the while what color or shape the object actually is. By contrast, when one says to the clerk in the used furniture shop that the table in a dimly lit corner "looks black" or "looks oval," one does so because one is unable to see clearly what color or shape the table actually is. Here there *is* an interest in finding out something about the table, and there is reason to be hesitant or cautious or tentative. So one investigates. One brings the table out from behind the overstuffed chair or puts it in a better light or wipes the dust off of it. But having done so, that is, having *completed* the investigation, one is no longer free to go on using "looks so-and-so." By this I mean that we will fail if we try to invent a scenario in which, having gotten as good a look as one could possibly *want*, one goes on using "looks so-and-so" instead of saying, for example, "'Oh, it's round" or "Ah, ha, it *is* black!"

Let's try to invent such a scenario. The clerk has pulled the table out into the open where you can get a good look at it. Could you then say, "Well, it *looks* black"? You could if the light were poor or if the table were covered with a thick coat of dust. Suppose, then, that for these reasons you do say it. The clerk understands and accordingly pulls the table near to a window and dusts it off. Could you now say, "Well, it *looks* black"? What would you be getting at if you did? And what could the clerk take you to be saying? I should think that the clerk would stare at you in slack-jawed wonderment. You came in wanting to buy a black table. If we assume that this is still your purpose, we will understand that you wouldn't want to buy a table whose color you couldn't quite make out—one that *looked* black to you but whose color you couldn't see clearly. But once you have gotten as good a look as one could want, there is nothing further to investigate. And at that point "looks black" ceases to be appropriate. The same goes for "looks round" or "looks oval." When part of the table's surface is no longer obscured by the overstuffed chair, when you've got it in the middle of the room under good lighting, the investigation is complete, and the clerk wouldn't know what you were getting at if you said, "Out here in the middle of the room it looks round." Perhaps the clerk will wonder if you suffer from severe astigmatism, in which case he might ask, "Do you want to measure it?" But suppose you say, "Oh, no, I can see it well enough." Can we really suppose that you would carry on in this way? Surely not!

In cases such as these, then, once there remains nothing further to do to complete the investigation, "looks black" and "looks round" must, on pain of unintelligibility, give way to "is ___."

We can now summarize the difference between these uses of "looks" in the following way. In the instructional cases there does not come a point at which the use of "looks so-and-so" must, on pain of unintelligibility, give way to "is ___," that is, the instructor could say the same thing day after day as she initiates the unending supply of new students, and this is because the use of "looks" in such cases is not connected with an investigation of the table or the vase or whatever. In cases of the other sort, in which there's a question about the color or the shape of something, there comes a point at which it would no longer make sense to say "looks so-and-so" rather than "is so-and-so."

Russell, pretty clearly, failed to notice this difference. And having failed to distinguish carefully these very different uses of "looks," he then combined incompatible features of these uses. The feature he draws from the instructional use is that there does not come a point at which one is obliged to shift from "looks" to "is." The feature he draws from cases of the other sort is that so long as one is saying "looks black" or "looks oval" to the clerk in the furniture shop, one is unable to see clearly (or is uncertain whether one is seeing clearly) what color or shape the table actually is. It is almost as though Russell had reasoned as follows:

> We can go on indefinitely saying "looks so-and-so" in cases of the first sort. Therefore, in cases of the other sort, where we want to find out what color or shape the table is, we can never get from "looks" to "is" (or: can never complete our investigation).

I do not, of course, want to say that Russell explicitly reasoned in this way, as though he had noticed that there *are* the two different sorts of cases. The correct explanation has to be that he failed to notice the differences to which I have called attention and as a result conflated the different cases. This unwitting conflation led him to say: "[T]he senses seem not to give us the truth about the table itself, but only about the appearance of the table."[3] This thought could also be put as follows: "We can never see what color or shape a thing is but only what color or shape it appears to be." And it is this thought that, in turn, finds expression in Russell's conclusion that "to avoid favoritism, we are compelled to deny that, in itself, the table has any one particular colour."

At last I think I understand that remark. It is not, as at first it appeared, a plainly false statement, in which Russell is saying that tables are like iridescent taffeta. On the contrary, Russell is not telling us *anything* about tables. He has, so to speak, lost his way in the language. That is how we must understand his peculiar conclusion.

If I am right about this, our invoking Ramsey's maxim has paid off. By challenging the assumption shared by Moore and the skeptic, that is, the assumption that what we really see is not a table but an appearance of a table (or a sense-datum), we have found that this assumption is, at best, problematical. So we aren't obliged to address the question that troubles both Moore and the skeptic: "Is there really a table?" (or "Is there a real table?"). That question is generated by an assumption we have found reason to distrust. There are, of course, other ways of trying to breathe life into it, but that just means that we have to employ once more the sort of technique I have tried to illustrate in regard to Russell's discussion.

Conclusion

This technique is what I have called "Investigative Ordinary Language Philosophy." And I want to point out here that it is a technique which, when properly used, cannot be accused of begging philosophical questions by assuming that English is an ideal, or a philosophically privileged, language. My use of the technique was not aimed as discovering some metaphysical truth which another philosopher might dispute. The technique was appropriate just because anyone who reasons like Russell—and that probably includes most of us—has fallen into confusion *about* some feature of our language. If someone were to say to me that I should consult other languages before dismissing Russell's conclusion that we don't see tables, I would think he had dropped a stitch somewhere along the way, had missed the point of what I was doing. He is evidently assuming that there *is* such question as "Do we see such things as tables?" But as Wittgenstein once said, "This is the essence of a philosophical problem. The question itself is the result of a muddle. And when the question is removed, this is not by answering it" (LSD, p. 139). Wittgenstein may not have had the very best reasons for saying this, but he did say it, and that has made an enormous difference.

Russell's *Our Knowledge of the External World* and Its Relation to Wittgenstein's Philosophy

Russell's book *Our Knowledge of the External World* played an unusually important role in Wittgenstein's thinking. I do not mean that he borrowed Russell's philosophical views, for he dismissed most of those views quite emphatically. But Wittgenstein borrowed something else: he borrowed Russell's way of posing or framing certain philosophical problems, especially in the area of epistemology. He came to share with Russell certain assumptions or premises of the sort to which Ramsey's maxim (see chapter 5) can be applied. Moreover, Wittgenstein continued to accept these premises uncritically throughout his life; they remained as influential in his later writings as in his earliest. An awareness of this influence is important, for it can save one from wildly mistaken interpretations of Wittgenstein's work.[1]

The earliest evidence of Wittgenstein's familiarity with Russell's book is found in his pre-*Tractatus* notebooks. There are several entries, for April and May 1915, in which Wittgenstein is obviously commenting on *Our Knowledge of the External World*. In fact, the wording of these passages is so similar to some of Russell's wording as to suggest that Wittgenstein had read Russell's book only days—or hours—before committing his thoughts to paper. Moreover, there is unmistakable evidence that Wittgenstein received Russell's book in the spring of 1915, just prior to writing these remarks.

Russell's book, which was published in the summer of 1914, was written during January of that year,[2] when Wittgenstein was no longer in England. At his family's urging he had gone to Austria in December 1913, and did not set foot again in England until after the war. So if, as I've suggested, he obtained a copy of the book by late April 1915, it is most likely that someone sent it to him, and the evidence points to John Maynard Keynes as the sender.

Early in 1915 Wittgenstein received from Keynes a letter in which the latter remarked: "Russell, by the way, brought out a nice book at about the beginning of the war."[3] In reply Wittgenstein wrote: "I'm very interested to hear that Russell has published a book lately. Could you possibly send it to me and let me pay you after the war? I'd so much like to see it."[4] Presumably, Keynes would have received this request in February or early March, which would have left him sufficient time to get the book to Wittgenstein by late April.

1

The entries in Wittgenstein's notebooks that I have referred to are dated April 23 and 27 and May 1, 1915 (NB, pp. 42, 43, and 44). Among these are the following four, which occur together in a group dated May 1:

(i) "Scepticism is *not* irrefutable, but *obvious nonsense* if it tries to doubt where no question can be asked."

(ii) "My method is not to sunder the hard [data] from the soft, but to see the hardness of the soft."

(iii) "Russell's method in his 'Scientific method in philosophy' is simply a retrogression from the method of physics."

(iv) "All theories that say: 'This is how it must be, otherwise we could not philosophize' or 'otherwise we surely could not live', etc. etc. must of course disappear."[5]

A fifth passage, written four days earlier (27.4.15), appears also to have been prompted by Russell's book. It reads:

(v) "The freedom of the will consists of the fact that future events *cannot* be KNOWN NOW" (NB, p. 43).

A sixth passage, written on April 23, concerns Occam's razor and appears to be a criticism of what Russell said about it in his book. The passage begins:

(vi) "Ockham's razor is, *of course,* not an arbitrary rule or one justified by its practical success. What it says is that unnecessary sign-units have no reference" (NB, p. 42).

There are, as I will show, many other connections between Russell's book and Wittgenstein's philosophy, but I will begin by commenting on the passages I have just cited.

2

(i) Russell says: "Universal scepticism, though *logically irrefutable*, is practically barren."[6] The idea is repeated a few pages later: ". . . that universal scepticism which, as we saw, is as barren as it is irrefutable."[7] Wittgenstein retorts: "Scepticism is *not* irrefutable, but *obvious nonsense*" (italics Wittgenstein's).

(ii) "My method is not to sunder the hard [data] from the soft, but to see the

hardness of the soft." Wittgenstein is disputing Russell's view that one can separate hard data from soft data by subjecting the data (i.e., our prephilosophical beliefs) to methodological doubt.[8] Wittgenstein is saying that *his* method enables
one to see that (contrary to Russell) *none* of our prephilosophical beliefs fall into
Russell's category of soft data, that is, none prove to be unknowable when subjected to methodological doubt. (Russell gives two examples of "data" he regards
as being inherently "soft," as lacking philosophical respectability: "Certain common beliefs are undoubtedly excluded from hard data. Such is the belief . . . that
sensible objects in general persist when we are not perceiving them. Such also is
the belief in other people's minds.")[9] As I have already explained and discussed
this in detail in chapter 2, I will say no more about it here.

(iii) "Russell's method in his 'Scientific method in philosophy' is simply a retrogression from the method of physics." What was Wittgenstein alluding to in this
remark? Since in his original (German) notebook entry he left the phrase "Scientific method in philosophy" in English, it is reasonable to assume that he was citing a source in English. And the best candidate is Russell's book, whose complete
title is *Our Knowledge of the External World as a Field for Scientific Method in
Philosophy.*[10]

What did Wittgenstein mean when he said that Russell's scientific method in
philosophy is simply "a retrogression from the method of physics"? He appears to
have been referring to Russell's remarks about philosophical method in the final
pages of *Our Knowledge of the External World.* I will not quote all of what Russell said, but the following sample will, I think, suffice to identify the target of
Wittgenstein's remarks:

> [A]s physics, which from Plato to the Renaissance was as unprogressive, dim, and
> superstitious as philosophy, became a science through Galileo's fresh observation
> of facts and subsequent mathematical manipulation, so philosophy, in our own
> day, is becoming scientific through the simultaneous acquisition of new facts and
> logical methods.[11]

Russell goes on to say that philosophers, by practicing methodological doubt and
confessing how little can be known, must try to emulate the humility of scientists.[12] He concludes:

> The one and only condition, I believe, which is necessary in order to secure for
> philosophy in the near future an achievement surpassing all that has hitherto been
> accomplished by philosophers, is the creation of a school of men with scientific
> training and philosophical interests, unhampered by the traditions of the past, and
> not misled by the literary methods of those who copy the ancients in all except
> their merits.[13]

One can find in Wittgenstein's writings many remarks that have a direct connection with what Russell says in this passage. (He was very much opposed, for example, to Russell's idea that philosophy is on the verge of making great progress;
this idea, he thought, reveals a misconception about the nature of philosophy.)[14]
Perhaps Wittgenstein was still thinking of Russell's remarks in this passage when
he said in The Blue Book: "Philosophers constantly see the method of science before their eyes, and are irresistibly tempted to ask and answer questions in the way

science does" (BB, p. 18). In lectures he reacted directly to Russell's idea that "philosophy, in our own day, is becoming scientific through the simultaneous acquisition of new facts and logical methods." Wittgenstein said: "All I can give you is a method; I cannot teach you any new truths" (WL35, p. 97). In the same lecture he said that philosophical problems have been

> attacked in the way scientific problems are, and are treated perfectly hopelessly, as if we had to find out something new. The problems do not appear to concern questions about language but rather questions of fact of which we do not yet know enough. It is for this reason that you are constantly tempted to think I am . . . discussing the problems of a science called metaphysics. (WL35, p. 99)

It is noteworthy that although Wittgenstein disputed Russell's idea that philosophy needs "new truths," his attitude toward Russell was quite different as regards the needed "logical method." I will not go into that here as I have already pointed out (chapter 3, note 10) that Wittgenstein said quite a number of things that echo Russell's remarks about logical method.

(iv) Wittgenstein writes: "All theories that say: 'This is how it must be, otherwise we could not philosophize' or 'otherwise we surely could not live', etc. etc. must of course disappear." This is apparently a reaction to Russell's remark: "While admitting that [philosophical] doubt is possible with regard to all our common knowledge, we must nevertheless accept that knowledge in the main *if philosophy is to be possible at all.*"[15] A few pages later Russell repeats this thought in a sentence which begins: "If we are to continue philosophizing, we must make our bow to the sceptical hypothesis, and . . . proceed to the consideration of other hypotheses which, though perhaps not certain, have at least as good a right to our respect as the hypothesis of the sceptic."[16] Wittgenstein, always the purist, very likely thought that this was an irresponsible way of dealing with skepticism.[17]

(v) "The freedom of the will consists of the fact that future events *cannot* be KNOWN NOW" (NB, p. 43). Here Wittgenstein is emphatically rejecting Russell's view of the matter as stated in *Our Knowledge of the External World.* Russell frames the issue as follows: "It is a mere accident that we have no memory of the future. We might—as in the pretended visions of seers—see future events immediately, in the way in which we see past events." And he asks: "If we saw future events in the same immediate way in which we see past events, what kind of free will would still be possible?"[18] Following a brief discussion, Russell concludes that "we might be free . . . even if we could now see what our future volitions were going to be. Freedom, in any valuable sense, demands only that our volitions shall be, as they are, the result of our own desires, not [the result] of an outside force compelling us to will what we would rather not will." Wittgenstein was clearly disputing this. And he continued to do so in the *Tractatus,* where he said: "The freedom of the will consists of the impossibility of knowing actions that still lie in the future" (5.1362).

(vi) This brings us to Wittgenstein's remark about Occam's razor and another aspect of Russell's method. Russell writes:

> The above extrusion of permanent things [i.e., things that exist at moments when no one perceives them] affords an example of the maxim which inspires

all scientific philosophizing, namely "Occam's razor": *Entities are not to be multiplied without necessity.* In other words, in dealing with any subject-matter, find out what entities are undeniably involved, and state everything in terms of these entities. Very often the resulting statement is more complicated and difficult than the one which, like common sense and most philosophy, assumes hypothetical entities whose existence there is no good reason to believe in. . . . but it is a mistake to suppose that what is easy and natural in thought is what is most free from unwarrantable assumptions, as the case of "things" very aptly illustrates.[19]

On a later page Russell alludes to this method, saying: "[O]ur method has secured us against error. . . . [T]he method we have adopted is the only one which is safe, and which avoids the risk of introducing fictitious metaphysical entities."[20] What Wittgenstein would have found unacceptable in this is that Russell, quite clearly, thought that a philosopher can allow that there *may* be entities "whose existence there is no good reason to believe in," that is, entities whose existence can be successfully called into question by a philosophical skeptic. As I pointed out above, Russell explicitly places in this category both other minds and objects that exist while unperceived.

So Russell regarded Occam's razor as offering advice as to how philosophers can play it *safe.* But this means that taking risks (with hypothetical entities) is *possible,* although unnecessary. Wittgenstein thought of the matter quite differently. He says of Occam's razor:

> Ockham's razor is, *of course,* not an arbitrary rule or one justified by its practical success. What it says is that unnecessary sign-units have no reference.
>
> It is clear that signs fulfilling the same purpose are logically identical. The purely logical thing just *is* what *all* of these are capable of accomplishing (NB, p. 42).[21]

Wittgenstein's version of Occam's razor is thus very different from Russell's: It declares that "unnecessary sign-units have no reference." A sign would be unnecessary, presumably, if we could get by without it. But Wittgenstein, instead of saying with Russell that we would be *safer* without such signs in our language, says that such signs "have no reference"—meaning that if anyone *tried* to use such a sign he would not be talking about anything. So if we could get by without, say, words that purport to be names of "other minds" (personal names that can't be analyzed behavioristically), then anyone who tried to use such a name would be talking, not about another person, but about nothing at all. And that means that it is logically impossible to be skeptical about "other minds," for you can't be skeptical about the existence of something unless you can speak of (refer to) it.

Russell failed to realize this. In response to the skeptic he was prepared to say only that "*in so far* as physics or common sense is verifiable, it must be capable of interpretation in terms of actual sense-data alone."[22] Russell, in other words, allowed that perhaps part of what plain men say and believe cannot be defended against the skeptic's claim that they believe in things, such as chairs and other people, whose very existence is unknowable.

3

There are many things in *Our Knowledge of the External World* that Wittgenstein, throughout his career, reacted to in one way or another. In my book, *Wittgenstein's Metaphysics,* I mentioned not only some of the points made above (see chapter 1, pp. 4–5 and 7) but also the following:

(vii) I pointed out (in chapter 13, note 4) that Russell's discussion of induction[23] contains elements (e.g., the remarks about animals) that seem to have influenced Wittgenstein.

(viii) I pointed out (in chapter 16, note 5) that Russell's discussion of time[24] contains elements that Wittgenstein adopted as his own.

(ix) Russell's discussion of visual perspective and of how it gives each sighted person a "private world"[25] contains ideas that Wittgenstein explicitly criticized (see *Wittgenstein's Metaphysics*, pp. 72–74).

Although I did not explicitly call attention to the fact, *Our Knowledge of the External World* contains (in chapter 4) Russell's account of how a phenomenalistic language might be constructed. I will not try to summarize his account, except to call attention to his remark that in such a language

> a 'thing' will be defined as a certain series of aspects, namely those which would commonly be said to be *of* the thing. To say that a certain aspect is an aspect *of* a certain thing will merely mean that it is one of those which, taken serially, *are* the thing.

By defining things in this way "our language is so interpreted as to avoid an unnecessary metaphysical assumption of [a thing's] permanence."[26]

In a later discussion of the *Tractatus,* Wittgenstein described the Tractarian idea of analysis thus: "I used to think that . . . one would be able to use visual impressions etc. to define the concept of a sphere" (PG, p. 211).

4

There are other points of relevance that I did not discuss in *Wittgenstein's Metaphysics*. I will here mention five of these.

(x) Wittgenstein's remarks in The Blue Book about the "geometrical eye" (BB, pp. 63–64) seem to be related to what Russell says (pp. 99–100) about the meaning of "here" (in perspective space).

(xi) Russell's account in *Our Knowledge of the External World* of the difference between waking life and dreaming seems to have become—and remained—Wittgenstein's view as well.[27] Russell writes:

> The first thing to realize is that there are no such things as "illusions of sense." Objects of sense, even when they occur in dreams, are the most indubitably real objects known to us. What, then, makes us call them unreal in dreams? Merely the unusual nature of their connection with other objects of sense. I dream that I am in America, but I wake up and find myself in England

without those intervening days on the Atlantic which, alas! are inseparably connected with a "real" visit to America. Objects of sense are called "real" when they
have the kind of connection with other objects of sense which experience has led
us to regard as normal; when they fail in this, they are called "illusions." But what
is illusory is only the inferences to which they give rise; in themselves, they are
every bit as real as the objects of waking life. And conversely, the sensible objects
of waking life must not be expected to have more intrinsic reality than those of
dreams. Dreams and waking life, in our first efforts at construction, must be
treated with equal respect.[28]

The crucial idea here is that "objects of sense are called 'real' when they have the
kind of connection with other objects of sense which experience has led us to regard as normal; when they fail in this, they are called 'illusions.'" So we call certain experiences "illusions" or "dreams" because of their aberrant content. On
this view, then, what constitutes a "real" chair is not something that transcends
"immediate experience." This is why Wittgenstein, in his lectures of 1931–32,
could say: "Idealists were right in that we never transcend experience. Mind and
matter is a division *in* experience" (WL32, p. 80), adding that "the world is not
composed of sense-data and physical objects. The relation between them is one in
language" (Ibid., p. 81). There are passages in *On Certainty* that depend on
Wittgenstein's thinking in this way.

(xii) In his discussion of methodological doubt Russell says that until our
"naive beliefs" have undergone skeptical scrutiny,

they are mere blind habits, ways of behaving rather than intellectual convictions.
And although it may be that a majority will pass the test, we may be sure than
some will not, and that a serious readjustment of our outlook ought to result. In
order to break the dominion of habit, we must do our best to doubt the senses,
reason, morals, everything in short. In some directions, doubt will be found possible; in others, it will be checked by that direct vision of abstract truth upon which
the possibility of philosophical knowledge depends."[29]

This passage contains two ideas Wittgenstein was to rebel against in later years.
One is Russell's disdain for "mere blind habits." (Compare: "I obey the rule
blindly" (PI, §219) and "'But, if you are *certain*, isn't it that you are shutting your
eyes in face of doubt?' They are shut" (PI, p. 224).) The other is Russell's saying
that philosophy ought to bring about "a serious readjustment of our outlook."
Wittgenstein says: "Philosophy may in no way interfere with the actual use of language; it can in the end only describe it. . . . It leaves everything as it is" (PI,
§124).

(xiii) In drawing his distinction between hard and soft data, Russell says that
soft data are beliefs that are "psychologically derivative" while also being "logically primitive."[30] Such beliefs are psychologically derivative in that they arise
from something we perceive; they are logically primitive in that they are "not arrived at by a logical inference." Russell gives the following as an example:

From the expression of a man's face we judge as to what he is feeling: we say we
see that he is angry, when in fact we only see a frown. We do not judge as to his
state of mind by any logical process: the judgement grows up, often without our

being able to say what physical mark of emotion we actually saw. . . . There may or may not be a possible deduction leading to the same result, but whether there is or not, we certainly do not employ it.[31]

Russell adds: "If we call a belief 'logically primitive' when it is not actually arrived at by a logical inference, then innumerable beliefs are logically primitive which psychologically are derivative."

Russell goes on to say, in regard to such beliefs, that "unless they can on reflection be deduced by a logical process from beliefs that are also psychologically primitive [e.g., that are immediately verifiable], our confidence in their truth tends to diminish the more we think about them." As an example, he cites the belief that "tables and chairs, trees and mountains, are still there when we turn our backs on them," saying that "as soon as the question is seriously raised whether . . . we have a right to suppose that they are still there, we feel that some kind of argument must be produced, and that if none is forthcoming, our belief can be no more than a pious opinion."[32] In other words, so long as a belief remains logically primitive it is not philosophically respectable.

On Russell's view, then, the job of philosophy is to try to produce grounds to support beliefs of this sort or, where this effort fails, to show how the common-sense belief—or the language in which it's expressed—can be replaced with a logical construction that eliminates from the original anything that can't be verified by sense impressions. Neither of these alternatives was acceptable to Wittgenstein.

His alternative was to view the philosopher's job as that of interpreting the things we all say in such a way as to show that they *can* survive skeptical scrutiny. In the *Tractatus* he held that such an interpretation can be provided by logical analysis, in other words, by showing that what is said in ordinary language can be analyzed into explicitly phenomenological propositions. In later years he dropped the idea of analysis and proposed another way of providing the required interpretation.

I will mention here two elements of his new approach to skepticism: his concept of a criterion and his concept of a language-game. The role of Wittgenstein's criteria has already been indicated in what I said in chapters 2, 7, and 8 about the linkage of verification and interpretation. When Wittgenstein declares that such-and-such is the criterion for p, he is telling us both (a) how we come to *know* that p and (b) *what* it is we are coming to know, that is, how to interpret "p." Since this was Wittgenstein's way of trying to remove the temptation to skepticism, it is clear that the criterion for p must itself be something no skeptic would regard as unknowable. So nothing can be a criterion unless it is given in immediate experience, even though in our everyday language we may not describe our criterion in explicitly phenomenological terms. Wittgenstein strongly suggests, in fact, that if we tried to so describe it, we would find ourselves unable to do so.

So the situation is this: we say things about tables and chairs and other people in language that is not explicitly phenomenological, but in doing so, the concepts we employ somehow grow out of the phenomenal world we perceive, that is, we have certain *experiences* and then *say* certain things, such as "He is suffering terribly" and "The jewels are locked in the safe." That we say such things poses no special problem for the *Tractatus* view of language, because on that view these things we say can be traced back, analytically, to elementary propositions, which describe immediate experience in phenomenological terms. So according to the *Tractatus* there is no logical hiatus between what we perceive and what we say. But this unbroken logical chain was lost when Wittgenstein later abandoned analytic reductionism. So it now looked as though our concepts have come into being out of nowhere, unaccountably. They certainly do not have the logical (analytic, definitional) basis in experience that was alleged in the *Tractatus*.

Wittgenstein needed to acknowledge this, and he did so by saying that our language-games simply emerge "spontaneously" (PI, p. 224; see also RFM (revised), IV, 23). Speaking in the same vein, he said, "You must bear in mind that the language-game is so to say something unpredictable. I mean: it is not based on grounds. It is not reasonable (or unreasonable). It is there—like our life" (OC, §559).

This is the same as to say that there is no accounting for our saying the things we say, for our having these particular concepts. "Our mistake," said Wittgenstein, "is to look for an explanation where we ought to look at what happens as a 'proto- phenomenon'. That is, where we ought to have said: this language-game is played" (PI, §654). "What has to be accepted, the given, is—so one could say— *forms of life*" (PI, p. 226).

This could be made to look terribly irresponsible. For it would be inexcusable for Wittgenstein to propose this way of thinking if he shared Russell's realist interpretation of the things we commonly say, for in that case he would be saying that philosophers must simply *ignore* skepticism, must learn to live with it. I will explain this by turning again to the problem of other minds.

Wittgenstein agreed with part of what Russell said about this. In a passage quoted above, Russell said: "We do not judge as to [another person's] state of mind by any logical process: the judgement grows up, often without our being able to say what physical mark of emotion we actually saw. . . . There may or may not be a possible deduction leading to the same result, but whether there is or not, we certainly do not employ it." So far Wittgenstein and Russell were agreed that our judgments are not supported by any deductions we make from more secure propositions. But Russell found this unsatisfactory and declared that "unless [the things we commonly say] can on reflection be deduced by a logical process from beliefs that are also psychologically primitive [e.g., that are immediately verifiable], our confidence in their truth tends to diminish the more we think about them." Wittgenstein disagreed, saying that philosophy "cannot give [language] any foundations" (PI, §124). And my point is that if Wittgenstein had stopped at *this* point and said that philosophers must content themselves with saying "This language-game is played," he would be conveying a message of resignation. He would have been telling Russell and others to resign themselves to skepticism and not fret about it. But this was *not* Wittgenstein's message. Rather, as I pointed out above, he also said that no foundations are *needed* for rendering philosophically respectable the things we commonly say. Foundations aren't needed because the things we say are not to be interpreted as Russell interpreted them, namely, as being about things that transcend experience.

My point here is that Wittgenstein's advice about accepting language-games as the given and not hankering after justifications (foundations) can escape the charge of being irresponsible only *because* he was a reductionist. His followers, by contrast, want to accept what Wittgenstein says about language-games, while at the same time *dismissing* reductionism. (Newton Garver, for example, says that Wittgenstein "assume[s] the existence of an external world."[33]) But to depict Wittgenstein in that way is to make him look either perverse or irresponsible.

Two clarifications may be useful here. The first pertains to the fact that Wittgenstein says both that philosophy is purely descriptive and that philosophy cannot provide foundations for our language-games. These remarks are addressed to the same point in a philosophical problem, but it is useful to think of them as being addressed—primarily, at least—to different audiences. The first remark is best thought of as spoken by Wittgenstein, qua phenomenalist, to his former Tractarian self; the second remark is best thought of as spoken by Wittgenstein, qua opponent of realism and skepticism, to a philosopher like Russell. When he says that philosophy is purely descriptive, he is telling himself, as I demonstrate in chapter 3, that the Tractarian ideal of a complete *analysis* of concepts in terms of experience must be replaced with descriptions of the *use* of words. Whereas, when he says that philosophy can provide no foundations for our language-games, he is telling a philosopher like Russell to abandon his search for justifications. But, as I said above, Wittgenstein also held that there is no *need* for foundations because the things we say are not to be interpreted as Russell interpreted them, namely, as being about things that transcend experience.

My second clarification pertains to the fact that although Wittgenstein repeatedly said that no *explanations* can be provided for our having the concepts we have, he also at times seems to offer explanations. For example, near the end of his life he said: "Life can educate one to a belief in God. And *experiences* too are what bring this about. . . . Experiences, thoughts,—life can force this concept on us. So perhaps it is similar to the concept 'object' *[dem Begriff 'Gegenstand']*" (CV, p. 86). Since I have elsewhere explained in detail *(Wittgenstein's Metaphysics,* pp. 146–147) how Wittgenstein was thinking of the concept "object," I will here simply quote a passage in which he makes the point in a very compressed way. He writes: "What holds the bundle of 'sense-impressions' together is their mutual relationships. That which is 'red' is also 'sweet' and 'hard' and 'cold' and 'sounds' when one strikes it" (RPP, I §896). Here Wittgenstein is explaining that it is *because* of such regularities amongst our sense-impressions that we have concepts like *apple* and *cat.* And he is offering an analogy for this in his remark about the concept of God being forced on one by life's experiences. So why is this not in conflict with his insistence that philosophers are not to offer explanations?

The answer, I believe, lies in Russell's discussion of hard and soft data, where he introduces the distinction between a belief's being psychologically derivative (in that it arises from something we experience) and a belief's being "logically primitive" (in that it is not arrived at by a logical inference). When Wittgenstein says that philosophy provides no *explanations,* he means to say that our belief in (for example) "other minds" is not arrived at by a logical inference, but he is quite prepared to allow that such a belief arises from something we experience—and that philosophers can describe (or otherwise allude to) such experiences. For example, in the case of "other minds" he says that a "primitive reaction" is involved: "It is a primitive reaction to tend, to treat, the part that hurts when someone else is in pain; and not merely when oneself is . . ." (Z, §540), and adds: "My relation to the appearances here is part of my concept" (Z, §543). This is meant to be explanatory but not in the sense of providing a deductive justification of our concepts.[34] And the same holds for his explanation for our having the concept of an object.

Returning now to Wittgenstein's main points, they can be summed up as follows: (1) We have criteria for various things—for another's state of mind, for example, and these criteria show that what we are speaking of are *not* things that transcend experience; (2) the fact that we say the things we do (employ certain concepts, play certain language-games) is a "proto-phenomenon," that is, language-games emerge spontaneously; (3) philosophers can describe all of this but they must stop searching for foundations since foundations can seem to be *needed* only on the false assumption that we are speaking of things that transcend immediate experience. A fourth item can be added to these three, but it needs some explaining.

Russell maintained that so long as a belief remains logically primitive, in other words, unproved, it is not philosophically respectable, and it is obvious that Wittgenstein rejected this. But he did more than reject it; he took the opposite view and became, in various ways, a champion of that which is primitive. For example, in *On Certainty* he writes:

> I want to regard man here as an animal; as a primitive being to which one grants instinct but not ratiocination. As a creature in a primitive state. Any logic good enough for a primitive means of communication needs no apology from us. Language did not emerge from some kind of ratiocination. (§475)[35]

One can picture Wittgenstein wagging his finger at Russell as he wrote the line: "Any logic good enough for a primitive means of communication needs no apology from us."

It is in this connection that Wittgenstein speaks repeatedly of language-games being something *primitive*. To understand this, one must bear in mind that he always makes this point in conjunction with dismissing a philosophical attempt at providing a justification for what we say, such as attempted justifications of induction or so-called "proofs" of an external world.

This is clearest, perhaps, in his remarks bearing on the so-called "problem of other minds":

> You say you attend to a man who groans because experience has taught you that you yourself groan when you feel such-and-such. But as you don't in fact make any such inference, we can abandon the justification by analogy. . . . (Z, §537)
>
> It is a help here to remember that it is a primitive reaction to tend, to treat, the part that hurts when someone else is in pain; and not merely when oneself is. . . . (Z, §540)
>
> But what is the word "primitive" meant to say here? Presumably that this sort of behaviour is *pre-linguistic:* that a language-game is based on it. . . . (Z, §541)

My relation to the appearances here is part of my concept. . . . (Z, §543)

Being sure that someone is in pain, doubting whether he is, and so on, are so many natural, instinctive, kinds of behaviour towards other human beings, and our language is merely an auxiliary to, and a further extension of, this relation. Our language-game is an extension of primitive behaviour. (For our *language-game* is behaviour.) (Instinct). (Z, §545)

And in general: "The origin and primitive form of the language-game is a reaction; only from this can more complicated forms develop. Language—I want to say—is a refinement, 'In the beginning was the deed'" (CV, p. 31).[36]

These ideas are sometimes referred to as Wittgenstein's naturalism, and he has been praised for pursuing this line of thought. Newton Garver, for example, declares that Wittgenstein introduced "a brilliant innovation" when he insisted that "the uses of language which structure our lives can only be accepted, not justified or explained."[37] But as I have pointed out—not only here but also in *Wittgenstein's Metaphysics* (p. 125)—Wittgenstein's so-called "naturalism" is the result of his taking several wrong turns. It is not something we should want to emulate.

Garver also says that "Wittgenstein did not share Russell's belief in the primacy of epistemology."[38] I find this an astonishing assertion, but I can see how Garver came to think about Wittgenstein in this way. He did so by divorcing epistemology from logic and metaphysics (as when he says that Wittgenstein's "main achievement . . . has been to overcome the three-hundred-year hegemony of epistemology over logic and metaphysics in Western philosophy")[39] and by thinking that a philosopher's theory of knowledge and his theory of meaning are unrelated (as when he explains that "Wittgenstein did not have a theory of knowledge" partly because "he was more interested in problems of meaning than in problems of knowledge.")[40] What Garver has failed to realize is that Wittgenstein's *way* of dealing with epistemological problems was to *turn them into* problems of logic and meaning. Garver even goes so far as to say that "it distorts Wittgenstein to conceive him as . . . endorsing the idea that meaning is to be determined in terms of verification," because "such a view puts epistemology back in the center of the philosophical stage."[41] Garver has failed to realize that Wittgenstein concerned himself with interpretation and verification and criteria and meaning and use and language-games *because* he was doing battle with skepticism.

I have tried to summarize the points on which Wittgenstein's philosophical views developed by adapting or reacting against ideas that Russell put forward in *Our Knowledge of the External World.* Most important in all this was his determination to "see the hardness of the soft"—to show that none of the things we commonly say fails to survive the ordeal of skeptical scrutiny. But in carrying out this project Wittgenstein was failing to challenge the skeptic in the right place. Instead of challenging skepticism at its source, he conceded to the skeptic everything that goes into making the skeptic skeptical, such as the idea that we perceive sense-data and that what we perceive of another person is a body and its behavior.

This is what I had in mind when, in the first paragraph of this appendix, I said that Wittgenstein borrowed Russell's way of posing or framing certain philosophical problems, especially in the area of epistemology. His way of dealing with these issues appears analogous to the way he thought one should react to Otto Weininger's *Sex and Character.* Writing to Moore in August 1931, he sympathized with Moore's lack of enthusiasm for Weininger, but then added:

> It is true that he is fantastic but he is great and fantastic. It isn't necessary or rather not possible to agree with him but the greatness lies in that with which we disagree. It is his enormous mistake which is great. I.e., roughly speaking if you add a ~ to the whole book it says an important truth.[42]

But if you simply negate what another thinker says, you are retaining the *categories* in which he thinks and states things. This, it seems to me, is the kind of relationship that existed between Wittgenstein and Russell's *Our Knowledge of the External World.* Perhaps Wittgenstein was, in a way, acknowledging this when he wrote: "Doing philosophy is turning bad arguments around" (WR, p. 264). If you simply turn an argument around, for instance, turn a *modus ponens* into a *modus tolens* (as philosophers often do in disagreeing with one another), the argument revolves about a fixed point, which means that the philosophical categories are left in place. Accordingly, if you do philosophy in the manner Wittgenstein describes, you make yourself a hostage to those categories, and that insures that you will make no progress.

Notes

Introduction

1. *Philosophical Investigations*, vol. 3 (Fall 1980), pp. 15–36. See also *Philosophical Investigations,* vol. 4 (Spring 1981) for Malcolm's criticism of my essay, pp. 61–71, and my response to Malcolm, pp. 72–90.

2. This is explained in my essay, "The Metaphysics of Wittgenstein's *On Certainty,*" *Philosophical Investigations,* vol. 8 (April 1985), pp. 81–119.

3. See chapter 1, pp. 4–5, 7; chapter 13, note 4; and chapter 16, note 5.

Chapter 1

1. *Some Main Problems of Philosophy* (New York: Macmillan, 1953), pp. 1–2.

2. Bertrand Russell, *My Philosophical Development* (London: George Allen and Unwin, 1959), p. 230.

3. Ibid., pp. 216–217.

4. Elsewhere he said, in a somewhat more radical tone: "While thinking philosophically we see problems in places where there are none. It is the job of philosophy to show that there are no problems" (PG, p. 47).

5. Max Black, commenting on this passage, says: "One might object that there is nothing for seeing the world 'right' *(richtig)* to be contrasted with; as one cannot see wrongly" *(A Companion to Wittgenstein's Tractatus,* Ithaca, N.Y.: Cornell University Press, 1964, p. 377). But Wittgenstein certainly thought that philosophers very often see the world wrongly—when they "look at the facts through the medium of a misleading form of expression" (BB, p. 31).

6. "The Rise and Fall of the Picture Theory," in *Perspectives on the Philosophy of Wittgenstein,* ed. Irving Block (Cambridge: MIT Press, 1983), p. 85.

7. In lectures he said: "Whenever we try to talk about the essence of the world [i.e., try to state an a priori matter in the material mode of speech] we talk nonsense" (WL32, p. 110). The importance Wittgenstein attached to this is shown by a remark he made in a letter to Russell, dated 19 August 1919: "The main point is the theory of what can be expressed by propositions—i.e., by language—(and, which comes to the same, what can be *thought)* and what cannot be expressed by propositions, but only

shown; which, I believe, is the cardinal problem of philosophy" *(Letters to Russell, Keynes and Moore,* ed. G. H. von Wright (Oxford: Blackwell, 1974), p. 71).

8. In the *Tractatus* he had written:

> What finds its reflection in language, language cannot represent.
>
> What expresses *itself* in language, *we* cannot express by means of language.
>
> Propositions *show* the logical form of reality.
>
> They display it. (TLP, 4.121)

He goes on to say: "What *can* be shown, cannot be said" (TLP, 4.1212), meaning presumably that there are things a philosopher *can* show, although he can't *say* them. What can he show? This is where Wittgenstein's phrase "the logical form of reality" is needed: a philosopher can show the logical form of reality. As a synonym for this phrase he later used "essence of the world," "essence of what is represented," and sometimes simply "essence."

9. In lectures he said:

> Luther said that theology is the grammar of the word 'God'. I interpret this to mean that an investigation of the word would be a grammatical one. For example, people might dispute about how many arms God had, and someone might enter the dispute by denying that one could talk about arms of God. This would throw light on the use of the word. What is ridiculous or blasphemous also shows the grammar of the word. (WL35, p. 32)

Elsewhere Wittgenstein said: "The way you use the word 'God' shews, not *whom* you mean, but what you mean" (RPP, I, §475).

10. His very next sentence reads: "A recognition of what is essential and what inessential in our language if it is to represent, a recognition of which parts of our language are wheels turning idly, amounts to constructing a phenomenological language"—but this gets us ahead of the story.

11. Quoted by O. K. Bouwsma in *Wittgenstein: Conversations 1949–1951* (Indianapolis, Ind.: Hackett, 1986), p. 37.

12. The questions, of course, are rhetorical. Wittgenstein once said that philosophy could be taught solely by asking questions (WL35, p. 97).

13. Quoted by M. O'C. Drury, "Conversations With Wittgenstein," in *Recollections of Wittgenstein,* ed. Rush Rhees (Oxford: Oxford University Press, 1984), p. 158. It is noteworthy that Wittgenstein chose as his motto for the *Investigations* a passage from Nestroy that can be translated: "It is in the nature of progress that it appears much greater than it actually is." The significance of this lies in the fact that Wittgenstein intended (see PI, p. x) that the *Tractatus* and the *Investigations* should be published in a single volume, so that this motto, sandwiched between them, would serve as a warning that the difference between the two books is not as great as it may appear.

14. The phrase "essence of the world" ("Wesen der Welt") appears in the *Tractatus* (3.3421) where we are told that the essence of the world is revealed to us when we realize that a particular mode of signifying is a *possible* mode of signifying. But 3.3421 seems to make sense only when taken together with the surrounding passages, for example, with 3.344, which tells us that "what signifies in the symbol is what is common to all those symbols by which it can be replaced in accordance with the rules of logical syntax." (See also TLP 5.4711.) The same idea is found in PR, pp. 51 and 85. See chapter 6 below for further discussion of this.

15. See chapter 6, esp. note 5.

16. *Meaning and Saying: Essays in the Philosophy of Language* (Washington, D.C.: University Press of America, 1979), p. ix.

Chapter 2

1. *Our Knowledge of the External World,* (London: George Allen and Unwin, 1952), pp. 74, 78.

2. These sentences were retained in the *Tractatus* at 6.51. In 1930 Wittgenstein said in his conversations with Waismann: "[I]t is only the method of answering a question that tells you what the question was really about. Only when I have answered a question can I know what it was aimed at. (The sense of a proposition is the method of its verification.)" (WVC, p. 79).

3. Russell, *Our Knowledge,* pp. 72–80.

4. Ibid., pp. 242–243.

5. Ibid., p. 79.

6. I am using the word *realist* as Wittgenstein did in his later years (see Z, §§413–414 and PI, §402), that is, to designate philosophers like Russell and Moore, who hold that we constantly speak of things that transcend experience. These are the philosophers Wittgenstein was criticizing when he said: "If I had to say what is the main mistake made by philosophers of the present generation, including Moore, I would say that it is that when language is looked at, what is looked at is a form of words and not the use made of the form of words" (LC, p. 2).

7. The letter is quoted by Brian McGuinness in *Wittgenstein, A Life* (Berkeley: University of California Press, 1988), p. 106.

8. Reprinted in *Logic and Knowledge,* ed. Robert C. Marsh (London: George Allen and Unwin, 1956), pp. 133–134.

9. G. E. Moore, "Wittgenstein's Lectures in 1930–33," reprinted in *Philosophical Papers,* (London: George Allen and Unwin, 1959), p. 311.

10. Quoted from his conversations with Wittgenstein by Bouwsma, *Wittgenstein: Conversations 1949–1951,* p. 13.

11. Wittgenstein's next sentence, placed in quotation marks, is a line that most readers won't recognize. It is a quotation from the philosopher Hans Driesch and reads: "I have, knowing of my knowledge, consciousness of something." Twenty years later Wittgenstein was still thinking about solipsism of the present moment and mentioned Driesch by name:

> "The ideal clock would always point to the time 'now'." This also connects up with the language which describes only my impressions of the present moment. Akin is the primal utterance that is only an inarticulate sound. (Driesch.) The ideal name, which the word 'this' is (RPP, I, §721).

12. Schopenhauer begins *The World as Will and Representation* with the sentence "The world is my representation" and goes on to say: "If any truth can be expressed *a priori,* it is this." He adds that "this truth is by no means new. It was to be found already in the sceptical reflections from which Descartes started. But Berkeley was the first to enunciate it positively, and he has thus rendered an immortal service to philosophy" ((New York: Dover, 1969), trans. E. F. J. Payne, vol. 1, p. 3). On a later page Schopenhauer writes: "[T]he individual is the bearer of the knowing subject, and this knowing subject is the bearer of the world. This is equivalent to saying that the whole of nature outside the knowing subject, and so all remaining individuals, exist only in his representation; that he is conscious of them always only as his representation, . . .

and as something dependent on his own inner being and existence" (p. 332). He adds: "Everyone looks on his own death as the end of the world . . ." (pp. 332–333). The relevance of this is that we know from several sources that Schopenhauer was the earliest philosophical influence on Wittgenstein (see my *Wittgenstein's Metaphysics*, p. 3). And in the *Tractatus* Wittgenstein declares that "what the solipsist *means* is quite correct" (5.62) and says, echoing Schopenhauer, that "at death the world does not alter, but comes to an end" (6.431). Wittgenstein also shared Schopenhauer's high opinion of Berkeley, saying that Berkeley was a "very deep thinker" (quoted by M. O'C. Drury, "Conversations with Wittgenstein," in *Recollections of Wittgenstein,* p. 157).

13. "Ludwig Wittgenstein: A Portrait," in *Ludwig Wittgenstein: Philosophy and Language,* eds. Alice Ambrose and Morris Lazerowitz (London: George Allen and Unwin, 1971), pp. 20–21; emphasis added. The sentence within brackets was added by Ambrose.

14. In *Philosophical Grammar* Wittgenstein said: "Doing philosophy is turning bad arguments around" (WR, p. 264). This is what he does in the present case. Russell trusted the looks of our language, gave it a realist interpretation, and concluded that much that we say is vulnerable to skepticism. Wittgenstein simply turned this around. To show that what we say is *not* vulnerable to skepticism, he declared that the looks of our language is *not* trustworthy and that the proper interpretation is quite different from the realist interpretation which naturally suggests itself.

15. Russell, *Our Knowledge,* pp. 88–89.

16. Along with these remarks Waismann makes the point that a proposition can't be verified in several different ways:

> I cannot . . . say 'I shall verify this proposition in this way *or* that way.' A method of verification, after all, is not something that is added to a sense. A proposition already *contains* the method of its verification. . . . A statement has sense, not because it is constructed in a legitimate way, but because it can be verified." (WVC, p. 244)

In discussion with Schlick and Waismann, Wittgenstein had said (WVC, pp. 158–159) that there are cases in which "it seems as if I had verified the same sentence in ways that were different every time. But this is not so." He explains that what might look like several different ways of verifying something are, instead, different *symptoms* of it. (See also Waismann's further explication of this point on pp. 258–259.) These remarks are of interest because they tell us something important about the way in which Wittgenstein was to use the term *criterion* when he introduced it two years later as an alternative to speaking of verification. They tell us that although there can be several *symptoms* of the same state of affairs, there cannot be several different *criteria* for the same state of affairs, whether at the same or at different times. That is , if Wittgenstein were to say, for example, that at one time X was the criterion for S and at another time Y was the criterion for S, he would mean that in the one case "S" means one thing and in the other "S" means something different. Thus he says: "Nothing is commoner than for the meaning of an expression to oscillate, for a phenomenon to be regarded sometimes as a symptom, sometimes as a criterion, of a state of affairs" (Z, §438). In other words, the meaning of an expression does not remain constant when first one thing and then another is taken as a criterion.

17. Moore's record of Wittgenstein's lectures contains the following:

> Near the beginning [of his 1930 lectures] he made the famous statement, 'The sense of a proposition is the way in which it is verified'; but in [his lectures of

1932] he said this only meant 'You can determine the meaning of a proposition by asking how it is verified' and went on to say, 'This is necessarily a mere rule of thumb, because "verification" means different things, and because in some cases the question "How is that verified?" makes no sense'. He gave as an example of a case in which that question 'makes no sense' the proposition 'I've got toothache', of which he already said that it makes no sense to ask for a verification of it—to ask 'How do you know you have it?' . . . . He went on to say 'Verification determines the meaning of a proposition only where it gives the grammar of the proposition in question.' ("Wittgenstein's Lectures in 1930–33," in *Philosophical Papers*, p. 266)

18. "Did Wittgenstein Have a Theory of Hinge Propositions?" *Philosophical Investigations*, vol. 12 (April 1989), pp. 135–136.

19. Ibid., p. 135. Notice the curious use of the word *accuse*. I didn't think I was making accusations. Is it an accusation to say that Hume was an empiricist?

Chapter 3

1. *The Philosophy of Wittgenstein* (Englewood Cliffs: Prentice-Hall, 1964), pp. 253–254.

2. Ibid., p. 319.

3. Ibid., p. 321.

4. Ibid., p. 329.

5. Pitcher is not alone in leaving this impression. For example, G. P. Baker and P. M. S. Hacker write: "Philosophy, Wittgenstein insists, . . . only describes. . . . The correct description of our linguistic practices will show where and why we have gone wrong in our philosophizing." What would this include? We are told that "it is the task of philosophy to articulate and clarify grammatical connections that are embedded in common forms of speech and inference (e.g. 'How do you know it was red?'—'Because I could see it'.)" *(Wittgenstein: Meaning and Understanding* (Chicago: Chicago University Press, 1985), pp. 280–281 and 276).

6. Here it may be objected that Wittgenstein explicitly says that "one must always ask oneself: is the word ever actually used in this way in the language-game which is its original home?" (PI, §116). Am I not ignoring this? No, I want only to say that when Wittgenstein undertook to answer questions about the *use* of words, he employed certain special procedures for doing so. In this chapter I am concerned with one of those procedures: his substitution method. I will discuss his other procedures in later chapters.

7. The relevant passages in The Blue Book are the following:

[T]he solipsist asks: "How *can* we believe that the other has pain; what does it mean to believe this? How can the expression of such a supposition make sense?"

. . . the answer of the common–sense philosopher is that surely there is no difficulty in the idea of supposing, thinking, imagining that someone else has what I have. But the trouble with the realist is always that he does not solve but skip[s] the difficulties which his adversaries see. . . . The realist answer, for us, just brings out the difficulty. . . . (BB, pp. 48–49)

Now when the solipsist says that only his own experiences are real, it is no use answering him: "Why do you tell us this if you don't believe that we really hear it?" Or anyhow, if we give him this answer, we mustn't believe that we have answered his difficulty. There is no common sense answer to a philosophical problem. One can defend common sense against the attacks of philosopher only by solving their puzzles, i.e., by curing them of the temptation to attack common sense; not by restating the views of common sense (BB, pp. 58–59)

8. Wittgenstein was openly antagonistic to ordinary language, saying at one point: "The whole of language must be thoroughly ploughed up" (WR, p. 277). He also said that people are so enmeshed in "grammatical confusions" that, in order to help them, "you have as it were to reconstitute their entire language. . . . [Y]ou can only succeed in extricating people who live in an instinctive rebellion against language; you cannot help those whose entire instinct is to live in the herd which has created this language as its own proper mode of expression" (WR, p. 272–273). Wittgenstein's sympathies clearly lay with those "people who live in an instinctive rebellion against language." They have good reason, he thought, to rebel.

We find that there is puzzlement and mental discomfort, not only when our curiosity about certain facts is not satisfied . . . , but also when a notation dissatisfies us. . . . Our ordinary language, which of all possible notations is the one which pervades all our life, holds our mind rigidly in one position, as it were, and in this position sometimes it feels cramped, having a desire for other positions as well. Thus we sometimes wish for a notation which stresses a difference more strongly, makes it more obvious, than ordinary language does, or one which in a particular case uses more closely similar forms of expression than our ordinary language. Our mental cramp is loosened when we are shown the notations which fulfill these needs. (BB, p. 59)

Wittgenstein regarded these needs as legitimate, and he was ready to satisfy them by inventing alternative symbolisms. At the same time, however, he wanted to temper such dissatisfaction with our language by saying something like the following:

You need to realize that the things we say in ordinary language are *only* misleading, that they do not actually imply the things that realists think they imply. For example, when I tell someone, 'I think about her often,' the words 'I think' do *not* imply that there is an ego which thinks. And when we say, "The pot boiled over while no one was watching," this does *not* imply that the pot existed while unperceived. If you think otherwise, you are treating the superficial grammar of our language as though it determines meaning, which it does not. Meaning is determined by use, which includes the way we verify a proposition. Notice that we treat "The pot boiled over while no one was watching" as verifiable, whereas it would not be possible to verify that something existed while no one perceived it. Realists, therefore, are wrong.

9. In Wittgenstein's conversations with Waismann something at least quite similar to this method was mentioned in December 1931. See WVC, p. 184. The guiding idea was already present in the *Tractatus,* although not as a method. I am referring to 3.344, which tells us that "what signifies in the symbol is what is common to all those symbols which can be substituted for it in accordance with the rules of logical syntax."

10. In The Blue Book Wittgenstein said something that suggests that his method of substitution may owe something to Russell. He said: "The cases in which particularly we wish to say that someone is misled by a form of expression are those in which we would say: 'He wouldn't talk as he does . . . *if he were aware of this other possi-*

bility of expression'" (BB, p. 28; emphasis added). Wittgenstein thought it vital to philosophy, although rare among philosophers, to be able to think of other possibilities of expression, alternative grammatical forms. (That is why he compared himself to "a man who is inventing a new calculus (say the differential calculus) and is looking for a symbolism.") In a passage written in 1949 Wittgenstein said that "the philosopher's task [is] imagining possibilities" (LW I, §807). Presumably, that's what he was alluding to when, in the same period, he wrote: "Merely recognizing philosophical problems as logical ones is an advance. With it come the proper attitude and the method" (LW, I, §256). This seems to echo something Russell said in *Our Knowledge of the External World.* Using the word *hypotheses* in a peculiar way, to mean "logical possibilities" or "imaginable forms of words," he said that although it has "been lacking hitherto in philosophy," a vital part of "the mental training required for a philosopher" is that one should "cultivate logical imagination, in order to have a number of hypotheses at [one's] command. . . . [I]t is necessary to acquire fertility in imagining abstract hypotheses. . . . It is in this way that the study of logic becomes the central study in philosophy: it gives the method of research" (pp. 242–243). Because of their falling out in later years, it is often forgotten that in the *Tractatus* period, when these lines were written, Wittgenstein and Russell were very close. In 1949 Wittgenstein, in conversation with Oets Bouwsma, said: "Now Russell was different in his good days. He was wonderful" (Bouwsma, *Wittgenstein: Conversations 1949–1951,* p. 49).

    11. CE, Appendix B, p. 435; my translation.

    12. *The Lichtenberg Reader,* ed. and trans. by Franz H. Mautner and Henry Hatfield (Boston: Beacon Press, 1959) p. 19.

    13. *The Analysis of Matter* (New York: Dover, 1954), pp. 151–152.

    14. In plain opposition to Russell's view, Wittgenstein wrote: "Bad influence of Aristotelian logic. The logic of language is immeasurably more complicated than it looks" (WL, II, p. 44).

    15. London: George Allen and Unwin, 1937, 2nd ed., p. 1.

    16. Ibid., p. xi; emphasis added.

    17. "The Philosophy of Logical Atomism, reprinted in *Logic and Knowledge,* ed. Charles C. Marsh (London: George Allen and Unwin, 1956), pp. 269–270.

    18. In his later years Wittgenstein used the word *analysis* to include his substitution method. (See PI, §90, 2nd para.). In this connection see the discussion of the word *soul* in chapter 6 of this book.

    19. Notice how many of the opening themes of the *Investigations* were already present in 1933 in the opening passages of The Yellow Book:

> Frege ridiculed people for not seeing that the meaning of the signs "1", "2", "3", etc. was the important thing, not the scratches on paper. It is a queer thing, however, that people have a propensity, on hearing the substantive "the number 1", to think of its meaning as being something beyond the sign and corresponding to it, in the way that Smith corresponds to the name "Smith". . . .
>
>   . . . The question ["What is the number 1?"] is misleading because, although it is correct to reply "There is no object corresponding to '1' in the sense that there is an object corresponding to Smith", we then look for an object in *another* sense. This is one of about a half-dozen traps we constantly fall into. When we hear the substantive word "number" used in the question "What is number?" our propensity is to think of an ethereal object. . . . As a way out of the difficulty posed by this question I suggest that we do not talk about the meaning of words but rather about the use of words (WL35, pp. 43–44).

He went on to say:

> Our language is constructed on an apparently simple scheme, so that we are inclined to look at language as being much simpler than it is: we look for an object when we see a sign of the language. . . .
>
> One important source of difficulty in philosophy is that words look so much alike. They are brought together in a dictionary like tools in a box, and like the tools, which look pretty much alike, they may have enormously different uses. . . . When we talk of words and their meanings we tend to compare them with money and the things it buys rather than money and the uses it has. . . .
>
> I have remarked that we are inclined to view our language as much simpler than it is. Cf. Augustine, who said that he learned Latin by learning the names of things. Surely he learned also such words as "not", "or", etc. We can criticize his view in either of two ways: that it is wrong, or that it describes a simpler thing than we call language (WL35, pp. 45–46).

Wittgenstein goes on to imagine "a person learn[ing] a language by having people tell him the names of things after pointing to them" and imagining that "the language served one purpose only, say, for building a house with different shaped materials" (WL35, p. 47).

20. The Brown Book begins with Wittgenstein citing Augustine's account of learning language and commenting that whoever gives such an account "does not primarily think of such words as 'today', 'not', 'but', 'perhaps'" (BB, p. 77). Then in §2 he writes:

> [B]y introducing numerals we have introduced an entirely different *kind* of instrument into our language. The difference of kind is much more obvious when we contemplate such a simple example than when we look at our ordinary language with innumerable kinds of words all looking more or less alike when they stand in the dictionary." (BB, p; 79)

Several paragraphs later, in §6, Wittgenstein comments on the fact that many kinds of words are called "names" (as in the expressions "names of numbers," "names of nations," and so on), and proceeds to comment that one reason for this may be that "we imagine the functions of proper names, numerals, words for colours, etc., to be much more alike than they actually are. If we do so we are tempted to think that the function of every word is more or less like the function of the proper name of a person." Yet once we see how different are the functions of various words, we will see no reason why we shouldn't call many kind of words "names" (BB, p. 82; compare PI, §10 and §13). Is this perhaps why, at one point, Wittgenstein considered using as a motto for the *Investigations* a line from "King Lear": "Let me teach you differences"? He may have been thinking: once you have been made to see the *differences* among words you will no longer be tempted by realism.

21. I do not intend to discuss in this book Wittgenstein's account of sensation words, but I want to call attention to the fact that what he says about them carries forth his antirealist view that words can have a use without standing for (or referring to) something. For example, his discussion opens with the question: "How do words *refer* to sensations?" (PI, §244). Rather than wanting an answer to this question, he wants us to see that the question arises from the realist's mistaken assumption that nouns always stand for things. Accordingly, he remarks in a later passage that the

problems about sensations arise when, *mistakenly,* "we construe the grammar of the expression of sensation on the model of 'object and designation'" (PI, §293). See my discussion of this in *Wittgenstein's Metaphysics,* chapters 19 and 20.

22. "Empirical Propositions and Hypothetical Statements," *Mind,* vol. 61 (July 1950), pp. 291, 296, 301.

23. What, then, becomes of common sense, as described by Isaiah Berlin? Clearly, Wittgenstein would have thought that Berlin had misjudged the plain man and given an erroneous account of common sense. Accordingly, we find him saying: "A philosopher is a man who has to cure many intellectual diseases in himself before he can arrive at the notions of common sense" (CV, p. 44). Wittgenstein undoubtedly thought that realists—Moore, for example—suffer from intellectual diseases that prevent them from arriving at the notions of common sense. In fact, he explicitly said, in an obvious reference to Moore, that "the common-sense philosopher . . . is not the common-sense man" (BB, p. 48).

24. "There isn't a further process hidden behind [a person's behavior], which is the real understanding [of a word], accompanying and causing these manifestations . . ." (PG, p. 80). "In our study of symbolism [i.e., language] there is no foreground and background; it isn't a matter of a tangible sign with an accompanying intangible power or understanding" (PG, p. 87).

25. Why do I say in (iii) that S is to be inspected *in imagination?* Because that's the way philosophers do this, and it's the only way they could. Ask yourself what Hume is actually doing in the following thought–experiment.

> We can conceive of a thinking being to have either many or few perceptions.
> . . . Suppose it to have only one perception, as of thirst or hunger. *Consider it in that situation.* Do you conceive of anything but merely that perception? Have you any notion of *self* or *substance?* . . . For my part, I have a notion of neither. *(A Treatise of Human Nature,* ed. L. A. Selby–Bigge (Oxford: Oxford University Press, 1951), p. 634–635)

I have italicized the relevant sentence, the one that brings out what I meant by "in imagination." Now compare what Hume says with Wittgenstein's saying: "The experience of feeling pain is not that a person 'I' has something. I distinguish an intensity, a location, etc. in the pain, but not an owner" (PR, p. 94).

26. See *Wittgenstein's Metaphysics,* chapters 16–19. Someone may question my claim that what Wittgenstein says about rule-following has no other basis than his phenomenalism, for it might be thought that his phenomenalism is not responsible for *one* version of his problem, namely, that any rule can be interpreted in more than one way, so that a rule does not inexorably determine its application. But this version *is* a product of his phenomenalism, albeit indirectly. I mean, this version can't arise without relying on the idea of logical possibility, and that idea, in turn, is the product of phenomenalism (see *Wittgenstein's Metaphysics,* chapter 18, note 4). When one thinks about Wittgenstein's pupil learning arithmetic and does so without bringing in the idea of logical possibility, one is immediately led to a point made by A. C. Grayling, namely, that "to be in a *position* to understand 'add 2' one has to know enough arithmetic: there are holisms of understanding for a region (for a practice, say) which the teacher can draw upon in explanations of what is to be done, and the learner in vindication of what he is doing" ("Wittgenstein's Influence: Meaning, Mind and Method," in *Wittgenstein Centenary Essays,* ed. A Phillips Griffiths (Cambridge: Cambridge University Press, 1992), pp. 68–69). In response to Wittgenstein one wants to say: "But

there is, after all, a *point* to counting by twos or by tens—not just saying the numbers, but counting *things* that way. (Think of the way a pharmacist counts pills as she fills a prescription.) A pupil who has grasped *that* won't go off on a tangent."

27. This, surely, explains a matter to which John Hunter has called attention, namely, that

> while Wittgenstein often alludes to criteria, he rarely specifies them. He does in scientific examples like the criterion for angina; but in the case of such ordinary judgments as that a person is depressed or in pain or shamming or thinks he understands, the criteria are vaguely indicated as 'what he says and does', 'his behaviour', and so on. ("Critical Notice," *Canadian Journal of Philosophy*, vol. 4 (September 1974), p. 203)

This is an acute observation, but Hunter, unfortunately, did not realize that when Wittgenstein spoke of 'behavioral criteria,' the behavior he had in mind is the movements of a (Cartesian) body, not the conduct of a person. As a result, Hunter went on to propose (ibid., p. 204) a mistaken explanation for the fact that Wittgenstein rarely specified criteria, namely, that he had two concepts of a "criterion"—one for scientific judgments and another for ordinary judgments.

28. In other words, when we use such words as *calculate* and "run away," we take a step beyond the purest form of behaviorism. This, I gather, is the point Wittgenstein was making when he wrote: "It is always presupposed that the one who smiles *is* a human being and not just that what smiles is a human body" (LW, II, p. 84). It was Wittgenstein's view that running away and calculating and smiling are not features of reality, that is, of immediate experience, as a twinge of pain or a flash of light is; rather, they are constructs of our language.

29. See my discussion of this in *Wittgenstein's Metaphysics*, pp. 129–130. Incidentally, when I speak (as I do in this paragraph) of the 'difficulty of describing bodily movements,' I am merely relating Wittgenstein's views, not my own. I don't mean to suggest that there are bodies moving around.

Chapter 4

1. Russell, *Our Knowledge of the External World*, pp. 89–90.

2. I have barely scratched the surface of this issue. For a more thorough treatment see "The Analysis of Human Actions" in Frank Ebersole, *Language and Perception* (Washington, D.C.: University Press of America, 1979), esp. pp. 212–222 and the chapter "The Complexity of Speech Acts" in Ebersole, *Meaning and Saying*, pp. 93–147. See also Kent Kedl, "Language: Sounds We Use to Communicate," *Philosophical Investigations*, vol. 3, no. 1 (Winter 1980), pp. 26–43. Both Ebersole and Kedl discuss in detail the views of John Austin and John Searle. In my essay "Wittgenstein and Religious Belief" *(Philosophy,* vol. 63 (October 1988), pp. 427–452) I have argued that Wittgenstein's view of language is behavioristic in a respect not discussed here.

3. Notice that this is the conclusion of Russell, who is a realist. It is the realist who ends up thinking that he may be the only one who has ever spoken, has ever used language. I call attention to this in order to correct an idea that seems to be quite common, namely, that when Wittgenstein attacked the idea of a private language, he intended his argument to undermine phenomenalists. But the phenomenalist, if he has carried his reductionism through to other people, does not think that he is (or may be) alone in the world. Wittgenstein, I think we can say, aimed his private language argument at realists, at philosophers like Russell, for whom other minds remain "soft data."

Chapter 5

1. *The Foundation of Mathematics* (London: Routledge and Kegan Paul, 1931), pp. 115–116.

2. This is a point which reviewers of my book, *Wittgenstein's Metaphysics,* failed to understand. For example, Oswald Hanfling was mystified by the fact that I not only declared that the later Wittgenstein was a phenomenalist, 'broadly understood,' but also quoted Wittgenstein's remark that "it can never be our job to reduce anything to anything" (BB, p. 18). Although I also pointed out (p. 87) that the reductionism Wittgenstein rejects here is *analytic* reductionism, Hanfling responded rhetorically: "How, we may ask, can the anti-reductionist Wittgenstein be described as a phenomenalist, even 'broadly understood'?" ("Critical Notice," *Philosophical Investigations,* vol. 19 (April 1996), p. 167). But to say that Wittgenstein, because he rejected analytic reductionism, is "anti-reductionist" is to assume that there can be no other version of reductionism.

3. This tendency is especially pronounced in Wittgenstein's later writings. Instead of seeing whether support can be found for his own position (e.g., for his claim that in speaking we make sounds), he undertook to practice a sort of therapy on anyone unsympathetic with his reductionist views. And instead of acknowledging that his views are beset with grave difficulties, he treated them as unavoidable and resorted to saying things like "This is what we do" or "This language-game is played." What he should have done, instead, was to take a close look at the assumptions which got him into these predicaments.

4. This, very likely, is why some philosophers find it hard to believe that reductionist views are just as metaphysical as their inflationist counterparts. A reviewer of my *Wittgenstein's Metaphysics,* D. C. Barrett, S. J., comments: "Some critics of Cook have even questioned the correctness of regarding phenomenalism and behaviorism as metaphysical" *(International Philosophical Quarterly* (September, 1995), p. 360).

5. This is discussed in detail in my *Wittgenstein's Metaphysics,* chapter 11, "Hume on Causation." I am not suggesting that Hume realized he was inventing an ersatz meaning. On the contrary, he imagined that he was explaining what we actually mean in saying that one thing caused another. He makes this plain when he writes:

> Thus upon the whole we may infer, that when we [i.e., philosophers] talk of any being, whether of a superior or inferior nature, as endow'd with a power or force, proportion'd to any effect; when we speak of a necessary connexion betwixt objects, and suppose that this connexion depends upon an efficacy or energy with which these objects are endow'd; in all these expressions, *so apply'd,* we have really no distinct meaning, and make use only of common words, without any clear and determinate ideas. But as 'tis more probable, that these expressions here lose their true meaning by being *wrongly apply'd,* than that they never have any meaning; 'twill be proper to bestow another consideration on this subject, to see if possibly we can discover the nature and origin of those ideas we annex to them. *(Treatise,* I, III, xiv)

It seems to me that this is fairly typical of reductionists: they insist that they are explicating our familiar terms and deny that they are inventing ersatz meanings for them. This is certainly what Wittgenstein claimed to be doing: clarifying the things we say. Although that is *not* what he was doing, some philosophers still do not recognize this. See, for example, Hanfling, "Critical Notice," pp. 164–177, esp. p. 175. Hanfling seems scandalized by my claim (in *Wittgenstein's Metaphysics,* chapters 16 and 17) that Wittgenstein was, unwittingly, inventing ersatz meanings for certain of our words, including those in which we speak of intellectual abilities, such as knowing how to play chess.

6. The high estimation of Hume among Wittgensteinians can be illustrated by some remarks by George Pitcher. Having quoted from Wittgenstein the line that "the aspects of things that are most important for us are hidden because of their simplicity and familiarity" (PI, §129), Pitcher continues:

> It takes a man of great philosophical skill and insight to pick out the obvious and to realize its profound importance. . . . To mention just one familiar example from the history of philosophy: there are no facts cited in Hume's famous analysis of causality that are not perfectly obvious, that we all did not already know. . . . [W]hat genius Hume displayed in noticing these 'trivialities,' in realizing their significance, and in presenting them to us in a way which makes us see it too! (Pitcher, *The Philosophy of Wittgenstein*, p. 323)

7. David Hume, *An Enquiry Concerning Human Understanding*, sec. VII, part II.

8. Frank Ebersole has urged me to clarify something here. I am interpreting Ramsey's phrase "some third possibility" in a way that he may not have had in mind. Whereas Ramsey may have supposed that the third possibility had to be a third philosophical view of the same general type as the other two, I am allowing that the third possibility may be of a *completely* different sort, namely, that one will find reasons for rejecting *all* such views.

9. In saying that Wittgenstein devised a new form of reductionism in his later years, I am not suggesting that *he* regarded it as a form of reductionism. On the contrary, as I said above, the term *reductionism* is typically used pejoratively, to characterize a misrepresentation, and that is how I intend to use it. One can recognize that a philosopher is a reductionist only by seeing that he has misrepresented something. Wittgenstein did not think he had done so.

10. In the past the old metaphysical rivalries often took on the form of ideological differences: reductionists were denounced as nihilists, while they, in turn, declared inflationists to be deluded victims of mindless religious indoctrination.

11. H. H. Price, writing in 1940, refers to "those [philosophers] who think that the business of Philosophy is to analyse the rules according to which ordinary language functions" and adds that "almost all contemporary empiricists are among them" ("The Permanent Significance of Hume's Philosophy," *Philosophy*, vol. 15 (1940), p. 36). The reconciliation of empiricism and ordinary language has become so common that a reviewer of my *Wittgenstein's Metaphysics* could say that he finds it "hard to understand why empiricism and ordinary language are in conflict," as I claim they are (Mark Addis, *Mind*, vol. 105 (January 1996), p. 169).

Chapter 6

1. Wittgenstein states this explicitly when he says: "Most of the propositions and questions of philosophers arise from our failure to understand the logic of our language. (They belong to the same class as the question whether the good is more or less identical that the beautiful.)" (TLP, 4.003). So if you ask, "Does anything exist outside my mind?" you are speaking nonsense. Despite appearances, you are not asking a genuine question.

2. Why doesn't this objection to analytic reductionism apply as well to Wittgenstein's substitution method, described in chapter 3? Wittgenstein's answer, I believe, would be rather complicated. He might begin by saying that the new sentence (the sub-

stitute) does not *already* have a use, and then tell us that if this new sentence were used in place of the original sentence, this switch would have no practical consequences, for instance, although we commonly say "The pot boiled over while no one was watching," it would make no practical difference if, instead, we used the counterfactual form "If you had been in the kitchen, you would have seen the pot boil over." So the substitution method does not *deprive* us of anything, whereas analytic reductionism does. Or, if you prefer, the substitution method substitutes genuine synonyms, whereas analytic reductionism only pretends to.

3. In his lectures of 1936 Wittgenstein repeated this point. Rush Rhees's notes of those lectures contain the following:

> If we think of contemplating the appearance of a (human) foot, we are inclined to make an error: the idea that the word "foot" would [should?] really be used in the same way as "*appearance* of a foot", which we can substitute for it—although we find that we *can't*. . . . We don't use the word "foot" as one of the arguments in a function of which some arguments are "*appearance* of a foot." (LSD, p. 29; see also p. 41)

What Wittgenstein is here calling an error is *analytic* reductionism, and again his point is that "foot" has a unique use.

4. It is significant that Wittgenstein at one point considered using as his motto for *Philosophical Investigations* Bishop Butler's aphorism: "Everything is what it is and not another thing." (Wittgenstein mentioned this to Oets Bouwsma, who in turn mentioned it to me in the 1950s. It is also mentioned by Ray Monk in *Ludwig Wittgenstein: The Duty of Genius* (New York: The Free Press, 1990), p. 451.) There was more than a bit of irony in this, for Moore—as Wittgenstein well knew—had used Butler's aphorism as the motto for *Principia Ethica,* which suggests that Wittgenstein, in contemplating his own use of Butler's aphorism, meant to wrest from Moore the claim to be the defender of "common sense." If we should wonder how Wittgenstein could have thought that his reductionist views are consistent with Butler's aphorism, the answer is that he thought of his mature views as striking a neat compromise between Moore's realism, on the one side, and the analytic reductionism of the *Tractatus,* on the other. In other words, he thought that his rejection of the linguistically eliminative aspect of analytic reductionism (so as to retain the unique *grammar* of certain words) was sufficient warrant for his appropriating Butler's aphorism. The trouble is, of course, that this was not Butler's meaning, so that Wittgenstein's use of the aphorism would have been deceptive. Perhaps that is why he decided against using it.

5. Near the beginning of the *Investigations* Wittgenstein compares words to the many kinds of tools in a tool box, saying that "the functions of words are as diverse as the functions of these objects" (§11). It is commonly supposed that Wittgenstein meant to employ this comparison in order to draw attention to something we can see straightaway, without having to introduce anything like metaphysics. But as I pointed out in chapter 3, Wittgenstein intended the comparison to prepare the reader for his rejection, in later sections, of analytic reductionism. In this connection see especially §§60–64, where Wittgenstein turns the question whether one form of words can replace another into the question: "How far is it even *possible* to replace this language-game by [the other one]?" To which Wittgenstein responds that the other one just is "*another* language-game" (§64). My point is that philosophers could save themselves a lot of unnecessary grief if only they would recognize that Wittgenstein's comparison of words and tools in PI §11 is a part of his revised reductionist metaphysics and *not* a straightforward contribution to the philosophy of language.

6. "We remain unconscious of the prodigious diversity of all the everyday language–games because the clothing of our language makes everything alike" (PI, p. 224).

7. I am here quoting from Cora Diamond, *The Realistic Spirit* (Cambridge: MIT Press, 1991), pp. 211–212, where Professor Diamond is quoting Margaret Macdonald's unpublished notes of Wittgenstein's lectures on "Personal Experience," 1935–1936, lecture of 19 February 1936. See note 3, this chapter.

8. "Wittgenstein, Mathematics, and Ethics: Resisting the Attractions of Realism," in *The Cambridge Companion to Wittgenstein,* eds. Hans Sluga and David G. Stern (New York: Cambridge University Press, 1996), p. 255.

9. For the background to this see my discussion in chapter 3 of Wittgenstein's remark that "man has until recently used the symbols for numbers without knowing . . . that they signify nothing" (NB, pp. 95–96).

10. This seems to be, also, one of the merits he found in comparing language to games. If "grammar is not accountable to any reality," then just as we can make up new card games to suit ourselves, so we are free to invent new concepts to suit our purposes. This is why, no doubt, he thought that several cultures could not only have *different* concepts, but that these cultures could make no telling criticisms of one another's concepts. This is also why he thought that we could, without neglecting any facts, simply give up what he called "the cause and effect schema," that is, give up thinking that there are causes of, for example, various diseases. He thought of science as a "language-game," and since its rules (such as the one permitting us to ask and to try answering the question "What causes that?") are manmade (rather than being dictated by reality), we could simply drop or alter them without coming into conflict with "how the world is." (See *Wittgenstein's Metaphysics,* pp. 188–191.) Wittgenstein also thought of religion as a "language-game," which no doubt shaped the ways in which he thought about religion, for instance, that Christianity depends on no historical facts.

11. We should bear in mind here that Schopenhauer spoke of a philosopher regarding "only his own person as a real person, and all others as mere phantoms" *(The World as Will and Representation,* vol. 1, book 2, §19). So other "people" are phantoms. Notice that in Z, §543, Wittgenstein's use of the word *Erscheinung* in speaking of human behavior: "My relation to the appearances *[Erscheinung]* here is part of my concept."

12. See note 15, this chapter.

13. *An Introduction to Wittgenstein's Tractatus,* (London: Hutchinson University Library, 1959), p. 78.

14. Of relevance here are two facts that I discussed in chapter 1: that Wittgenstein in 1948 remarked to his friend Drury that his fundamental ideas came to him very early in life and that he chose as his motto for the *Investigations* a passage from Nestroy which can be translated: "It is in the nature of progress that it appears much greater than it actually is." Consider also in this connection Wittgenstein's remark: "It is very difficult to describe paths of thought where there are already many lines of thought laid down—your own or other people's—and not get into one of the grooves. It is difficult to deviate from an old line of thought *just a little*" (Z, §349; italics in the original).

15. The two sentences immediately preceding those I have quoted here are as follows: "There is no trouble at all with primitive languages about concrete objects. Talk about a chair and *a human body* and all is well: talk about . . . the human mind and things begin to look queer" (ibid., emphasis added). It is the phrase "a human body" that is of interest here, for it shows that Wittgenstein thought that what we see of other people are their *bodies*. It shows, in other words, that he failed to apply Ramsey's

maxim (see chapter 5) in such a way as to find the right way out of the problem of other minds. This is why he is obliged to introduce (PI, p. 178) the idea of having a special *attitude* towards human bodies. Without the attitude, they would just be things, like dolls.

16. The sentence which follows this has been translated, confusingly, as follows: "For what is hidden, for example, is of no interest to us." The German gives no warrant for "for example." The correct translation is: "For what happens to be *[etwa]* hidden does not interest us." Something that happens to be hidden, such as people's brains (since our skulls aren't transparent) or the backside of the moon (since it never rotates toward the earth), may be of interest to scientists but not to philosophers. Thus, in the next paragraph Wittgenstein says that philosophy is concerned with "what is possible *before* all new discoveries." It was his view that we can arrive at correct philosophical results even if we are ignorant of all scientific discoveries. An example of this attitude is his remark: "The best prophylactic against this [philosophical confusion] is the thought that I don't know at all whether the humans I am acquainted with have a nervous system" (RPP, I, §1063). He means: if, when I philosophize about thinking or memory, I bear in mind that the people I talk to may have no nervous system, that is, if I think of them as being like Pinocchio (a piece of wood), I will avoid certain philosophical mistakes.

17. In her published notes of an earlier lecture Alice Ambrose interpolates the following lines from The Yellow Book: "[W]e think we describe phenomena incompletely if we leave out personal pronouns. . . . But we can leave out the word 'I' and still describe the phenomenon formerly described [by saying 'I think']" (WL35, p. 22).

18. It seems that on one occasion, in an early lecture, Wittgenstein did put the matter in a very Humean way. He said: "Sense–data are the source of our concepts" (WL32, p. 81), thus implying that where there is no experience (no sense–datum) there is no concept.

19. If someone thinks that Wittgenstein, by the time he wrote the *Investigations,* must have abandoned this mission, I will simply point out that in the late 1940s, not long before his death, he wrote: "How far do we investigate the use of words? Don't we also judge it? Don't we also say that this feature is essential, that one inessential?" (RPP, I, §666). And of course even in the *Investigations* Wittgenstein employs this technique of substituting one "form of words" for another.

20. Having conducted in vain his search for a substantial self, Hume anticipated the resistance of unrepentant realists and said:

> If anyone upon serious and unprejudic'd reflexion, thinks he has a different notion of *himself,* I must confess I can reason no longer with him. All I can allow him is, that he may be in the right as well as I, and that we are essentially different in this particular. He may, perhaps, perceive something simple and continu'd, which he calls *himself;* tho' I am certain there is no such principle in me. *(Treatise,* book I, part IV, sec. vi)

Hume was no doubt being ironic here, but he had the serious purpose of telling the unrepentant realist: don't come telling me that you and I have different notions of the self unless you can honestly say that you *perceive* something simple and continued which you call "I."

21. It is clear that Wittgenstein did not appeal to what we actually say. He did not, for example, notice that we say such things as "I have learned from experience that I can't get to sleep if I have had coffee with dinner" and "I could see right away that I can't jump as high as Jack." Had Wittgenstein appealed to ordinary language, he

might have concluded that experience does show us what *cannot* happen or *cannot* be done.

22. A realist, of course, might complain that Wittgenstein does *not* leave everything as it is, that while he purports to put "back into circulation" the words he has "disinfected," what he puts back is not the word with its original meaning. For example, when Wittgenstein puts the word *soul* back into circulation, here is what he gives us:

> Religion teaches that the soul can exist when the body has disintegrated. Now do I understand this teaching?—Of course I understand it—I can imagine plenty of things in connexion with it. And haven't pictures of these things been painted? And why should such a picture be only an imperfect rendering of the spoken doctrine? Why should it not do the *same* service as the words? And it is the service which is the point. (PI, p. 178)

Wittgenstein is saying something like: "The meaning of the religious teaching is exhausted in its capacity to make a person take life seriously; it tells us nothing about what happens at death." And I am suggesting that other philosophers—and especially realists like Moore—might protest that this is *not* what the religious teaching comes to and that Wittgenstein has replaced what is actually *taught* about the soul with an ersatz reductionist account of that teaching. Wittgenstein's idea is that *in the conceptual world* one's soul can continue to exist after death. But the religious believer—with the exception of D. Z. Phillips and three of his friends—is hoping to survive death, not in the conceptual world, but in reality.

Chapter 7

1. In *Mysticism and Logic* (London: George Allen & Unwin, 1951), pp. 145–146.

2. Quoted from Ramsey's notes by Merrill and Jaakko Hintikka, *Investigating Wittgenstein* (Oxford: Blackwell, 1986), p. 77.

3. Someone may object to my gloss, thinking that idealists don't doubt or deny the existence of material things. But in *On Certainty* Wittgenstein wrote: "The idealist's question would be something like: What right have I not to doubt the existence of my hands?" (§24). The British idealist, J. M. E. McTaggart, compared material things to "the Gorgons and the Harpies"—as Moore was quick to point out in response to John Wisdom's remark that idealists "who have said that Matter does not exist did not mean to deny that you have two hands or a watch in your pocket." See "G. E. Moore" in John Wisdom, *Paradox and Discovery* (New York: Philosophical Library, 1965), p. 83.

4. This was not an uncommon view. See R. J. Hirst's discussion of naive realism in *The Encyclopedia of Philosophy,* vol. 7, ed. Paul Edwards (New York: Macmillan, 1967), in which he reports that naive realism "is usually alleged by philosophers to be [the view held by] the plain man" (p. 78).

5. The words *realist* and *realism* need some explaining. I have used—and will continue using—them in the way Wittgenstein did in his post-*Tractatus* years: as a label for philosophers like G. E. Moore. This must be sharply contrasted with Wittgenstein's earlier usage, which was influenced by the fact that in the early years of the century neutral monism was called "realism" or "the new realism." Wittgenstein, because he shared this philosophical orientation, spoke of his own position in the *Tractatus* as "realism" (NB, p. 85) and "pure realism" (TLP, 5.64). This view is also sometimes called "naive realism."

6. Edwin B. Holt et al., *The New Realism* (New York: Macmillan, 1912), pp. 4–5.

7. *Gestalt Psychology* (New York: New American Library, 1947), pp. 141–143.

8. There is internal evidence of Wittgenstein's having read Kohler's *Gestalt Psychology* in late 1929 or early 1930 (see *Wittgenstein's Metaphysics,* chapter 7, note 4). It is important to recognize that Wittgenstein's behaviorism, like Kohler's, pertains to what Kohler calls "perceptual bodies." The reason for this is that since Wittgenstein was a phenomenalist, he held a doubly reductionist view of other people's mental states: their mental states are reducible to bodily behavior and their bodies, in turn, are reducible to sense-impressions. So Wittgenstein's position could be described as phenomenalistic behaviorism. Such a view would have been long familiar to Wittgenstein from his reading of Schopenhauer, who said that "the whole of nature outside the knowing subject, and so all remaining individuals, exist only in his representation" *(The World as Will and Representation,* vol. I, bk. 4, §61).

9. Initially Wittgenstein spoke of verification, rather than criteria, and at that time he said: "How far is giving the verification of a proposition a grammatical statement about it? So far as it is [such a statement], it can explain the meaning of its terms. Insofar as [that which verifies a given proposition] is a matter of experience, as when one names a symptom, the meaning is not explained" (WL35, p. 31). Thus, when Wittgenstein later spoke of the *criteria* for p, his aim was to display the *meaning* of "p." Here it is important to realize that what Wittgenstein meant by "meaning" is something of concern only to philosophers, not to someone wanting to know the meaning of an unfamiliar word. What is explained by specifying the criteria (or verification) of a proposition is what *kind* of proposition it is, for instance, whether it is the kind of proposition inflationists think it is or, instead, the kind reductionists think it is.

Chapter 8

1. Anthony Kenney, for example, speaks of criteria as "evidence":

> Wittgenstein uses the concept of *criterion* especially to clarify certain problems in the philosophy of mind. Most commonly, in the *Investigations,* a criterion is an observable phenomenon which is, by logical necessity, evidence for a mental state or process which is not itself observable. ("Criterion," in *The Encyclopedia of Philosophy,* ed. Paul Edwards (New York: MacMillan, 1967), vol. 2, p. 260)

Kenny is implying here that a mental state or process, which is not observable, is something distinct from the (observable) behavior which is the criterion for it. To emphasize this point, Kenny adds in the next paragraph that Wittgenstein's concept of criteria does not make him a behaviorist.

2. I do not mean to imply here that Wittgenstein never used the word *evidence* where he would have thought *criterion* was appropriate. See in this regard LW I, §§951–952, and LW II, p. 67. In both places Wittgenstein used "evidence"—or "sufficient evidence"—instead of the word *criteria.* But the context in both cases suggests that his wording was dictated by his attempt to reply to his opponent in terms that his opponent would find congenial, rather than in the terms he himself preferred. For that reason—as well as others—I would dismiss any attempt to cite these passages as proof that Wittgenstein regarded criteria as evidence, in any *ordinary* sense of "evidence." One must bear in mind that Wittgenstein had a reason for introducing the term *criterion.* Such ordinary terms as *evidence* or *good evidence* or *conclusive evidence* did not, evidently, suffice for his purposes. Anything that would count as evidence he called "symptoms," thus marking off criteria as something else, something special.

3. Such considerations should be sufficient to rule out the explanation given by

Kenney (see note 1, this chapter). According to Kenny's explanation, X and Y are entirely distinct (the one being observable, the other not), even though the one is, as a matter of *logical necessity*, evidence for the other.

4. I have altered the translation of this passage. The German reads: "[S]chmerz-benehmen mit Schmerzen und Schmerzbenehmen ohne Schmerzen." Anscombe has translated this: "pain-behaviour *accompanied* by pain and pain-behaviour without any pain" (my italics). Plainly, the word *accompanied* gives altogether the wrong impression, suggesting as it does that Wittgenstein is prepared to allow that the behavior, if it is not pretense, can be *accompanied* by something, the pain. (See my discussion, under Rule #6, of Wittgenstein's phrase "nicht im Nebeneinander" from PI, p. 179.) A misunderstanding may arise also from the rhetorical question: "What greater difference could there be?" One may think that he is speaking of a qualitative difference, that is, a difference of the sort in which a headache is ranked as a *greater* discomfort than, say, a dizzy spell. But there is reason to believe (see my *Wittgenstein's Metaphysics,* pp. 130–131) that he meant something else, namely, that the greatest difference possible is that between *p* and *not-p*—regardless of what *p* may be. If that is what he meant, then this passage does not suggest that the great difference he was speaking of is a difference in something "inner" or "introspectable."

5. Most philosophers have fastened on #3 (the rule opposing *analytic* reductionism) to the exclusion of #2 and have thus taken Wittgenstein to be rejecting behaviorism. For example, Anthony Kenny says, "[I]t does not follow, because the criteria for the application of a concept are behavioral, that the concept itself is behavioral. To say that X is the criterion for Y is not—in the *Investigations*—to say that X is the definition of Y or that 'Y' means X" ("Criterion," *Encyclopedia of Philosophy,* p. 260). Kenny is saying here that because "criterion" is governed by Rule #3, Wittgenstein rejected behaviorism. (As I pointed out in note 1 of this chapter, Kenny explains "criterion" in such a way as to imply that a mental state, which is not observable, is something distinct from the (observable) behavior which is the criterion for it.) Similarly, P. M. S. Hacker observes that Wittgenstein's criterial relation is "distinct from entailment" *(Insight and Illusion,* (Oxford: Oxford University Press, 1975, p. 289) and also says that "one did not learn that 'toothache' means 'expression of toothache'" (p. 305), but from these correct observations (which are equivalent to Rule #3) he jumps to the mistaken conclusion that the criterial relation "enables Wittgenstein to refute behaviourism. . . . The behaviourist . . . . is wrong to think that psychological concepts are, in some way or other, *reducible* to behavioural ones" (p. 305). To understand "criterion" in this way is comparable to saying: since a flush is not identical with a group of five cards of the same suit, a poker player can't *draw* a flush by drawing five spades and when he *holds* a flush he is holding something other than (or more than) five cards of the same suit.

6. In The Blue Book he also said: "We talk of kinds of numbers, kinds of propositions, kinds of proof; and also, of kinds of apples, kinds of paper, etc. In one sense [of "kind"] what defines the kind are properties, like sweetness, hardness, etc. In the other the different kinds are grammatical structures" (p. 19). For Wittgenstein the concept "physical object" is the concept of a grammatical structure, which is another way of saying that physical objects belong to our *conceptual* world. In his lectures of 1946–47 he said that we have a "form"—meaning a grammatical form, namely, certain nouns—for "connecting up experiences with one another; we populate a space with sense-impressions. This is quite correct, because there is a relation between sense-impressions of two completely different spaces [i.e., visual space and tactile space]. Our impressions hang together" (WL47, p. 197). See WVC, p. 256, for the explanation that "an object is the way aspects are connected" by certain nouns of our everyday language.

7. *The Problems of Philosophy* (London: Oxford University Press, 1948), p. 16.

8. As I have defended this claim at length elsewhere, I will not do so here. See my *Wittgenstein's Metaphysics,* esp. chapters 9 and 10.

9. I have worded this rule so as to reflect what Wittgenstein says in PI, §183: "But did 'Now I can go on' in case (151) mean the same as 'Now the formula has occurred to me' or something different? We may say that, in those circumstances, the two sentences have the same sense, achieve the same thing. But also that *in general* these two sentences do not have the same sense."

10. "Two people are laughing together, say at a joke. One of them has used certain somewhat unusual words and they both break out into a sort of bleating. That might appear *very* extraordinary to a visitor coming from quite a different environment. Whereas we find it completely reasonable. (I recently witnessed this scene on a bus and was able to think myself into the position of someone to whom this would be unfamiliar. From that point of view it struck me as quite irrational, like the responses of an outlandish *animal.)*" (CV, p. 78). See also PI, p. 223.

11. On one occasion (BB, p. 55) Wittgenstein used the phrase "experiential criteria," but he no doubt regarded this as a pleonasm.

12. See in this connection chapter 7, note 8. See also Z §543, where Wittgenstein speaks of the behavior of other people as "Erscheinung."

13. It is worth noting here that Wittgenstein, in a somewhat different context, wrote the following:

The *facts* of human natural history that throw light on our [philosophical] problem are difficult for us to find out, for our talk *passes them by,* it is occupied with other things. (Thus we tell someone: 'Go into the shop and buy . . .'—not: 'Put your left foot in front of your right foot etc. etc., then put coins down on the counter, etc. etc.' (RPP, I, 78).

Here Wittgenstein is plainly saying that facts of the sort that are philosophically significant are bypassed by our ordinary forms of expression. And his example suggests that a philosophically *relevant* fact would be that someone put his left foot in front of his right foot, rather than that someone went into a shop and bought groceries.

14. The passages I have just discussed are immediately preceded by a paragraph in which Wittgenstein compares observations of human behavior with "observing the movements of a point (for example, a point of light on a screen)" (PI, p. 179). (See RPP, I, §§284–292, for the original.) How might one describe the movements of a point of light on a screen? One might say, for example, "It moved in spurts" or "It's movement was continuous"; "It moved in a circular fashion" or "It moved in straight lines, zigzag," etc. Or, if the movement was not regular, the description would have to be more complex. In any case, it is significant that Wittgenstein thought to compare human behavior to such movements, for that means that *descriptions* of human behavior would resemble descriptions of a point of light, that is, the *vocabulary* would be similar. (See RPP, I, 78, quoted in the preceding note.) It is no wonder, then, that Wittgenstein thought that it is very *difficult* to describe human behavior in a philosophically relevant way (see RPP, I, §257, quoted in note 12, chapter 9, this book).

15. The dictionary bears out what I have just written. The entry for "groan" in *The American Heritage Dictionary* reads as follows:

1. To voice a deep, wordless, prolonged sound expressive of pain, grief, annoyance, or disapproval. 2. To produce a similar sound expressive of stress or strain: *"I stretched out . . . hearing the springs groan beneath me"* (Ralph Elison).

16. Wittgenstein is surely mistaken about this. In our everyday lives we do not use language behavioristically even in a nonexplicit way. (Nor, of course, do we use language dualistically.) This is clear from the fact that what we say about other people is not predicated on the idea that we are speaking of Cartesian bodies. If we were using mentalistic terms behavioristically, we would have had to learn them by first mastering the idea of a Cartesian body, but how could children do that *first?* To get the hang of that idea, wouldn't they have to begin by repeating Descartes's *Cogito,* which is the spawning ground for Cartesian bodies? Instead of this a child cries "Mamma!" and exclaims "Dadda!" but Mamma and Dadda are *not* Cartesian bodies.

17. Here we may recall a passage Wittgenstein wrote in the late 1940s: "My difficulty is altogether like that of a man who is inventing a new calculus (say the differential calculus) and is looking for a symbolism" (RPP, I, §134). What would warrant this comparison? Wouldn't it be what, if I'm right about Rules #1–#6, Wittgenstein was doing with his concept of criteria?

18. Wittgenstein was notoriously impatient with those who wanted him to spell things out for them as clearly as possible. An early letter to Russell reveals his exasperation. Responding to Russell's request for a clarification, he wrote: "I beg you to think about these matters for yourself, it is INTOLERABLE for me to repeat a written explanation which even the first time I gave only with the *utmost repugnance." Letters to Russell, Keynes and Moore,* p. 42, letter R23.

19. Wittgenstein's pessimism in this regard came out very clearly in remarks he made to F. R. Leavis, who recounted their conversation as follows:

> I was walking once with Wittgenstein when I was moved, by something he said, to remark, with a suggestion of innocent inquiry in my tone: 'You don't think much of other philosophers, Wittgenstein?' —'No. Those I have my use for you could divide into two classes. Suppose I was directing someone of the first to Emmanuel'—it was then my college—'I should say: "You see that steeple over there? Emmanuel is three hundred and fifty yards to the west-south-west of it." That man, the first class, would get there. Hm! very rare—in fact I've never met him. To the second I should say: "You go a hundred yards straight ahead, turn half-left and go forty . . ." and so on. That man would ultimately get there. Very rare too; in fact I don't know that I've met him." ("Memories of Wittgenstein" in *Recollections of Wittgenstein,* p. 50)

Chapter 9

1. In lectures Wittgenstein introduced an analogous case to explain this. Having said that the grammar of "Moore has toothache" is very different from that of "I have toothache," he went on to say:

> The sense of "Moore has toothache" is given by the criterion for its truth. For a statement gets its sense from it verification. The use of the word "toothache" when I have toothache and when someone else has it belongs to different games. (To find out with what meaning a word is used, make several investigations. For example, the words "before" and "after" *mean something different* according as one depends on memory or on documents to establish the time of an event.) (WL35, p. 17; emphasis added)

In other words, the meaning of "before" will not be the same if I say "I distinctly remember that Jack arrived before Jill" and if you say "I see by the log book that Jack arrived before Jill—he at 10:20, she at 10:40." As the reader will rightly infer from this, Wittgenstein had his reasons for taking such a view of the meaning of temporal terms. He was intent upon finding a way to dismiss skepticism regarding the past, and his way of doing so was, typically, to resort to a reductionist solution: statements about the past are reduced to statements about something immediately given, such as seeing something in a log book or having a distinct memory. See my discussion of this in chapter 16 of *Wittgenstein's Metaphysics*.

2. The *Investigations* contains a translation error that seriously distorts Wittgenstein's meaning. In §79 we find (in translation) "The fluctuation of scientific definitions: what today counts as an observed concomitant of a phenomenon will tomorrow we used to define it." Here it looks as though one and the same phenomenon is mentioned twice: once when X was an observed concomitant of it and again when X was used to define it. But Wittgenstein's German sentence tells a different story: "Das Schwanken wissenschaflicker Definitionen: Was heute als erfahrungsmässige Begleiterscheinung des Phänomens A gilt, wird morgen zur Definition von 'A' benützt." So the translation should run: "[W]hat today counts as an observed concomitant of the phenomenon A will tomorrow be used to define 'A'." Wittgenstein undoubtedly meant that "A" does not have the same meaning in the two cases, that is, before and after "A" gets defined in a new way.

3. See Rogers Albritton, "On Wittgenstein's Use of the Term 'Criterion,'" reprinted in *Wittgenstein: The Philosophical Investigations,* ed. George Pitcher (South Bend: University of Notre Dame Press, 1968).

4. Ibid., p. 242. Instead of giving his simple negative answer, Albritton should have argued: in view of the frequency with which Wittgenstein says or implies that such-and-such behavior is what we *call* "toothache" or "worry," etc., we must conclude that he was a behaviorist.

5. Albritton writes: "But instead of making [his proper] conception clear, Wittgenstein distorts it . . . by representing the criteria for so-and-so's being the case as various things that may *be* what is called 'so-and-so's being the case'" (ibid., p. 244).

6. In correspondence a dozen years ago Albritton, in response to my claim that Wittgenstein was a phenomenalist, told me that he had long ago "made up for myself . . . a Wittgenstein who couldn't possibly not notice that phenomenalism is a metaphysical theory, and wouldn't be caught dead in its grip," adding that "I am more or less terminally reluctant to give up this 'projected' Wittgenstein of mine." In the same letter Albritton described his projected Wittgenstein as "the archenemy of metaphysics, the only real one in the history of philosophy (is there another?)" As I have tried to show, however, Wittgenstein was as deeply enmeshed in metaphysics as Moore or Russell. (He was, however, opposed to what empiricists regard as metaphysical: the material mode formulation of metaphysics and the idea that something might transcended experience.) As for Albritton's question whether there is another philosopher who has engaged philosophical issues without himself becoming enmeshed in metaphysics, the answer is: Yes, Frank Ebersole, whose contribution to philosophy, in my estimation, is the greatest of anyone this century, especially in the areas of philosophy of language, theory of knowledge, and perception.

7. Ibid.

8. Ibid., pp. 244–245.

9. Ibid., p. 246.

10. The same point can be made about the account given by Anthony Kenny in the passage quoted in note 1 of chapter 8. The mistake is extremely common. G. P. Baker and P. M. S. Hacker, for example, say that "the relation between outward behaviour and an inner state which Wittgenstein expresses by saying that pain-behav-

iour is a criterion for being in pain is laid down in grammar." *Skepticism, Rules and Language* (Oxford: Blackwell, 1984), p. 110.

11. Addressing the question whether philosophy is at all useful, and if so for what, Wittgenstein wrote: "Philosophy is a tool which is useful only against philosophers and *against the philosopher in us*" (MS 219, 11). Quoted by Anthony Kenny in "Wittgenstein on the Nature of Philosophy" in *Wittgenstein and his Times*, ed. Brian McGuinness (Chicago: University of Chicago Press, 1982), p. 13; emphasis added. It would go very much against Wittgenstein's spirit to proceed as though one could recognize the solution to a philosophical problem without being oneself in the grip of that problem. Unfortunately, many of Wittgenstein's would-be followers seem to think that one can do philosophy by *starting* from Wittgenstein's view that philosophical problems are nothing but intellectual muddles. Those who proceed in this manner tend to think that philosophical problems can be dealt with, as it were, from the *outside*, as if one could plant oneself firmly in some safe, uncontaminated region and hand down solutions in a pontifical manner. The 'solutions' thus arrived at typically fail to engage with the problems they are meant to solve, but they also, because of their glibness, infuriate philosophers who are grappling with those problems. Their glibness, which is merely annoying, is of less moment than the fact that they fail to engage with the targeted problems, which makes it appear that Wittgenstein, too, failed to address those problems.

12. Wittgenstein, well aware of the temptation to do as Albritton does, comments on the temptation as follows:

> Pure description is so difficult because one believes that one needs to fill out the facts in order to understand them. It is as if one saw a screen with scattered colour–patches, and said: the way they are here, they are unintelligible; they only make sense when one completes them into a shape.—Whereas I want to say: Here *is* the whole. (If you complete it, you falsify it.) (RPP, I, §257)

So what are to count as descriptions must not be 'filled out,' for doing so would falsify them. I take it that such a falsification would occur if a philosopher spoke, as Albritton does, of a man groaning *because* he had toothache—as if the toothache were something "inner," something "behind" the groaning. (Wittgenstein says that "the temptation is overwhelming to say something further, when everything has already been described" (Z, §313).) See in this connection RPP, I, §78, quoted above in chapter 3.

13. "Recollections of Wittgenstein" in *Ludwig Wittgenstein: The Man and His Philosophy*, ed. K. T. Fann, (New York: Dell, 1967), p. 84.

14. Mays may be right, however, in suggesting that Wittgenstein carried this through in a manner which betokened "something more than a philosophical position." If so, this would have nothing to do with his engineering background, but it might be connected with his family background, with whatever had led his brothers to commit suicide. We should bear in mind here that the position Wittgenstein staked out in the *Tractatus* was a form of solipsism (see my *Wittgenstein's Metaphysics*, pp. 65–66), a position someone might adopt as a refuge from a domineering or intimidating person. Wittgenstein, at the age of sixteen, read *The World as Will and Idea* and found Schopenhauer maintaining that whoever embraces solipsism "regards and treats only his own person as a real person, and all others as mere phantoms" (vol. I, bk. 2, §19). Perhaps, then, we shouldn't find it surprising that Wittgenstein, in his later work, continued to hold a position which afforded him some sort of refuge—which allowed him, as Mays puts it, "to regard other people as if they were inanimate objects." This

would be consistent with Von Wright's observation: "It is probably true that he lived on the border of mental illness. A fear of being driven across it followed him throughout his life" ("Biographical Sketch," in Norman Malcolm, *Ludwig Wittgenstein: A Memoir* (Oxford: Oxford University Press, 1977, p. 3). Bouwsma similarly reports Wittgenstein having said to him "in all seriousness with the kind of smile Dostoyevsky would suggest in such circumstances: 'But do you know, I think I may go nuts'" (Bouwsma, *Wittgenstein: Conversations 1949–1951*, p. 9).

Chapter 10

1. "Introduction," *The Cambridge Companion to Wittgenstein*, p.20.

2. "Wittgenstein," in *The Revolution in Philosophy*, eds. A. J. Ayer et al., (London: Macmillan, 1956), p. 88.

3. "Ludwig Wittgenstein," reprinted in *Ludwig Wittgenstein: The Man and His Philosophy*, pp. 122, 124.

4. Alan R. White, *G. E. Moore: A Critical Exposition* (Oxford: Blackwell, 1958), pp. 200, 213. He also says that Moore's "dominant method" is "close to Wittgenstein's search for the connexions, the similarities and dissimilarities . . . between the various uses of a given word and between these and the uses of other words" (p. 216).

5. *Wittgenstein's Conception of Philosophy* (Berkeley: University of California Press, 1971), p. 51.

6. The only exception I have been able to find is G. H. von Wright, who writes: "It is sometimes said that the later Wittgenstein resembles Moore. This is hardly true. Moore's and Wittgenstein's ways of thinking are in fact utterly different. Although their friendship lasted until the latter's death, I do not believe that there is any trace of an influence of Moore's philosophy on Wittgenstein" ("Biographical Sketch," p. 15).

7. *Insight and Illusion*, p. 305.

8. *The Cambridge Companion to Wittgenstein*, p. 21.

9. This dualistic interpretation of Wittgenstein is epitomized by Merrill B. and Jaakko Hintikka in *Investigating Wittgenstein*, where they say that "in the famous 'private language argument' . . . Wittgenstein was thus not essentially modifying the Cartesian account of our inner life. . . . He was . . . criticizing Cartesian semantics, not Cartesian metaphysics" (p. 250).

10. See my *Wittgenstein's Metaphysics*, pp. 18, 133.

11. Pitcher, *The Philosophy of Wittgenstein*, pp. 195–197. Pitcher attaches to the penultimate sentence in this passage a footnote quoting Moore's remark that philosophers often hold views inconsistent with that they *know* to be true.

12. *Philosophy in the Twentieth Century* (New York: Vintage, 1984), p. 155.

13. Bouwsma, *Wittgenstein: Conversations 1949–1951*, pp. 48–49.

14. F. R. Leavis, "Memories of Wittgenstein," in *Recollections of Wittgenstein*, p. 51. Leavis indicates that he is uncertain whether Wittgenstein said these exact words or only said something that could be expressed in these words.

15. Drury, "Conversations with Wittgenstein," in *Recollections of Wittgenstein*, p. 115.

16. *Ludwig Wittgenstein: A Memoir*, p. 66.

17. "Portrait of a Philosopher," in *Ludwig Wittgenstein: The Man and His Philosophy*, p. 56.

18. "An Autobiography," in *The Philosophy of G. E. Moore*, ed. Paul Arthur Schilpp (New York: Tudor, 1942), p. 33.

19. Quoted by Alice Ambrose, in "Ludwig Wittgenstein: A Portrait," in *Ludwig Wittgenstein: Philosophy and Language,* p. 16.

20. "Biographical Sketch," in Malcolm, *Wittgenstein: A Memoir,* p. 1.

21. See, for example, the quotation from D. A. T. Gasking and A. C. Jackson in chapter 13, note 12.

22. "Moore and Ordinary Language," in *The Philosophy of G. E. Moore,* pp. 365, 368.

23. Ibid., pp. 354–355.

24. Ibid., pp. 357–358.

25. Ibid., p. 360.

26. Ibid., p. 361.

27. "George Edward Moore," in Norman Malcolm, *Knowledge and Certainty* (Englewood Cliffs: Prentice-Hall, 1963), p. 179.

28. Ibid., p. 183.

29. Quoted from Bouwsma's notebooks by the editors, J. L. Craft and Ronald E. Hustwit, in their introduction to Bouwsma, *Wittgenstein: Conversations 1949–1951,* p. xxvii.

30. Ibid., p. 181.

31. Ibid., p. 182.

32. From this developed the popularity of what came to be called "the paradigm case argument," which Anthony Flew explained as follows:

> The clue to the whole business [of philosophy] now seems to lie in mastering what has recently been usefully named, The Argument of the Paradigm Case. Crudely: If there is any word the meaning of which can be taught by reference to paradigm cases, then no argument whatever could ever prove that there are no cases whatever of whatever it is. Thus, since the meaning of 'of his own free will' can be taught by reference to such paradigm cases as that in which a man, under no social pressure, marries the girl he wants to marry (how else *could* it be taught?), it cannot be right, on any grounds whatsoever, to say that no one *ever* acts of his own free will. . . .
>
> What such arguments by themselves will certainly not do is to establish any matter of value, moral or otherwise. . . .
>
> To see the power, and the limitations, of the Argument of the Paradigm Case is to realize how much of common sense can, and how much [namely, values] cannot, be defended against philosophical paradoxes by simple appeal to the ordinary use of words. ("Philosophy and Language," in *Essays in Conceptual Analysis,* ed. Anthony Flew (London: Macmillan, 1956), pp. 19–20)

33. This idea, expressed in various ways, has been around for a long time. William James put the matter as follows:

> My thesis now is this, that *our fundamental ways of thinking about things are discoveries of exceedingly remote ancestors, which have been able to preserve themselves throughout the experience of all subsequent time.* They form one great stage of equilibrium in the human mind's development, the stage of *common sense.* . . .
>
> In practical talk, a man's common sense means his good judgment, his freedom from eccentricity. . . . In philosophy it means something entirely different, it means his use of certain intellectual forms or categories of thought. Were we lobsters, or bees, it might be that our organization would

have led to our using quite different modes from these of apprehending our experiences. It *might* be too (we can not dogmatically deny this) that such categories, unimaginable by us to–day, would have proved on the whole as serviceable for handling our experiences mentally as those which we actually use.

. . . . Experience merely as such doesn't come ticketed and labelled, we have first to discover what it is. . . . What we usually do is first to frame some system of concepts . . , and then use this as a tally by which we 'keep tab' on the impressions that present themselves. . . . There are many conceptual systems of this sort. . . . [O]bviously you can rationalize [sense-impressions] by using various conceptual systems.

The old common–sense way of rationalizing them is by a set of concepts of which the most important are these:

Thing
The same or different
Kinds
Minds
Bodies
One Time
One Space
Subjects and attributes
Causal influences
The fancied
The real

. . . . With these categories in our hand, we make our plans and plot together, and connect all the remoter parts of experience with what lies before our eyes. Our later and more critical philosophies are mere fads and fancies compared with this natural mother-tongue of thought.

Common sense appears thus as a perfectly definite stage in our understanding of things, a stage that satisfies in an extraordinarily successful way the purposes for which we think. 'Things' do exist, even when we do not see them. Their 'kinds' also exist. Their 'qualities' are what they act by, and are what we act on; and these also exist. . . . [T]his stage of philosophy . . . suffices for all the necessary practical ends of life; and, among our race even, it is only the highly sophisticated specimens, the minds debauched by learning . . . who have ever even suspected common sense of not being absolutely true.

. . . [Our] common sense categories . . . may have been verified by the immediate facts of experience which they first fitted; and then from fact to fact and from man to man they may have spread, until all language rested on them and we are now incapable of thinking naturally in any other terms.

James goes on to say that although the common sense categories "amply suffice" for practical purposes, when you subject them to intellectual scrutiny by comparing them with scientific or philosophical categories, "you find it impossible to say within just what limits of fact any one of them shall apply." It may well be that common sense categories are best for practical purposes, but it is not possible to determine whether common sense is "truer absolutely." James concludes:

We have seen reason to suspect [common sense], to suspect that in spite of their being . . . so universal and built into the structure of language, its categories may after all be only a collection of extraordinarily successful hypotheses . . . by which our forefathers have from time immemorial unified . . . their immediate experiences. . . . Retain, I pray you, this suspicion about common sense. *(Pragmatism* (New York: Longmans, Green & Co., 1949), pp. 170–193)

The foregoing remarks show us two things about James. First, from the fact that he speaks of the categories of common sense being "built into the structure of language," we can see that he thought of ordinary language as being a conceptual scheme. Second, he would have thought it a serious mistake to try to solve philosophical problems by appealing to ordinary language.

34. *An Inquiry into Meaning and Truth* (London: George Allen and Unwin, 1951), p. 124.

35. Thomas Reid, *Essays On the Intellectual Powers of Man,* essay 1, chapter 1.

36. *The Mind and Its Place In Nature* (London: Trench, Trubner & Co., 1925), p. 148; see also pp. 184–186.

37. Perhaps the most detailed exposition of this criticism was made by Stuart Hampshire in his essay "The Interpretation of Language: Words and Concepts," in *British Philosophy in the Mid-Century,* ed. C. A. Mace (London: Allen and Unwin, 1957), pp. 267–279. See also Jerry Fodor and Jerrold Katz, "The Availability of What We Say," *The Philosophical Review,* vol. 72 (January 1963), esp. pp. 68–70. Hampshire's article is reprinted in *The Linguistic Turn,* ed. Richard Rorty (Chicago: University of Chicago Press, 1975).

38. This can be illustrated by recounting a symposium at the 1960 meeting of The American Philosophical Association, Midwest Division. The leading paper of the symposium, entitled "Must Philosophers Reform Ordinary Language?" was authored by Herbert Feigl and Grover Maxwell, who held not only that ordinary language is a conceptual scheme but that Broad had been right in denouncing philosophical appeals to what people say. Their paper (delivered by Maxwell) argued that when philosophers examine the conceptual scheme of our language, they may find "inadequacies . . . in our conceptualization of the 'normal' cases" of a term's employment ("Why Ordinary Language Needs Reforming," reprinted in *The Linguistic Turn,* p. 195.) Our conceptualization may be defective, they explained, because "the implicit rules that are present in the ordinary language game may indirectly reflect beliefs that are false" (Ibid., p. 198). That there are "somewhat primitive theories presupposed by ordinary language" is owing to the fact that "our everyday concepts grew and evolved as a result of the facts and beliefs deemed most important throughout the history of mankind" (Ibid., pp. 197 and 198). One of the respondents to this paper was Oets Bouwsma, an ordinary language philosopher, who proceeded to point out that in the ordinary affairs of life (he gave as an example ordering shirts from Sears & Roebuck) the terms of ordinary language give us no trouble at all, that is, we aren't constantly falling into confusion and misunderstandings ("The Terms of Ordinary Language are . . ." in O. K. Bouwsma, *Philosophical Essays* (Lincoln: University of Nebraska Press, 1965), pp. 203–209). As Bouwsma summed up the matter elsewhere: "Ordinary language is all right? Of course [it is], we understand one another" ("The Blue Book," reprinted in Bouwsma, *Philosophical Essays,* p. 199.) Maxwell, in response, observed that Bouwsma's criticism failed entirely to address the point at issue, which is *not* that our language is inadequate for shopping at Sears and the like. The issue, rather, is that the conceptual scheme of ordinary language is a defective map of the ontological terrain. My point is that those who join in Broad's criticism of Standard Ordinary Language

Philosophy can agree with Bouwsma that our language is adequate for *practical* purposes. They can do so, I mean, without retracting their claim that it is (or may be) a *philosophically* inadequate language, for they need only agree with J. J. C. Smart that a conceptual scheme that "has proved useful in the history of the race" is not necessarily "metaphysically adequate"; on the contrary, "an incorrect theory can sometimes be more useful, practically, than a correct one" *(Between Science and Philosophy* (New York: Random House, 1968), p. 329).

39. I am not being original in using the map metaphor. The idea came to me, I believe, after reading the following remarks by Renford Bambrough:

> It is clearly necessary . . . to distinguish between those features of a map that correspond with features of the land that is mapped by it and those that are features conferred on the map by the mode of its projection and do not correspond simply and straightforwardly with any feature of the land that is being mapped. . . . There is [for example] a systematic distortion of relative size and distance in a map on Mercator's projection. Land masses near the poles are made relatively larger and those near the equator relatively smaller than they actually are. . . .
>
> If we know and understand the projection, we do not have any serious trouble with a map; and since the projection was deliberately devised, it is quite easy to come to understand and use it. But the modes of projection by which our language portrays the world are not set out for us in any elementary textbook; and although they are human products, they were not deliberately devised by any human being. It is therefore a matter of the most stubborn difficulty to know and to explain at what points and in what respects our language does and does not represent the world that it is used to describe. The struggle with this difficulty is a very large part of the task of metaphysics. The group of treatises that we know as Aristotle's *Metaphysics* is primarily concerned with this central problem. . . .
>
> Aristotle himself does give prominence to one particular use of the subject-predicate form, namely, that in which the subject is a particular concrete substance such as a horse or a statue; and he has been criticized by later philosophers for failing to see that there in no *necessity* for giving primacy to this use. He has been accused, with some plausibility, of reading into the world itself a structure that is suggested by the structure of his language but that need not be supposed to be the actual metaphysical structure of the world. . . . But his critics forget that if the structure of language bore no relation to the nature of the world in and of which it is used, then it would not be a viable and effective instrument for the purposes of its speakers. Aristotle's metaphysical doctrine is an account of the-world-as-we-know-it, and he was right in supposing that this is closely connected with the-world-as-we-describe it. His mistake consisted in supposing that the relation between language and the world is simpler and more direct than it is, not in supposing that there is such a relation. (Introduction, *The Philosophy of Aristotle* (New York: New American Library, 1963), pp. 32, 35)

40. I suspect that Malcolm failed to realize that there is an issue here that needs to be addressed. I can't believe that he would have argued in the way he did had he recognized what his critics generally think it means to "repudiate ordinary language." They would *not* mean that some quite ordinary thing we all say is never true, meaning that it's always false in the way that "I saw a unicorn" is always false. They would mean,

rather, that our ordinary conceptual scheme is the wrong one, that it misrepresents the ontological structure of the world. Malcolm appears not to have realized this, for when he attacked philosophers' conclusions, he treated them as though they were "repudiating ordinary language" in the former, rather than the latter, way.

41. In doing so, Schwyzer is not being perverse. J. O. Urmson, commenting on John Austin and others at Oxford who practiced a form of ordinary language philosophy, writes:

> If one asks these philosophers what such minute description [of our language] is good for, and why they attempt so close a study of ordinary language, they will answer, first of all, that they consider it interesting in itself and useful for discovering the conceptual resources of our language. They will add that one thereby gains a better understanding of the world to which these concepts are applied. ("The History of Philosophical Analysis," reprinted in *The Linguistic Turn*, p. 300)

42. "Thought and Reality: The Metaphysics of Kant and Wittgenstein," *The Philosophical Quarterly*, vol. 23 (July 1973), p. 204.

43. Ibid., pp. 204–205.

44. Ibid., pp. 193–194.

45. Schwyzer, in attributing this Kantian view to Wittgenstein, is undoubtedly right so far as Wittgenstein's *conceptual world* is concerned. The same can be said of P. M. S. Hacker when he writes:

> In the *Tractatus* the structure of language or thought provided the insight into the structure of reality. In the *Investigations* the structure of language is still the subject of investigation. Moreover it is still isomorphic with the structure of reality, not because language must mirror the logical form of the universe, but because the apparent 'structure of reality' is merely the shadow of grammar. *(Insight and Illusion, p. 145)*

When Hacker says that on Wittgenstein's later view "the apparent 'structure of reality' is merely the shadow of grammar," it is clear that he means that our *conceptual world* is the shadow of grammar. At times Hacker talks as though, for Wittgenstein, our conceptual world is all that there is, that it's identical with reality. One result is that Hacker, in expounding Wittgenstein's view of philosophy, writes: "The task of philosophy is to eradicate misconceptions by giving us a perspicuous representation of our grammar, to designate the way we look at things—our form of representation" (ibid.). This suggests that Wittgenstein was concerned exclusively with our conceptual world, which (as Hacker puts it) "changes as we change, and it can be altered" (ibid.). And this, in turn, seems to imply that Wittgenstein might have allowed that certain philosophical views which he denounces as conceptual confusions—dualism, for example— could, if we made certain changes in our "form of representation," be defended. Such an interpretation of Wittgenstein is, as I see it, profoundly mistaken. On my interpretation, Wittgenstein held that reality itself doesn't alter as conceptual schemes come and go, that reality is never anything other than "experience," the essence of which is made clear by restating in the formal mode the account which neutral monists have given in the material mode. Schwyzer, too, seems not to realize that Wittgenstein makes a distinction between reality and our conceptual world. The nature or essence of that which belongs to our conceptual world—the nature of God, for example—is determined by the way we use words, by what we do and do not say. (See chapter 1, note 9, for Wittgenstein's remarks about "God.") But Wittgenstein would not say the same of reality, of the phenomenal world. What *that* is like is not a matter of our linguistic conventions. In other words, he would not allow that the theses of neutral monism are acceptable only because—and only so long as—our language makes them acceptable.

46. "Thoughtless Brutes," in Norman Malcolm, *Thought and Knowledge* (Ithaca: Cornell University Press, 1977), p. 49,

47. Malcolm (in a private communication) expressed considerable annoyance with me when, for the very same purpose, I called attention to this passage in a published article. He objected that I misrepresented him by failing to mention that in the paper from which I quoted he had not only given the above argument but had *also* examined Descartes' reasons for claiming that animals don't think. That objection, however, does not address the point I was making then and am making now.

48. "A Reply to My Critics," in *The Philosophy of G. E. Moore,* p. 675.

49. Ibid., p. 673.

50. Malcolm says that a philosophical skeptic is in a peculiar position because, on the one hand, "he will agree that the facts of the situation are what we should ordinarily describe by the expression 'seeing a cat in the tree,'" and yet, on the other hand, he insists that no one *really* sees a cat, but sees only some sense-data of a cat. This, says Malcolm is "a great absurdity; for [the skeptic] implies that a person can use an expression to describe a certain state of affairs, which is the expression ordinarily used to describe just such a state of affairs, and yet be using incorrect language." But try saying this to, for example, someone who is deeply impressed by Descartes' dream argument. *That* person won't accept what Malcolm says here, namely, that "he [the skeptic] will agree that the facts of the situation are what we should ordinarily describe by the expression 'seeing a cat in the tree,'" Far from agreeing to that, the skeptic will insist that he can't tell whether he's seeing a cat or only *dreaming* that he is seeing a cat. He will insist that the *only* relevant facts he's aware of are consistent with both his seeing a cat and his *not* seeing a cat but dreaming that he is. In other words, he would reject Malcolm's claim that his skepticism involves him in the absurdity that someone could "use an expression to describe a certain state of affairs, which is the expression ordinarily used to describe *just such a state of affairs,* and yet be using incorrect language." The skeptic will reply: "If I were to say just now that I see a cat in the tree, the facts which make this a conventionally correct use of words are the visual facts which are consistent with both my seeing a cat and my only dreaming that I see one. So the visual facts *can* obtain even when there is no cat in a tree, and therefore if those facts do presently obtain, then if I say, 'I see a cat in the tree,' I am using words in a conventionally correct way despite the fact that I am saying something that is (contrary to Malcolm) untrue."

51. Alan White has argued, quite correctly in my view, that Moore never did attempt to refute the conclusion of a philosophical argument by pointing out that it conflicted in some way with ordinary language. White says:

> Having established what is the philosophical view and what the common sense view and that the two conflict, he [Moore] can then use the appeal to the latter to refute the former. The appeal to ordinary language is, for him, mainly subsidiary to the appeal to common sense. Malcolm and those who agree with him have reversed the correct relative position of the two [in Moore's reasoning]. *(G. E. Moore: A Critical Exposition,* p. 7.)*

52. White makes this point very clearly when he says that Moore's

> ultimate ground for holding the statements of common sense to be true is that they simply and self–evidently are true. Quite often he simply asserts as a final

answer that such and such a common sense belief is just quite certain. (Ibid., p. 15)

An example of this is the following. Moore, in discussing the views of skeptical philosophers, wrote: "[I]t seems to me a sufficient refutation of such views as these, simply to point to cases in which we do know such things [as the skeptic denies we can know]. This, after all, you know, really is a finger: there is no doubt about it: I know it, you all know it" ("Some Judgments of Perception," reprinted in G. E. Moore, *Philosophical Studies* (New York: Humanities Press, 1951), p. 228).

53. "Philosophy and the Analysis of Language," reprinted in *The Linguistic Turn*, p. 279.

54. Ibid., Fn. 9.

55. "Wittgenstein on Certainty" in *Understanding Wittgenstein*, ed. Godfrey Vesey (Ithaca: Cornell University Press, 1976), p. 242; emphasis added.

56. An adequate reason would not be that ordinary language is perfectly serviceable for ordinary purposes. See note 38 above.

57. It appears that A. C. Grayling shares this idea with Malcolm. He says that Wittgenstein held that philosophical problems arise "only because we misunderstand the working of language." He then adds that, *because* Wittgenstein thinks of philosophical problems in that way, his "approach represents an attempt at a shortcut, for if one adopts it one disposes of all the problems of philosophy in one blow . . . without having to become involved in analysis of its various problems" ("Wittgenstein's Influence: Meaning, Mind and Method," in *Wittgenstein Centenary Essays*, ed. A. Phillips Griffiths (Cambridge: Cambridge University Press, 1992), pp. 62–63). But unlike Malcolm, Grayling is not in sympathy with Wittgenstein. He declares that "on this fundamental matter [Wittgenstein] has failed to persuade," for the simple reason that his diagnosis of philosophical perplexity "seems implausible" (p. 63).

58. Not Wittgensteinian? Someone may be inclined to dispute this by calling attention to Wittgenstein's remark, in The Blue Book, that "ordinary language is all right" (p. 28). It may be thought that this remark comes to the same as Malcolm's praising Moore for realizing that "any philosophical statement which violates ordinary language is false" and for "defend[ing] ordinary language against its philosophical detractors." But this interpretation is entirely mistaken. When Wittgenstein said that ordinary language is "all right," he meant that it is usable for practical purposes, despite the fact that many of our normal forms of expression are extremely misleading. (Our language is all right because *grammar is arbitrary*, it doesn't determine meaning.) In order to think that Wittgenstein's remark is an endorsement of Standard Ordinary Language Philosophy, one would have to have in mind the wrong contrast, namely, "When philosophers propose an alternate form of expression, thinking that it's preferable to our normal grammatical form, they have got matters exactly backward; it is ordinary language that's all right and the philosopher's preferred form is not." For Wittgenstein, however, the proper contrast is this:

When philosophers propose an alternate form of expression, thinking that it's preferable to our normal grammatical form, they are partly right and partly wrong. They are right because their alternative form of expression *is* philosophically superior to our ordinary one. They are wrong because they think that our normal form of expression says something false (see PI, §402) and therefore needs to be replaced by a more suitable form of expression. If they had realized that grammar is arbitrary, they would have realized that ordinary language is all right.

A few paragraphs before remarking that "ordinary language is all right" Wittgenstein says: "We shall try to construct new notations in order to break the spell of those which we are accustomed to" (p. 23), and then explains that "whenever we make up 'ideal languages' it is not in order to *replace* our ordinary language by them" (BB, p. 28; emphasis added). Clearly, Wittgenstein's sympathy (unlike Malcolm's) lay with the philosopher who is critical of ordinary language, but he saw no need to remove it from daily life.

Chapter 11

1. "A Defence of Common Sense" in *Contemporary British Philosophy, Second Series,* ed. J. H. Muirhead (London: George Allen and Unwin, 1925), and "Proof of an External World," *Proceedings of the British Academy,* 25 (1939). Both papers are reprinted in Moore's *Philosophical Papers,* and my page references will be to this volume.

2. "Some Judgments of Perception," reprinted in Moore, *Philosophical Studies,* p. 228.

3. "The Conception of Reality," reprinted in Moore, *Philosophical Studies,* p. 209.

4. *Some Main Problems of Philosophy,* p. 135.

5. Ibid., p. 1.

6. Ibid., p. 19.

7. "Moore's 'Defence of Common Sense,'" in *The Philosophy of G. E. Moore,* p. 316.

8. "The Status of Sense–data," reprinted in Moore, *Philosophical Studies,* p. 196.

9. "Four Forms of Skepticism," in Moore, *Philosophical Papers,* pp. 225–226.

10. Ludwig Wittgenstein, *On Certainty,* §§10, 347, 348, 412, 423, 461, and 464.

11. In *Philosophical Papers,* pp. 242–243.

12. "A Defence of Common Sense," *Philosophy of G. E. Moore,* p. 33.

13. Descartes, *Philosophical Writings,* eds. E. Anscombe and P. Geach (Edinburgh: Nelson, 1954), pp. 62 and 65.

14. Bertrand Russell, *Philosophy* (New York: Norton, 1927), pp. 243–244.

15. Some years after writing this I found that A. J. Ayer had made this same point in his "Metaphysics and Common Sense," in *Metaphysics,* eds. W. E. Kennick and Morris Lazerowitz (Englewood Cliffs: Prentice-Hall, 1966), pp. 317–330.

16. *Philosophical Writings,* p. 62.

17. "Proof of an External World," p. 146.

18. "Certainty," pp. 227–228.

19. In "Four Forms of Scepticism" Moore says: "I do not think it is *rational* to be as certain of [the premises of a skeptic's argument] as of the proposition that I do know that this is a pencil" (p. 226).

20. There is, it seems, such a form of lunacy. See "Doubting Mania" in *Dictionary of Philosophy and Psychology,* ed. James Baldwin (New York: Macmillan, 1925), pp. 296–297.

21. Moore does not make this explicit in the passage quoted above, but several paragraphs later he writes: "If one of you suspected that one of my hands was artificial he might be said to get a proof of my proposition 'Here's one hand and here's another', by coming up and examining the suspected hand close up" ("Proof of an External World," p. 149).

22. Wittgenstein may have been recognizing this difference when he wrote in *On Certainty:*

I am sitting with a philosopher in the garden; he says again and again "I know that that's a tree", pointing to a tree that is near us. Someone else arrives and hears this, and I tell him: "This fellow isn't insane. We are only doing philosophy." (OC, §467)

Chapter 12

1. In G. E. Moore, *Philosophical Studies,* pp. 191, 195.
2. Ibid.
3. See my discussion of this in chapter 8 of *Wittgenstein's Metaphysics.*
4. Cora Diamond is a recent example of what I have in mind (see Diamond, *The Realistic Spirit: Wittgenstein, Philosophy, and the Mind,* pp. 46–47). Another recent example is Mary Midgley. In her discussion of empiricism she says that "the current form of linguistic philosophy which descends from British empiricism" is valuable "because it uses everyday language and directs attention strongly towards existing everyday thought as its starting point" *(Wisdom, Information, and Wonder* (London: Routledge, 1989), p. 208). As for Wittgenstein, Midgley says that although he produced in the *Tractatus* "the definitive version of the reductive, purifying enterprise" which typifies one strain of empiricism, he eventually came "to see its faults fully and to replace [his earlier reductionism] by . . . far richer, more flexible models [of philosophizing]" (Ibid., p. 27). The reductive aims of the *Tractatus,* she says, led empiricism away from "its other role of serving as the champion of ordinary, everyday thinking, and did not come back to [this nonreductive role] until Moore and the later Wittgenstein turned their attention back to ordinary language" (Ibid., p. 186). It is my contention that neither Moore nor the later Wittgenstein nor any empiricist ever paid much attention to ordinary language, except in the most trivial ways. Midgley is quite right to place both linguistic philosophy (or most of it) and the later Wittgenstein in the orbit of empiricism, but if she thinks that empiricism is not "reductive," I don't know what she means by "reductionism."
5. See *Wittgenstein's Metaphysics,* chapters 14 and 15.
6. See *Wittgenstein's Metaphysics,* chapters 16–19.
7. I have discussed this matter in three articles: "Religious Belief," in *Wittgenstein's Intentions,* eds. John V. Canfield and Stuart G. Shanker (New York: Garland Publishing, 1993), pp. 147–161; "Wittgenstein and Religious Belief," *Philosophy,* vol. 63, (October 1988), pp. 427–452; and "Kierkegaard and Wittgenstein," *Religious Studies,* vol. 23, (June 1987), pp. 199–219.
8. Bouwsma, having attended several informal discussions with Wittgenstein, wrote in his diary: "I have found W[ittgenstein] a great tonic, like a purge. And how I need it. How solid with the habits of long nonsense! I must do what I can to subject myself to his drubbing and to learn to speak freely so that I may expose my rags to him. If I can only speak!" (Bouwsma, *Wittgenstein: Conversations 1949–1951,* p. 8). Bouwsma later remarked to Frank Ebersole that he had never noticed a mistake in anything Wittgenstein had written or said.

Chapter 13

1. Letter to Huygens, in *Oeuvres Complete de Christian Huygens* (The Hague, 1905), vol. X, p. 681. My translation.
2. See my essay "A Reappraisal of Leibniz's Views on Space, Time, and Motion," *Philosophical Investigations,* vol. 2 (Spring 1979), pp. 22–63.

3. Letter to Leibniz, dated September 12, 1695, in *Die Philosophichen Schriften von G. W. Leibniz* (Berlin, 1875–1890), vol. VI, p. 128.

4. G. W. Leibniz, *The Monodology and Other Writings,* ed. and trans. Robert Latta (Oxford, 1898), p. 342.

5. Recall here Wittgenstein's remark: "If I had to say what is the main mistake made by philosophers of the present generation, including Moore, I would say that it is that when language is looked at, what is looked at is a form of words and not at the use made of the form of words" (LC, p. 2).

6. *Principles,* part I, secs. 51, 52.

7. Ibid., Introduction, sec. 20. Was this passage, perhaps, the source of Wittgenstein's account of the names of sensations?

8. Locke had maintained that "the chief end of language" is that "men learn names, and use them in talk with others, only that they may be understood: which is then only done when by use or consent the sound I make by the organs of speech excites in another man's mind who hears it, the idea I apply it to in mine when I speak it" (*An Essay Concerning Human Understanding,* III, iii, 3).

9. Was Wittgenstein perhaps thinking of this passage—especially the phrase "how false soever they may be"—when he wrote: "[W]e are tempted to say that our mode of expression does not describe the facts as they really are . . . . As if the form of expression were saying something false even when the proposition *faute de mieux* asserted something true" (PI, §402)?

10. *Essays on The Intellectual Powers of Man,* essay 2, ch. 18.

11. This—or something like it—could, I think, actually happen. If you have been sitting for a long time in an oddly cramped position, you can be mistaken about where exactly your feet are: they may be drawn up beneath you without your realizing it, and in that situation you might inadvertently point to a place in midair when asked "Where is that blister?" or "Where is that splinter you wanted removed?"

12. D. A. T. Gasking and A. C. Jackson, "Wittgenstein as a Teacher," reprinted in *Ludwig Wittgenstein: The Man and His Philosophy,* p. 54.

13. A year earlier, in 1947, he wrote: "Am *I* the only one who cannot found a school or can a philosopher never do this? I cannot found a school because I do not really want to be imitated. Not at any rate by those who publish in philosophical journals" (CV, p. 61).

14. I have given some details of this in earlier chapters. See chapter 5, note 11 and chapter 10, note 9.

15. Just as Wittgenstein claimed that his method was "purely descriptive," so Kierkegaard said that in his writings he had tried to provide an "exact description of Christianity." And yet his most important claims about Christianity rest on a philosophical assumption which has no place in Christianity. See my "Kierkegaard and Wittgenstein," *Religious Studies,* vol. 23 (June 1987), pp. 199–219.

Chapter 14

1. "A language can be known to be 'ideal' only by comparing its logical structure with the ontological structure of the world, *which must be known independently* if the comparison is to be significant." Irving Copi, "Language Analysis and Metaphysical Inquiry," reprinted in *The Linguistic Turn,* p. 131; emphasis added.

2. "The Interpretation of Language: Words and Concepts," p. 279.

3. Jerry Fodor and Jerrold Katz, "The Availability of What We Say," p. 68.

4. Ibid.

5. Ibid., pp. 69–70.

6. *Meaning and Saying,* p. x.

7. Ibid., p. x.

8. Ibid., p. viii.

9. *Meaning and Saying,* pp. vii–viii. Ebersole continues: "The desire to theorize, though, is often overwhelming, and when it is there is nothing to do except to face it for what it is. I know of no effective way to do this except to confront it with more and more examples, to present it with the details—the facts. For I know from many past experiences that these philosophical theories which rush in on me not only make me distort the facts, they make me blind to the very facts they have led me to distort."

10. See, for example, Ebersole's essay "The Family Resemblance Metaphor," in *Language and Perception,* pp. 1–78.

11. Near the end of his life Wittgenstein reflected on what his examples ought to be like. In 1949 he wrote: "The contexts in which a word appears are portrayed best in a play; therefore, the best example for a sentence with a certain meaning is a quote from a play" (LW, II, p. 7). He went on to say: "The best example of an expression with a specific meaning is a passage in a play" (LW, II, p. 8). I doubt that Wittgenstein when he wrote this was thinking of Shakespeare or Oscar Wilde. More likely he meant only that a philosophical example must consist, not of an isolated sentence, but of a bit of dialogue carried on by known characters. If so, Wittgenstein had come to realize something that is missing from most of his work. Even in *On Certainty,* where he seems to be working with examples, they are often specified as "propositions"—as when he writes:

> When Moore says he *knows* such and such, he is really enumerating a lot of empirical propositions which we affirm without special testing; propositions, that is, which have a peculiar logical role in the system of our empirical propositions. (OC, §136)

This talk of propositions sounds all too much like the *Tractatus* view of language. And throughout most of *On Certainty* Wittgenstein struggled to figure out how to describe the "peculiar logical role" of the propositions Moore had enumerated. Only at the very end (see OC §659) did he begin to see that something was wrong with that idea.

12. This, I think, is one of the ways in which Ebersole's work differs from Standard Ordinary Language Philosophy. Although he doesn't describe his method exactly as I have, he says something similar:

> I try to get a problem for philosophical investigation or inquiry isolated from history and from the doctrines of philosophers and get it "personalized," "internalized." . . . I do my best to tackle the problem as though it were the first time the problem had ever been considered; I try to think everything clean through as though none of it had been thought about before. *(Meaning and Saying,* p. vii)

Ebersole does not here speak of backtracking, but he clearly aims to get back to the beginning, to sources. And it is because his work takes this form that it cannot be dismissed by The Universal Dismisser, by the charge that ordinary language philosophy begs important questions.

13. The sort of examination I have in mind includes scrutiny of the thesis that a study of various natural languages lends support to the idea that language is a conceptual scheme. I have examined this thesis in two essays: "Whorf's Linguistic Relativism,

I" *Philosophical Investigations,* vol. 1 (Winter 1978), pp. 1–30, and "Whorf's Linguistic Relativism, II," *Philosophical Investigations,* vol. 1 (Spring 1978), pp. 1–37.

14. "Wittgenstein's Influence: Meaning, Mind and Method," p. 64.

15. *The Sovereignty of Good* (New York: Schocken, 1971), p. 29. Murdoch gives a variety of examples, including these: "Repentance may mean something different to an individual at different times in his life" (p. 26) and "we have a different image of courage at forty from that which we had at twenty" (p. 29).

16. I have discussed these issues in detail in *Morality and Cultural Differences* (New York: Oxford University Press, 1999).

17. See chapter 6, esp. note 22. I have discussed some aspects of this in my essay "Religious Belief," in *Wittgenstein's Intentions,* pp. 147–161.

18. *Theories of Primitive Religion* (Oxford: Oxford University Press, 1965), p. 12.

Chapter 15

1. *The Problems of Philosophy* (New York: Oxford University Press, 1912), p. 11.

2. Ibid., pp. 9–10.

3. Ibid., p. 11.

Appendix

1. I am thinking not only of the widespread view that Wittgenstein was some sort of ordinary language philosopher but also of the way Newton Garver interprets Wittgenstein in his recent book, *This Complicated Form of Life,* (Chicago: Open Court, 1994). Garver maintains that "Wittgenstein falls squarely within a philosophical tradition inaugurated by Kant" (p. xv) and also says that it is a "distortion of Wittgenstein's thought [to say] that he was an empiricist" (p. 78).

2. Russell, in his autobiography, writes: "I got back to Cambridge from Rome on New Year's Day 1914, and, thinking that the time had come when I really must get my [Lowell] lectures prepared, I arranged for a shorthand typist to come next day, though I had not the vaguest idea what I should say to her when she came. As she entered the room, my ideas fell into place, and I dictated in a completely orderly sequence from that moment until the work was finished. What I dictated to her was subsequently published as a book with the title *Our Knowledge of the External World as a Field for Scientific Method in Philosophy (The Autobiography of Bertrand Russell, 1872–1914* (Boston: Little, Brown and Company, 1951), p. 325). The next sentence reads: "I sailed on the *Mauretania* on March 7th." (The Lowell lectures were delivered in Boston in March and April of 1914.)

3. Quoted by Ray Monk, *Ludwig Wittgenstein: The Duty of Genius* (New York: The Free Press, 1990), p. 124.

4. *Letters to Russell, Keynes, and Moore,* ed. G. H. von Wright (Oxford: Blackwell, 1974), p. 111, letter K8. I am indebted to Harold Morick for calling this letter to my attention.

5. I will not comment on one other remark that is interspersed with the four I have just quoted. It reads: "It is one of the chief skills of the philosopher not to occupy himself with questions which do not concern him" (NB, p. 44). Wittgenstein may have thought that Russell occupied himself with such questions, but if so, it is not clear which questions these were.

6. *Our Knowledge of the External World,* p. 74.

7. Ibid., p. 78.

8. Ibid., pp. 72–80.

9. Ibid., p. 79.

10. It might be suggested that Wittgenstein could have been referring, instead, to Russell's Herbert Spencer Lecture "On Scientific Method in Philosophy," which also dates from 1914. But there is a good reason for rejecting this suggestion. The lecture was delivered on November 18, 1914 (see *The Philosophy of Bertrand Russell,* ed. Paul Schilpp, (New York: Todor, 1951), p. 756), by which time Wittgenstein had left England, not to return until after the war. If it be suggested that the lecture might have been composed at an earlier date, there is reason to dispute this. At the end of his lecture Russell explicitly refers to *Our Knowledge of the External World:* "A further defence and elaboration of the position which I advocate, but for which time is lacking now [i.e., in this lecture], will be found indicated in my book *Our Knowledge of the External World"* *(Mysticism and Logic,* pp. 123–124). This remark is in the text of the lecture, which suggests that the lecture was composed later, not earlier, than the book. I think we may conclude, then, that Wittgenstein was referring, not to the lecture, but to Russell's book.

11. *Our Knowledge of the External World,* p. 243.

12. Ibid., p. 244.

13. Ibid., p. 246.

14. Wittgenstein, in 1931, wrote: "People say again and again that philosophy doesn't really progress, that we are still occupied with the same philosophical problems as were the Greeks. But the people who say this don't understand why it has to be so. It is because our language has remained the same and keeps seducing us into asking the same question" (CV, p. 15).

15. Ibid., p. 73; emphasis added.

16. Ibid., p. 78.

17. Perhaps, too, he recalled that Schopenhauer had been equally cavalier in dealing with solipsism. Referring to solipsism as "theoretical egoism," Schopenhauer said that although it "can never be refuted by proofs," it needn't be taken seriously because "as a serious conviction . . . it could be found only in a mad house; as such it would then need not so much a refutation as a cure." Therefore, concluded Schopenhauer, we who "are endeavoring to extend our knowledge through philosophy . . . can pass it by and leave it in our rear without danger" *(The World as Will and Idea,* vol. I, bk. 2, §19).

18. Ibid., p. 238.

19. Ibid., p. 112.

20. Ibid., p. 134.

21. This passage is retained nearly verbatim in the *Tractatus,* but it ends as follows: "and signs that serve *none* [i.e., no purpose] are logically meaningless" (5.47321).

22. Ibid., pp. 88–89.

23. Ibid., esp. pp. 224–225.

24. Ibid., esp. pp. 121–126.

25. Ibid., pp. 94–100.

26. *Our Knowledge of the External World,* p. 112.

27. From his reading of Schopenhauer at an early age Wittgenstein would have been already familiar with the view of dreams that Russell espouses. See Schopenhauer's *The World as Will and Idea,* vol. 1, bk. I, §5.

28. *Our Knowledge of the External World,* pp. 92–93.

29. Ibid., pp. 242–243.

30. Ibid., p. 75–76.

31. Ibid., p. 76.

32. Ibid., p. 77.

33. *This Complicated Form of Life,* p. 10.

34. Notice here another of Wittgenstein's remarks: "If someone can believe in God with complete certainty, why not in Other Minds?" (CV, p. 73).

35. His idea here is related to such other passages as the following: "The squirrel does not infer by induction that it is going to need stores next winter as well. And no more do we need a law of induction to justify our actions or our predictions" (OC, §287) and "I might also put it like this: the 'law of induction' can no more be *grounded* [i.e., be given a foundation] than certain particular propositions concerning the material of experience [such as 'I see a red patch']" (OC, §499).

36. I have discussed this aspect of Wittgenstein's philosophy in "Wittgenstein and Religious Belief," *Philosophy,* vol. 63 (October 1988), pp. 427–452.

37. *This Complicated Form of Life,* p. 265.

38. Ibid., p. 102.

39. Ibid., p. 84.

40. Ibid., p. 159.

41. Ibid., p. 79.

42. Quoted by Ray Monk in *Ludwig Wittgenstein: The Duty of Genius,* p. 313.

Index